SAP - SALES & DISTRIBUTION AND LOGISTICS
EXECUTION

CONFIGURATIONS AND TRANSACTIONS

YOGI KALRA
SHEFARIA ENT INC.

ACKNOWLEDGMENTS

I am very thankful foremost to my clients and their employees who have given me the opportunity to work on their SAP systems, always learning from them and their Businesses; notable among them being, Stericycle, Shred-it, Kemira, Johnson & Johnson, BELL Industries, Chevron Phillips, Freightliner and many more. Without their support and my learning their Business Processes, this manual would not have been possible.

Finally, I am grateful to you, the reader for selecting this book among the thousands available, never an easy choice and I hope it met or exceeded your expectations. I am happy to answer any questions you may have on the topic or if, for better learning, you would like access to the demo system on which this book was written, you may contact us on shefariaentinc@gmail.com. The author will be grateful for your review and feedback on the public fora if the book helped you increase your understanding of the subject.

TABLE OF CONTENTS

FOREWORD

This manual, written with the objective of providing detailed training to both, consultants and users goes deep into the subject from initial sales cycle to the entire delivery process and invoicing the customers. The integration points of SD-LE with Accounting and Purchasing/Inventory are explained in detail and the chapters marked clearly if it is a Configuration (C) or Transaction (U) or both. Since most of the book has been written in standard SAP, once a company code and sales organization are set up, any SAP user, if so desires, can stay only with the areas marked 'U', by passing the 'C' since not everything in standard SAP depends on specific Sales Organization setups. Consultants or to-be consultants, of course, need to understand both sides of SAP. The effects of changes done in configuration are immediately shown by their effect on the transactions, thereby making the learning relational in real time for better understanding. From the user's perspective, not much from the subject has been left out in writing this manual and every effort has been taken to keep it relevant to the Sales and distribution related functions of daily working on SAP in an orderly flow.

This manual has been written keeping standard Business processes proposed by SAP. In writing this book, we have stayed away from all frills and concentrated on providing only useful subject matter with tips and tricks based on over my many years of experience in SAP implementations and consulting. This book is not a result of overnight arrangement but a composition of several years of training and understanding of Business processes across multiple industries in various disciplines. We believe it is as comprehensive as any book can be for users and consultants, new and old, to conducting any Sales and Logistics functions in SAP.

For New users: One of the primary learning curves in SAP is navigation. The data in SAP is so well organized that first time users are often astonished to see the integrative nature of this ERP system. It is no exaggeration to say that everything you need to know in SAP is at one, two or maximum three clicks away. Mastering navigation in SAP is half the battle won. Good navigation skills will guide you in finding sources of the data in the documents. It would be very worth the while to spend time on navigation on the different screens and get familiar with them as for the most part, there is a commonality in the way SAP is structured across different areas in terms of screen layouts. To get a better understanding of Navigation in a structured form, read the author's book **SAP Navigation & General Components.** Use the F1 key for help liberally – it will help you wade through the screens understanding everything thoroughly. As is the case with all seemingly multifaceted structures, the base is very simple. In spite of SAP's complexity as an ERP system, it's edifice is built on very elementary processes as you will notice while going through this book. Processes that are uniform, scalable and easily comprehensible. One of SAP's masterstrokes is the Transaction code and the philosophy that drives it. Usually a 4 alpha-numeric or alpha code (but can be often longer, especially in Finance reporting), it is used to invoke a program which will guide you through the entire process. Thus, a user need only to remember this transaction code for the function to be performed and entering it in the transaction window to begin your activity. This manual endeavors to cover over 350 such transactions; bear in mind, each of them will perform a related and unique business function. Further, to simplify learning, a transaction code is usually ended as 01, 02 or 03 signifying create, change or display respectively. Thus, VA01, VA02 and VA03 become Create Sales Order, Change Sales Order and Display Sales Order, respectively. Also, for the most part, transaction codes and configurable objects are case insensitive i.e. VA01 is same as va01.

For SAP Users and Process Owners: This book covers over 120 standard processes and transactions in SD and LE in depth in easily understandable language and with only relevant screen shots. It is unlikely that any organization will be required to call upon any other substantial transactions other than these in its normal functioning. Towards the end, the book also touches on some cross application components, which if you have access to, will simplify your work in SAP tremendously. Anyone new to the SAP world is advised to read the chapter on 'Variants' after getting a good feel of the first couple of transactions. Again, for users new to SAP, the best and perhaps fastest way to learn from this book is to think of what you do or did in your legacy system and look up this manual on how to perform the same process in SAP. The transaction code to perform that function is provided right in the beginning of the chapter.

For Consultants: This book covers all configurations relating to SD and LE in depth. The effect of the changes in configurations in real time is explained as you go along, making your learning easier. Also detailed are the relationship between SD-LE and MM/FI/PP wherever applicable to enable you to become more robust consultants. Most importantly, you will learn a lot by diving into the details of the transactions also as explained in this book and that will help you face the users more confidently. I can't recount the number of times I was embarrassed in my early days at client's sites when the experienced users explained to me navigation on the screens I did not know myself...

Your inputs and criticism are very welcome. If there is anything the author can do to help you understand the subject better or guide you in any way, please feel free to drop an email to shefariaentinc@gmail.com noting the name of the book and topic in the subject of the email. Since nothing is perfect, there may be some errors and omissions in the book. I will be very grateful for your comments and responses if you find them or even otherwise give your suggestions since they will work to make the next edition better.

SALES & DISTRIBUTION

Sales & Distribution Implementation begins with the Implementation Guide (aka IMG) screen. The transaction code to reach the screen is SPRO or it can be reached from the below path by clicking:

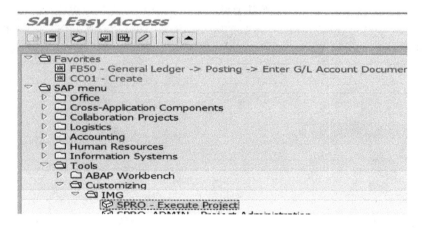

Fig 1

Fig 2

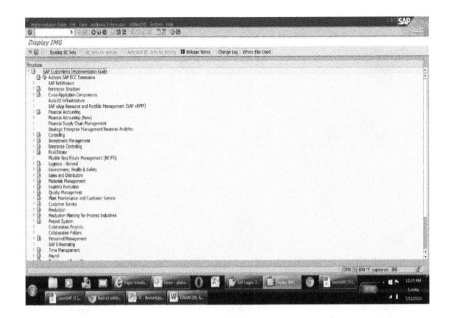

Fig 3

15

ORGANIZATIONAL STRUCTURE (C)

Activities in the different areas in SAP are carried on in/by 'structures'. Sales & Distribution module also has its own structure. This structure in SD comprises of many elements, the primary 3 being:

- Sales Organization. Coded as a 4-digit alpha numeric code, it is the highest level in the SD side of SAP. It represents the company code as its arm that does sales and distribution. It can be regarded as 'Who'
- Distribution Channel – are akin to the way the products or services will be delivered to the customers. Examples are retail, wholesale, direct sales, merchandiser sales etc. This can be referred to as the 'How'
- Division – usually representing the business areas of the organization – product lines like Chemicals, pumps, furniture etc. This can be called 'What' and is closely linked to the material master in SAP which we will understand to a fair detail as part of this training.

These three – Who, How and what combine to be called a 'Sales Area'. Everything on the SD side is done in a sales area. The sales area is unique i.e. for everything to be done in different sales areas, the products or customers need to be set up or 'extended' in all those sales areas.

All these objects must be created separately or configured and then connected with each other.

The path to set up the SO is:

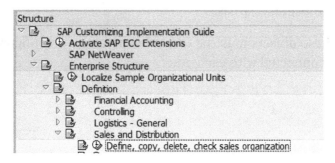

Fig 1

We can either copy from an existing one or create a new one. Double click on the option you want to follow (we will use the copying function here so use the 2nd one):

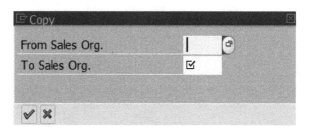

Fig 2

Use the Copy icon: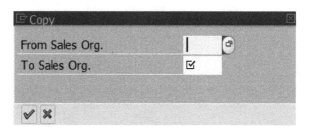

Fig 3

In the from field, pick up some standard SAP SO like 0001 and in the To your own SO's 4 digit alpha numeric code:

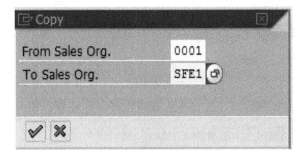

Fig 4

Click Enter to get to this window:

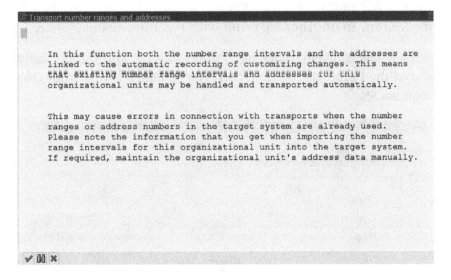

Fig 5

Hit Enter again.

You will come to a window that shows up like this:

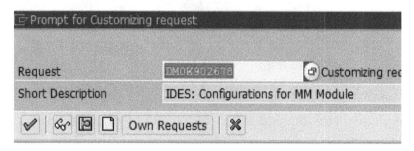

Prompt for Customizing request

Request	DM0K902678		Customizing rec
Short Description	IDES: Configurations for MM Module		

✔ ⟨⟩ 🖉 ☐   Own Requests   ✖

Fig 6

You must create a new transport if it proposes any transport number which is not your own. This transport number will be moved from one system to another carrying with it all the changes done. To create a new transport, click on ☐ if you want to add this change to your own pre-existing transport, you can choose that from Own Requests also.

Create Request

Request		Customizing request	
Short description	IDES: Configurations for SD-LE Module		
Project			
Owner	IDES0164	Source client	800
Status	New	Target	
Last changed	03.06.2016 20:13:30		

Fig 7

Give a description that will make sense to you or is specific to the change being done. Since we are starting from the beginning here, we will call it as above. Clicking on Save will give you a different (new) number as below:

20

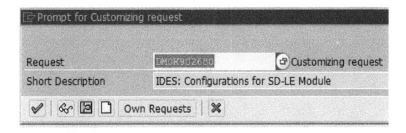

Fig 8

Hit Enter and the system will have saved your changes under this transport Number. As we go along, we will add more changes onto this same number so that we do not have to have multiple unnecessary numbers to remember and look for.

Click Enter to get to the message:

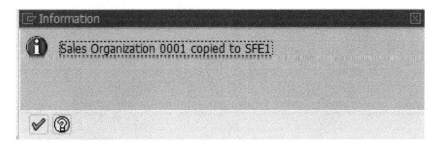

Fig 9

Click Enter again.

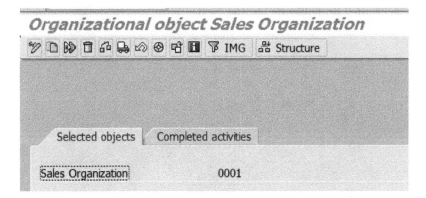

Fig 10

On the Completed Activities tab confirm the message:

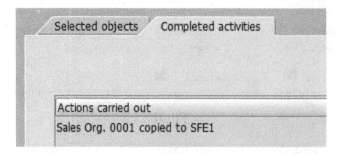

Fig 11

Step out to the previous screen to modify the details of your new SO – it would have copied all the data from 0001 and you will need to change the name, address etc. Click now on

Fig 12

Search for the new SO using the Position key:

Fig 13

Change View "Sales organizat

SOrg.	Name
SFE1	Sales Org. Germany
SL31	USA Los Angeles

Fig 14

Change the Name:

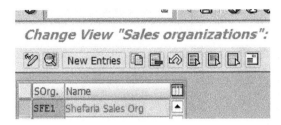

Fig 15

And then click on ⬛ :

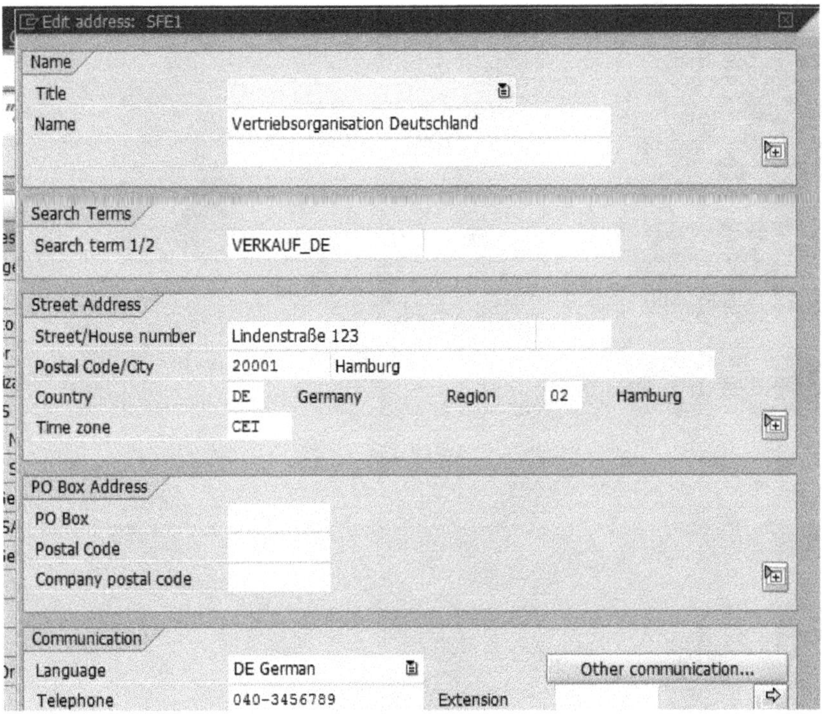

Fig 16

Replace the address with your SO's address, only the country is mandatory but it is advisable to put as much as you can. Save the data.

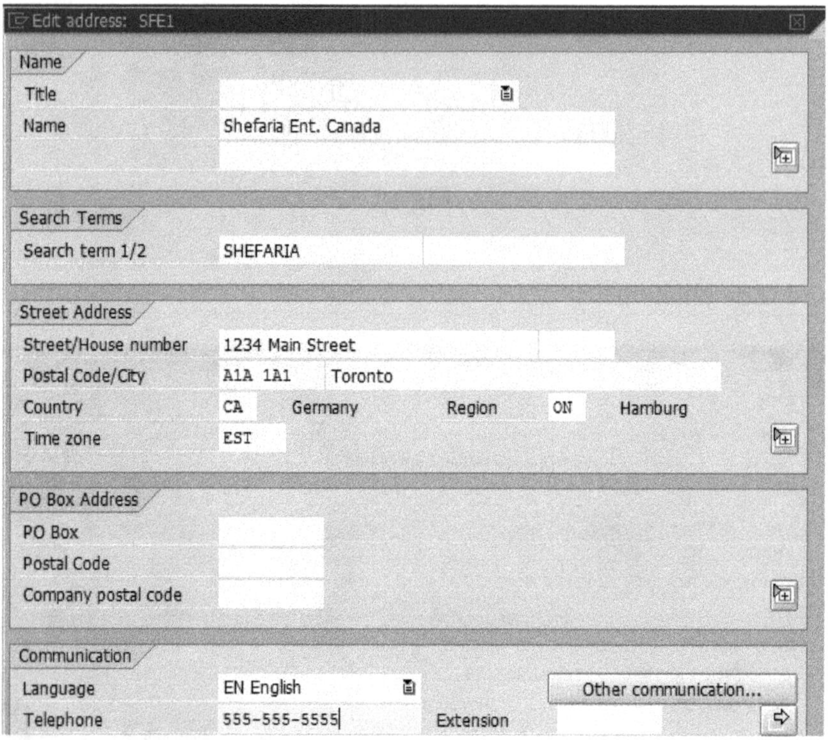

Edit address: SFE1				
Name				
Title				
Name	Shefaria Ent. Canada			
Search Terms				
Search term 1/2	SHEFARIA			
Street Address				
Street/House number	1234 Main Street			
Postal Code/City	A1A 1A1	Toronto		
Country	CA	Germany	Region	ON Hamburg
Time zone	EST			
PO Box Address				
PO Box				
Postal Code				
Company postal code				
Communication				
Language	EN English		Other communication...	
Telephone	555-555-5555	Extension		

Fig 17

Enterprise Structure
Localize Sample Organizational Units
Definition
Financial Accounting
Controlling
Logistics - General
Sales and Distribution
Define, copy, delete, check sales organization
Define, copy, delete, check distribution channel

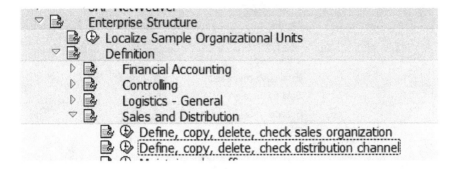

Fig 18

Again, we have the option to copy or Define our own:

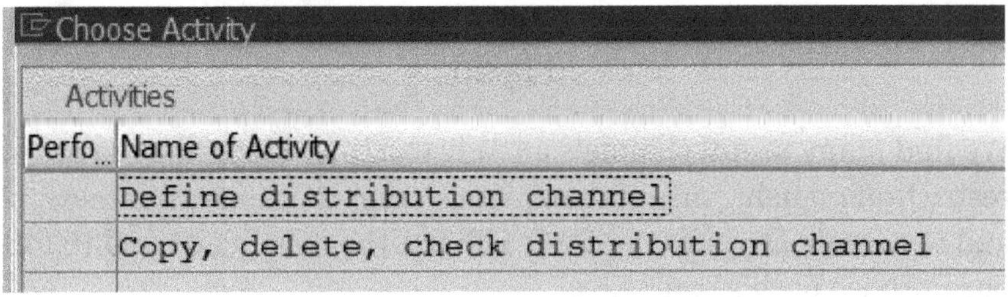

Choose Activity
Activities
Perfo...
Name of Activity
Define distribution channel
Copy, delete, check distribution channel

Fig 19

Let us choose Define this time:

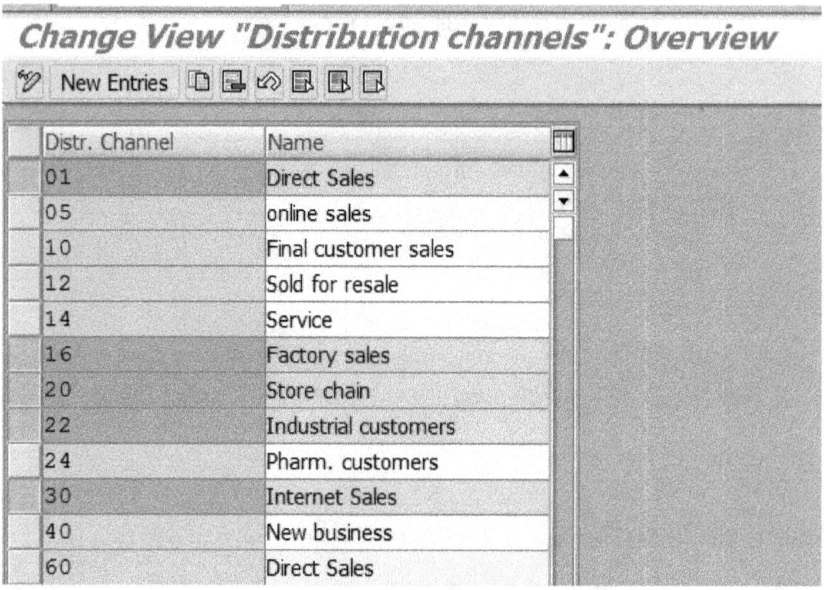
Change View "Distribution channels": Overview
New Entries
Distr. Channel
Name
01
Direct Sales
05
online sales
10
Final customer sales
12
Sold for resale
14
Service
16
Factory sales
20
Store chain
22
Industrial customers
24
Pharm. customers
30
Internet Sales
40
New business
60
Direct Sales

Fig 20

We find many useful channels already existing. Since there is no restriction on using any of them, let us restrict ourselves to these and not create any new ones. We will use the existing 01 and 16 for our purpose in this course.

3. DIVISION (C)

Division is configured under the module Logistics general because it relates to products, not only to sales. Path:

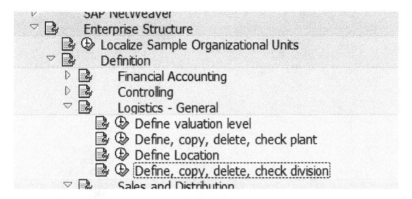

Fig 21

Choose Define Division so we can create one specific to our company's product line for example. Furniture:

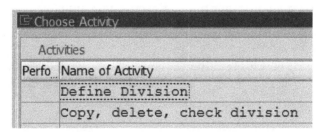

Fig 22

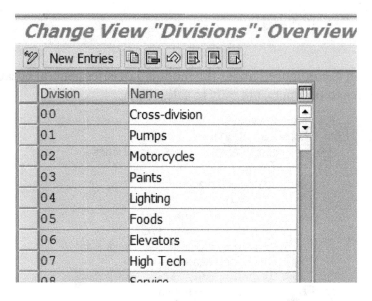

Fig 23

Click on New Entries

If we try to create another one with the same code, we get an error:

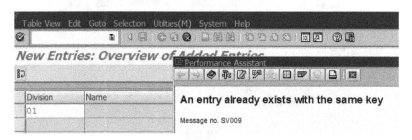

Fig 24

So, we create a new one using a code that has not been taken yet:

Click on ⬚ to release the columns for Entry:

Enter your code for the division and its description:

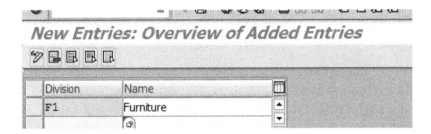

Fig 25

Hit Enter and Save:

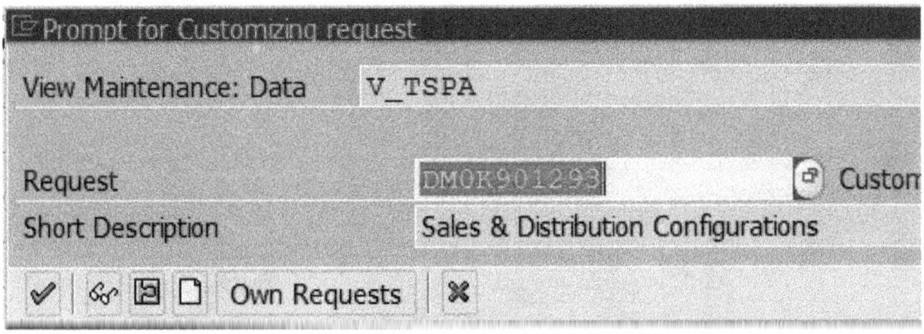

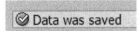

Fig 26

Save your data:

Fig 27

4. SALES OFFICE (C)

A sales office represents a geographical area which oversees the sales and distribution for the sales area. Since it is geographical and not functional, a sales office can be assigned to multiple sales areas. While it is not mandatory to have one, it is a very useful SD object as we will see later in the course so it is a good idea to set up at least one:

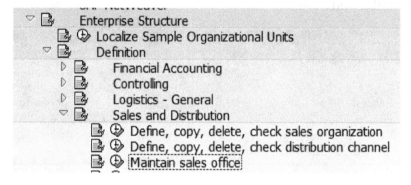

Fig 28

Again, click on New Entries and set up your sales office using a 4-digit alpha numeric code:

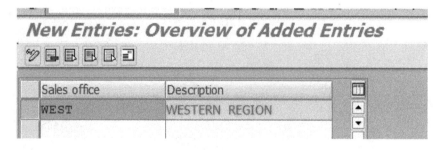

Fig 29

Hit Enter.

A window pops up asking you to enter the address:

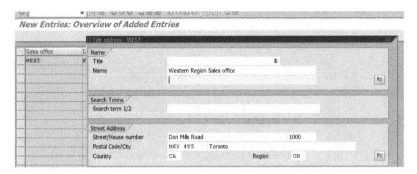

Fig 30

Hit Enter and Save.

5. SALES GROUP (C)

Companies often use Sales groups to represent employee/s that handle any business. Let us create one:

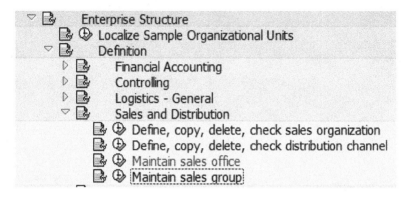

Fig 31

Fig 32

A sales group can be a 3-digit alpha numeric code:

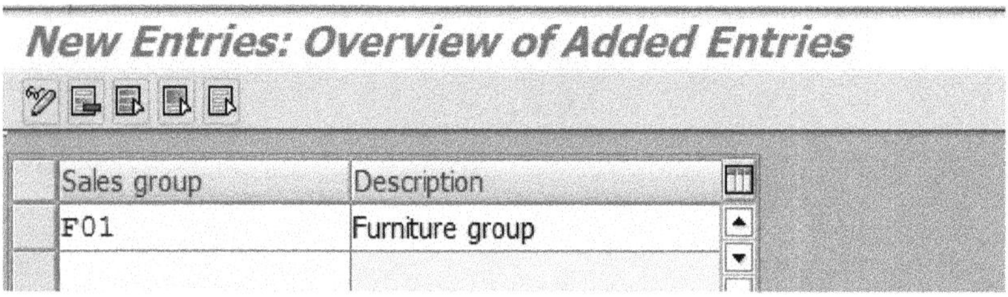

New Entries: Overview of Added Entries

Sales group	Description
F01	Furniture group

Fig 33

Save.

With this, we completed the basic organizational definitions of our sales and distribution module. In standard SAP, there is no limitation to how many sales areas one can have subject to if unique keys that can be used for the same.

6. PLANT (C)

Though a plant is a part of Logistics general, it is necessary for SD for some reasons:

- It is the org unit where stocks are kept fulfilling the sales orders
- It is the place from where taxes are calculated
- It is often a required address for transporters and shippers to show on the delivery notes and bills of lading when they pick up and transport goods to customers

Plant is configured in the path:

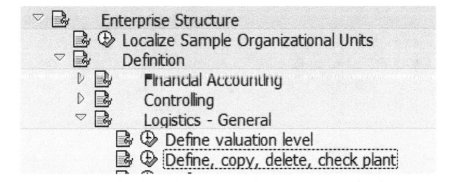

Fig 34

Fig 35

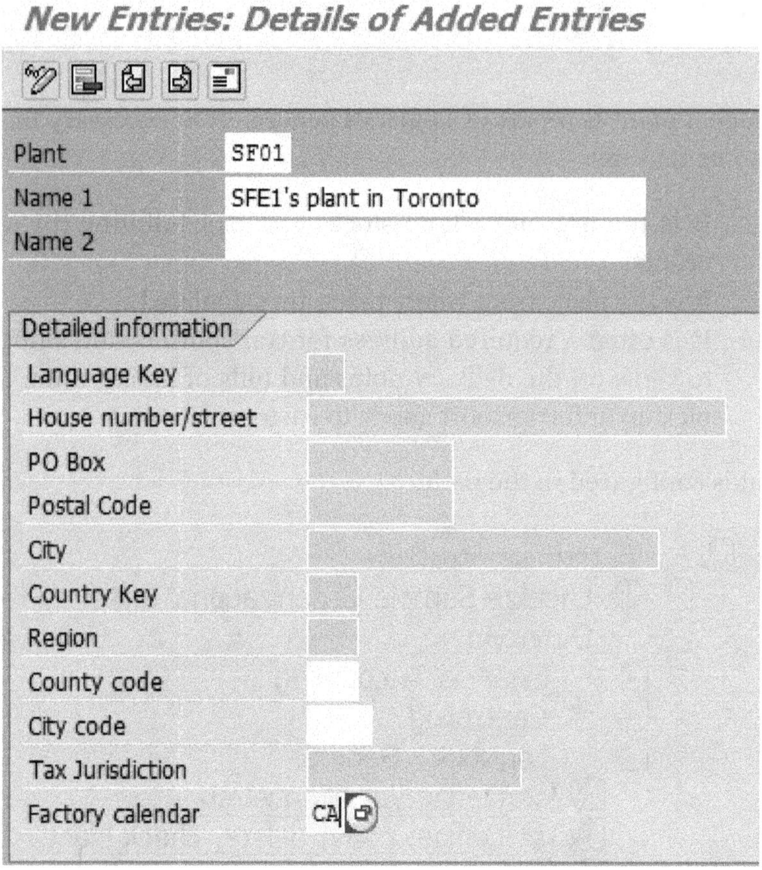

New Entries: Details of Added Entries

Plant	SF01
Name 1	SFE1's plant in Toronto
Name 2	

Detailed information

Language Key	
House number/street	
PO Box	
Postal Code	
City	
Country Key	
Region	
County code	
City code	
Tax Jurisdiction	
Factory calendar	CA

Fig 36

A plant requires a calendar for calculating delivery times so let us populate CA, Canada's calendar in it. Save and exit. If an address is asked for, enter as much as you can.

7. CREDIT CONTROL AREA (C)

CCA is a part of FI and used extensively in SD to finalize credit limits and exposures on customers. We will define one for our company:

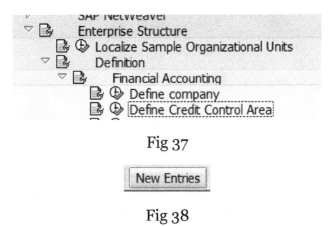

Fig 37

Fig 38

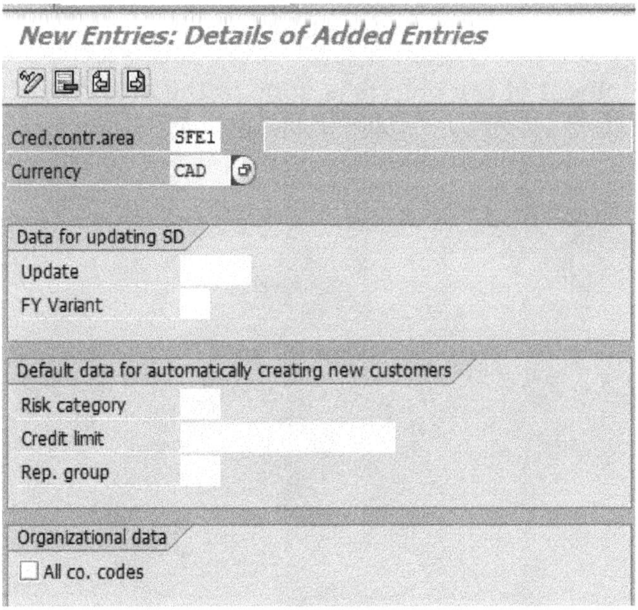

Fig 39

Save the object. We will re-visit this in more detail later.

ASSIGNMENTS OF ORG UNITS

The organizational units we created now need to be tied up with other objects and with each other so they can be used in SAP. Only then SAP can recognize their usage. The highest level of tie up is of linking the sales organization to the company code. Since the company code is set up in the Finance module, we will not set it up but instead, use a pre-existing one, and assign the sales org to it:

The assignment of org objects is done in the area Assignments in IMG:

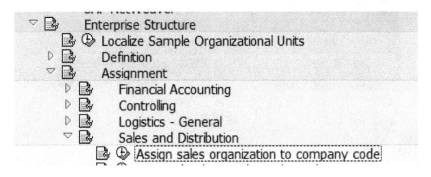

Fig 1

Using Position key 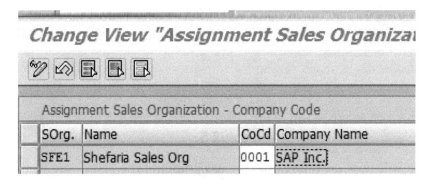 find our Sales org:

Fig 2

Replace 0001 with our new Co Cd (we see 0001 because we created our SO wrt the SO 0001):

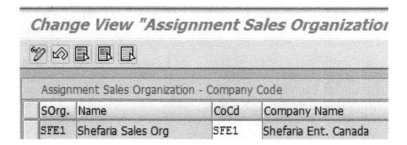

Fig 3

Save.

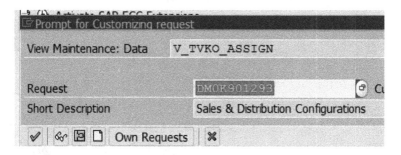

Fig 4

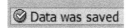

Fig 5

We will now do the rest of the assignments the same way in this order:

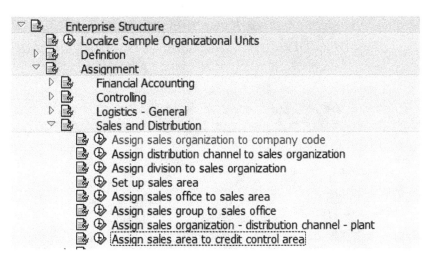

Fig 6

9. ASSIGN DISTRIBUTION CHANNEL TO SALES ORGANIZATION (C)

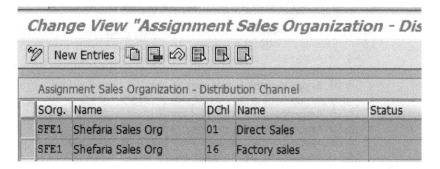

Fig 7

Save.

10. ASSIGN DIVISION TO DISTRIBUTION CHANNEL (C)

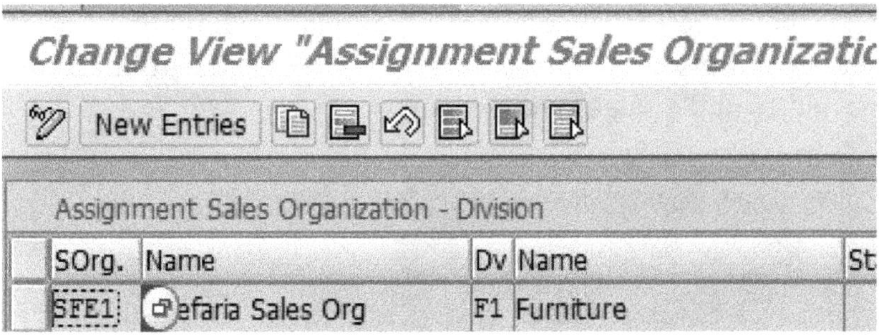

Change View "Assignment Sales Organizatic

New Entries

Assignment Sales Organization - Division

SOrg.	Name	Dv	Name	St
SFE1	efaria Sales Org	F1	Furniture	

Fig 8

Save

11. SET UP SALES AREA (C)

This is the highest level of organization relationship in SAP SD. Let us define our 2 sales areas because we have 2 distribution channels – 01 and 16 and a sales area is unique.

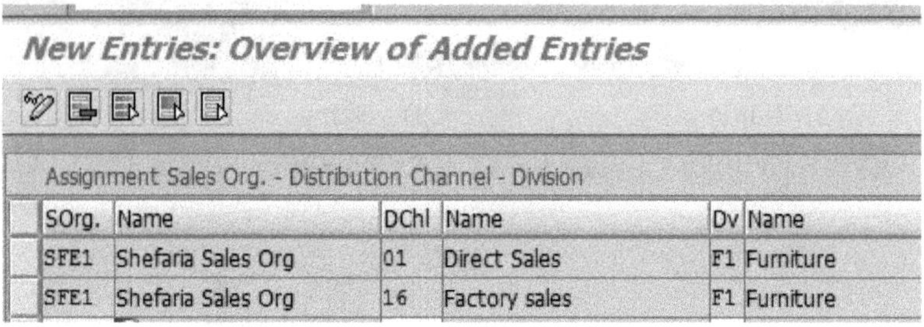

New Entries: Overview of Added Entries

Assignment Sales Org. - Distribution Channel - Division

SOrg.	Name	DChl	Name	Dv	Name
SFE1	Shefaria Sales Org	01	Direct Sales	F1	Furniture
SFE1	Shefaria Sales Org	16	Factory sales	F1	Furniture

Fig 9

Save.

12. ASSIGN SALES OFFICE TO SALES AREA (C)

Let's say our one sales office WEST will double up for both the sales areas so let us now assign it to both:

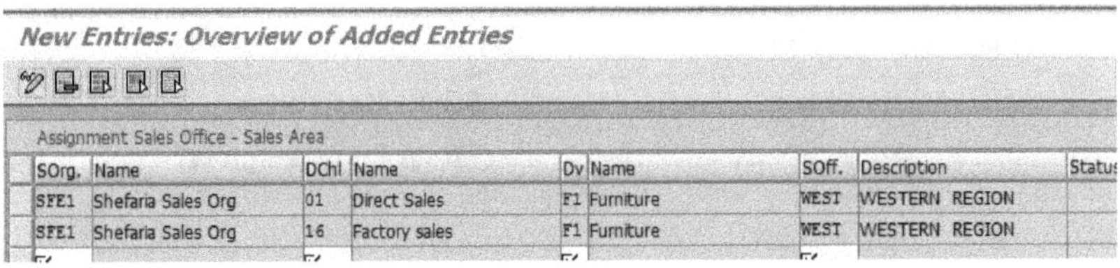

SOrg.	Name	DChl	Name	Dv	Name	SOff.	Description	Status
SFE1	Shefaria Sales Org	01	Direct Sales	F1	Furniture	WEST	WESTERN REGION	
SFE1	Shefaria Sales Org	16	Factory sales	F1	Furniture	WEST	WESTERN REGION	

New Entries: Overview of Added Entries

Assignment Sales Office - Sales Area

Fig 10

Save

13. ASSIGN SALES GROUP TO SALES OFFICE (C)

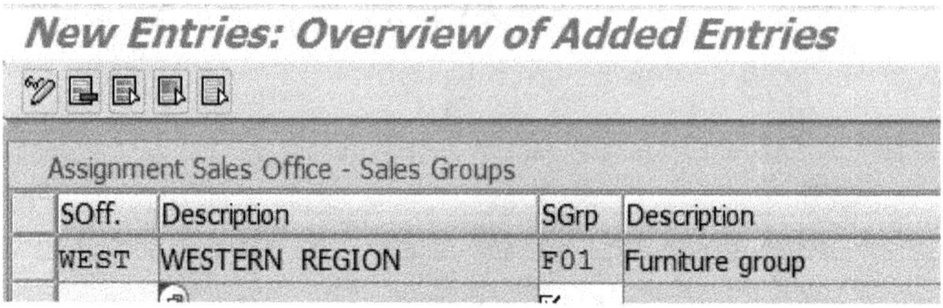

Fig 11

Save

14. ASSIGN SALES ORGANIZATION-DISTRIBUTION CHANNEL-PLANT (C)

SOrg.	Name	DChCust/Mt	Name	Plnt	Nai
		Assignment Sales Organization/Distribution Channel - Plant			
SFE1	Shefaria Sales Org	01	Direct Sales	SF01	
SFE1	Shefaria Sales Org	16	Factory sales	SF01	

Fig 12

15. ASSIGN SALES AREA TO CREDIT CONTROL AREA (C)

Scroll or search for your sales area and assign the CCA to it:

Fig 13

Save.

This completes our basic organizational assignments for SD and we are now ready to move to the actual SD elements.

MASTER DATA

Master data is a proposal of the most common or most expected data for any transaction. When the users create a transaction like a sales order, SAP proposes the necessary data from the customer master and material master which, for the most part, can be over written. The idea is that since it is the most often used data, it may not be required to enter it every time a transaction is created. This master data is usually created one time though it can be changed as needed. Since SAP requires data at every level, in SD, primarily at sales area level, it is necessary to maintain it so. To prevent maintenance of the same data at every sales area level, SAP provides the ability to 'replicate' this data from one distribution channel and division to the other DCs and divisions.

This is possible through configurations under the node Master data in Sales and Distribution module settings in IMG (C)

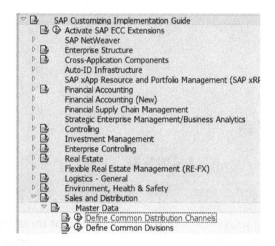

Fig 1

In the node Define Common Distribution Channels define the DCs:

Change View "Org.Unit: Dist.Channel per Sales Org.- Assign Master

SOrg.	DChl	Name	DCh-Conds	Name	DCh-Cust/Mt	Nam
SFE1		Direct Sales	01	Direct Sales	01	Direc
SFE1	16	Factory sales	16	Factory sales	16	Factc

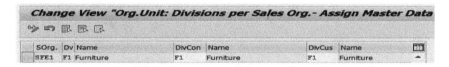

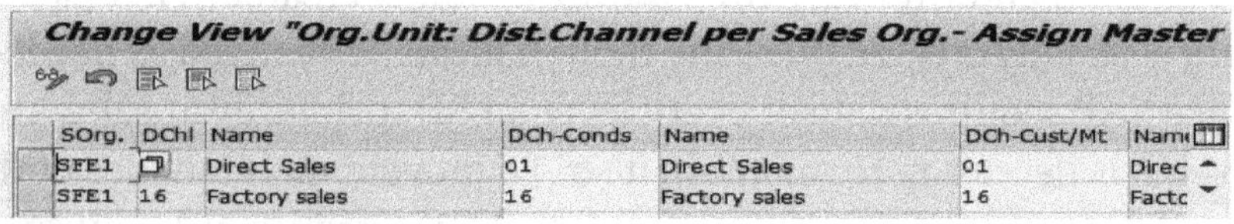

Fig 2

In the above configuration, we are asking SAP to use the pricing and material related data set up in SFE1-01 for all the other DCs also. Save.

Similarly, define the common division:

Change View "Org.Unit: Divisions per Sales Org.- Assign Master Data

SOrg.	Dv	Name	DivCon	Name	DivCus	Name
SFE1	F1	Furniture	F1	Furniture	F1	Furniture

Fig 3

Save.

CUSTOMER MASTER (C/U)

Customer Account groups

Customers in SAP are grouped into various grouping depending on their role vis-à-vis the vendor. A customer can be:

a) Sold to party – this is the highest level and the party regarded as the one with whom all the business transactions are done.
b) Ship to party – this is the customer where goods are shipped or services provided at
c) Bill to party – the one who will get invoiced
d) Payer – the one who will pay the invoice

In SAP, the sold to party can perform all the 4 functions. Apart from these 4, there can be other account groups like inter-company customers, one time customers, franchisees etc. New ones can be configured under financial accounting configurations.

The customer master in standard SAP is a composition of 3 distinct categories:

- General Data – this is the data specific to the customer and does not change whichever sales area the customer may be having business in.
- Company code data – this data stored information on the customer's banking records, who will be responsible for collections, payment methods, where the AR will post etc.
- Sales area data – the most important data for SD which can vary by each sales area. It contains information relating to pricing, credit, shipping etc.

Transaction XD01 or follow the path

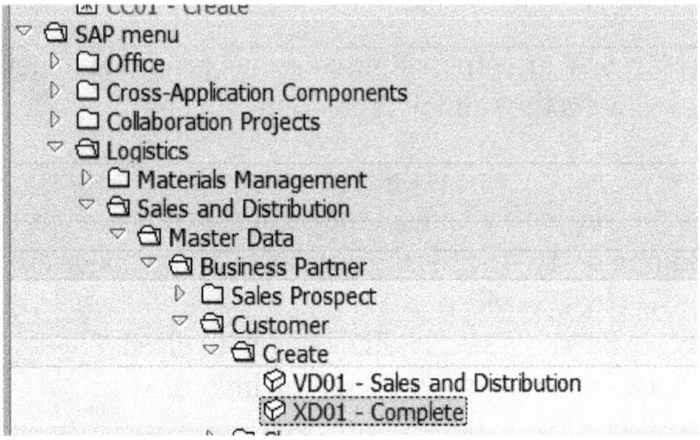

Fig 4

Since this is our first customer in SFE1-01-F1, enter the data as below and Hit Enter:

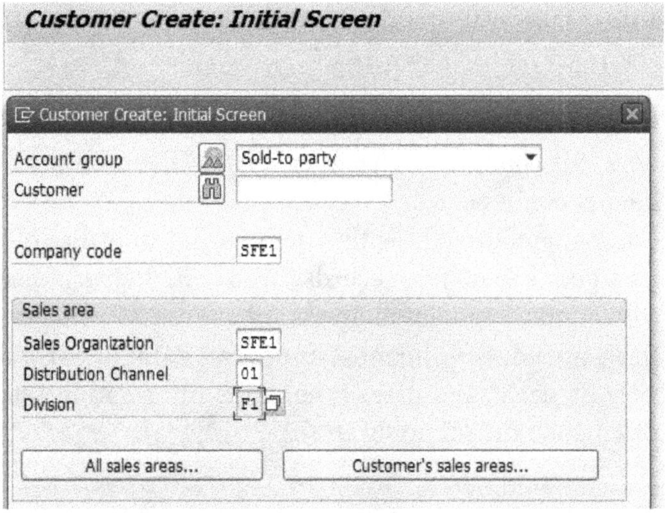

Fig 5

Alternatively, we can click on

All sales areas...

and select from among all the sales area that will come up in the window:

Sales Areas

Sales Org.	Name	Distr. Chl	Name	Division	Name
0001	Sales Org. Germany	01	Direct Sales	01	Pumps
0005	Germany Frankfurt	01	Direct Sales	00	Cross-division
0005	Germany Frankfurt	12	Sold for resale	00	Cross-division
0005	Germany Frankfurt	10	Final customer sales	00	Cross-division
0005	Germany Frankfurt	14	Service	00	Cross-division
0005	Germany Frankfurt	16	Factory sales	00	Cross-division
0006	USA Philadelphia	01	Direct Sales	00	Cross-division
0006	USA Philadelphia	12	Sold for resale	00	Cross-division
0006	USA Philadelphia	10	Final customer sales	00	Cross-division
0006	USA Philadelphia	14	Service	00	Cross-division
0007	Germany Frankfurt	01	Direct Sales	00	Cross-division

Sales Organization

Fig 6

General data

Give it a name and address:

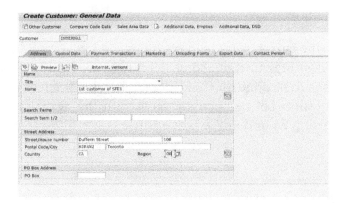

Fig 7

All the above different tabs belong to the general area data of the customer.

Sales Area Data

We can enter more data but since it is not necessary, we will proceed

to the sales area data **Sales Area Data**

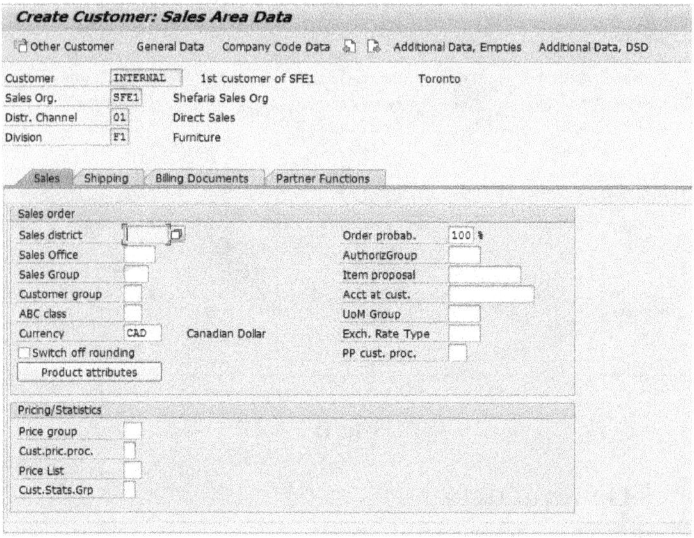

Fig 8

Note how the currency came in pre-populated. SAP could obtain it from the sales organization. Some fields here are very important for transactions to be done for the customer, notably pricing procedure and sales office. Let us populate them with the available data by selecting using F4 or doing a drop down:

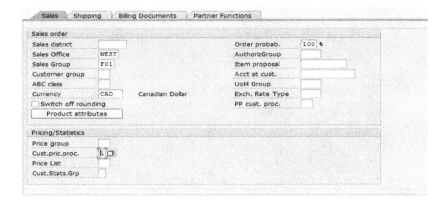

Fig 9

On the Shipping tab, enter some data that will help in delivering the goods for example. Plant and shipping conditions:

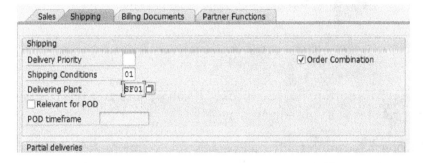

Fig 10

On the billing tab:

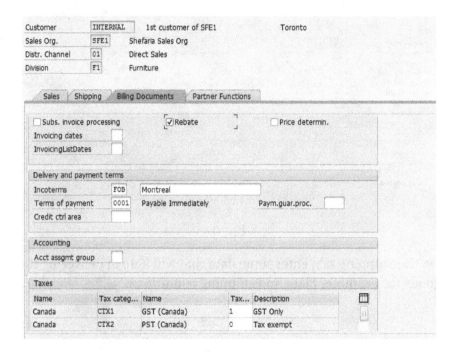

Fig 11

The rebate button must be checked if you want to give this customer any rebates at a subsequent date

Incoterms are internationally acceptable terms of shipping which essence, place the responsibility of the costs to the appropriate party

Terms of payment will determine when the customer will pay for the goods or services

Account assignment group is normally used by all companies to drive the G/L account to which this customer's revenue will be posted.

Tax classification will decide if the customer is taxable or not.

On partner function tab:

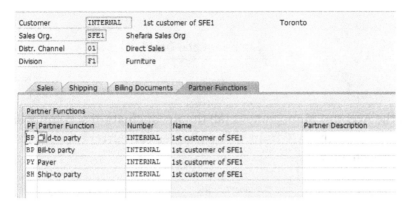

Fig 12

The account group is the main grouping under which the customer gets set up. What role the customer will play in the transaction is decided by the partner functions. We can set up the account groups in such a way that while a sold to may behave as sold to, ship to, payer and the bill to, a bill to can't behave as a ship to location. Or a ship to can't behave as a payer etc. thereby restricting their behavior in the system in terms of usage.

Company Code Data

Company Code Data

Fig 13

On the Account Management tab the Reconciliation account will be used to post the AR from this customer for current assets in the balance sheet:

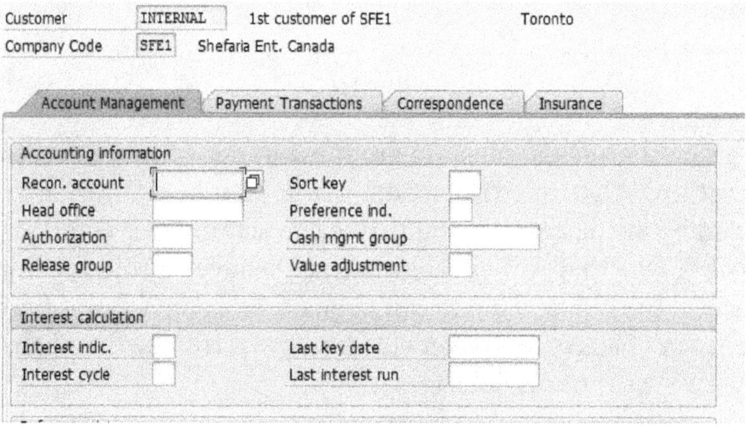

Fig 14

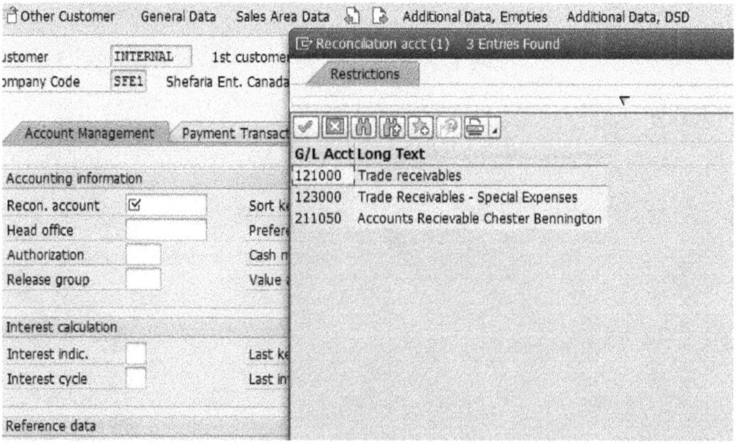

Fig 15

The rest of the 3 tabs carry data required from the financial and accounting angle and is usually the responsibility of the FI people to maintain. We will skip entering the data in these 3 other tabs – Payment transactions, Correspondence and Insurance.

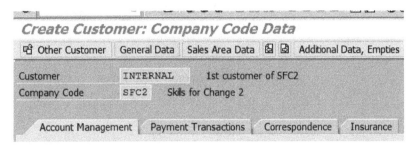

Fig 16

Save the customer.

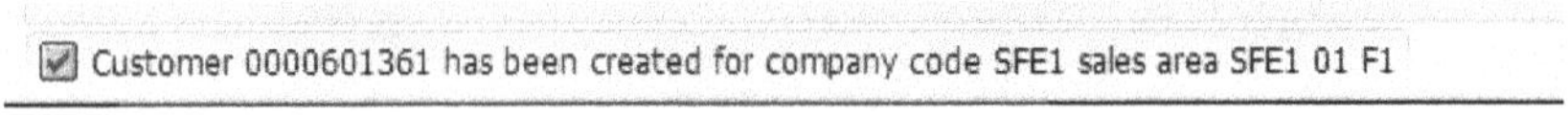

☑ Customer 0000601361 has been created for company code SFE1 sales area SFE1 01 F1

Fig 17

We can always go back and edit the data in XD02 or view it in XD03 centrally. To change or view only the sales area data, use VD02/VD03 respectively.

We now have our first customer ready to use subject to other configurations being complete.

MATERIAL MASTER (U)

We are now ready to create our first material and explore the fields and screens in the material master. The transaction to create a material is MM01 or follow the path:

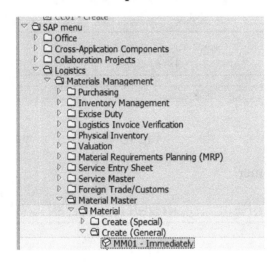

Fig 18

A typical screen will look like this:

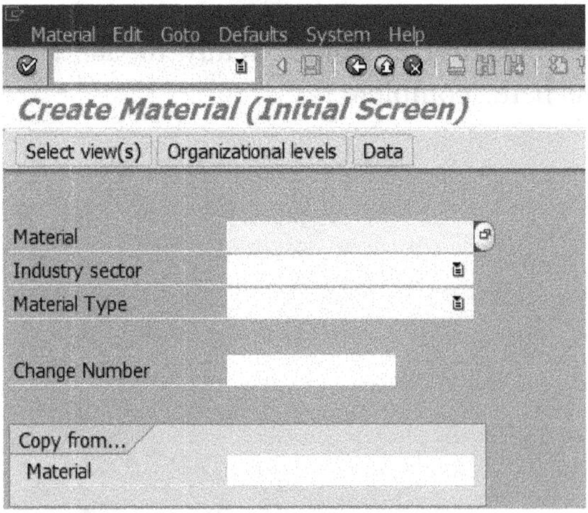

Fig 19

Choose the industry sector and material type (let's say FERT, finished goods):

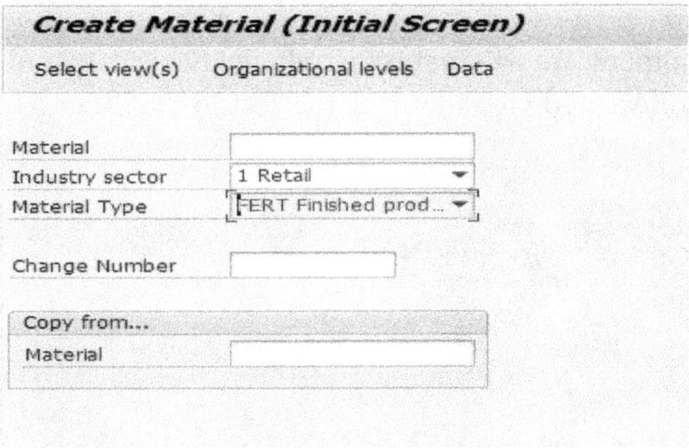

Create Material (Initial Screen)

Select view(s)   Organizational levels   Data

Material
Industry sector   1 Retail
Material Type   FERT Finished prod...

Change Number

Copy from...
Material

Fig 20

Hit Enter:

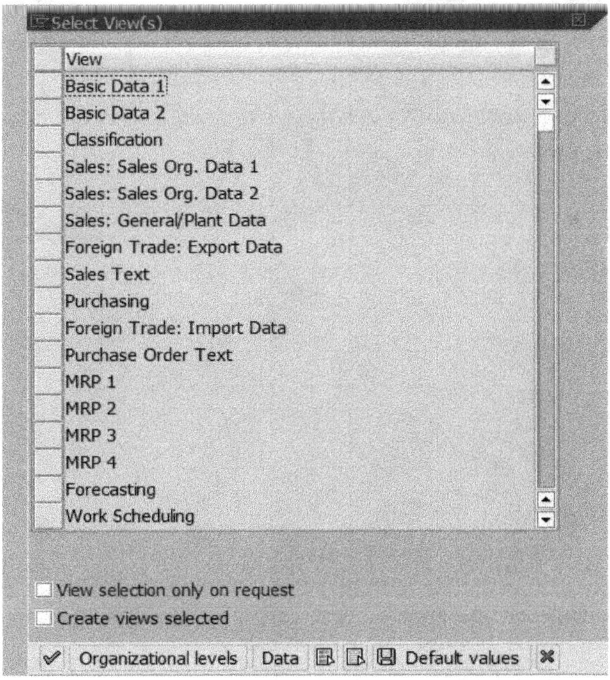

Select View(s)

View
Basic Data 1
Basic Data 2
Classification
Sales: Sales Org. Data 1
Sales: Sales Org. Data 2
Sales: General/Plant Data
Foreign Trade: Export Data
Sales Text
Purchasing
Foreign Trade: Import Data
Purchase Order Text
MRP 1
MRP 2
MRP 3
MRP 4
Forecasting
Work Scheduling

☐ View selection only on request
☐ Create views selected

✓ Organizational levels   Data Default values ✖

Fig 21

The above and more (available by scrolling down on the bar at the right) are the different screens available for different areas in a company to maintain data relevant to them.

For the moment, we will maintain only the Basic data and Sales and distribution related views leaving the rest to the other departments to fill.

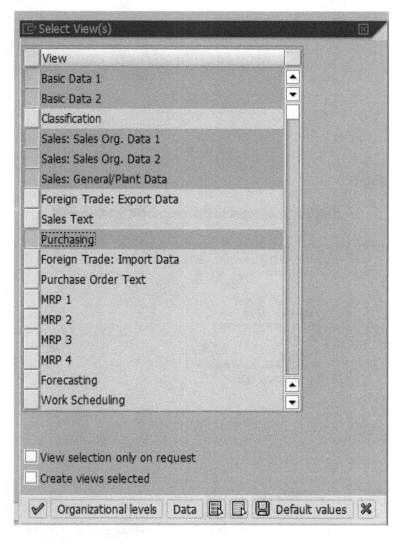

Fig 22

On clicking the green arrow, SAP will also ask to populate the plant/St Loc and sales org/DC:

Fig 23

Enter the data as below.

Tip: If you work in a certain sales org and DC most of the time, you can use the button [💾 Default values] to store your values as default values. The, when you come to the material master next time, it will auto-populate it with your default data:

Fig 24

Click on Enter to get into the first screen:

Basic data 1 & 2

Create Material 001000654 (Finished product)

⇨ Additional data   Organizational levels   Check screen data

| Basic data 1 | Basic data 2 | Classification | Sales: sales org. 1 | Sal |

Material   001000654

General data

Base Unit of Measure	☑		Material Group	☑	
Old material number			Ext. Matl Group		
Division			Lab/Office		
Product allocation			Prod.hierarchy		
X-plant matl status			Valid from		
☐ Assign effect. vals			GenItemCatGroup	NORM	Standard item

Dimensions/EANs

Gross Weight			Weight unit	KG
Net Weight				
Volume			Volume unit	
Size/dimensions				
EAN/UPC			EAN Category	

Packaging material data

| Matl Grp Pack.Matls | |

Fig 25

As we see, some fields are mandatory, marked with ☑ and some pre-populated which can be changed to other available values.

Basic Data 1 and Basic Data 2 are universal i.e. they always apply. We can't have the weight unit in kg for one sales org and in tons for another. We can define conversion units however and SAP will auto-convert to the appropriate unit in use.

Fill in as much data as you can:

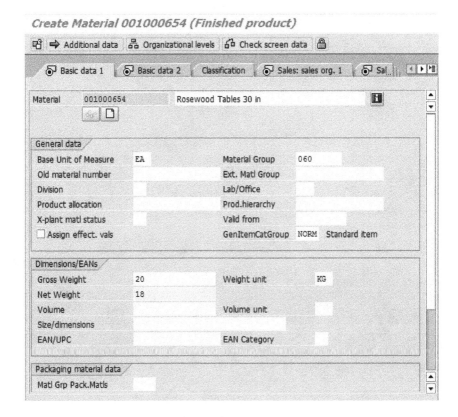

Fig 26

Filling the Division field will restrict this material to be sold only through that Division so best not to populate it.

It is not necessary to fill in all the data if it does not apply:

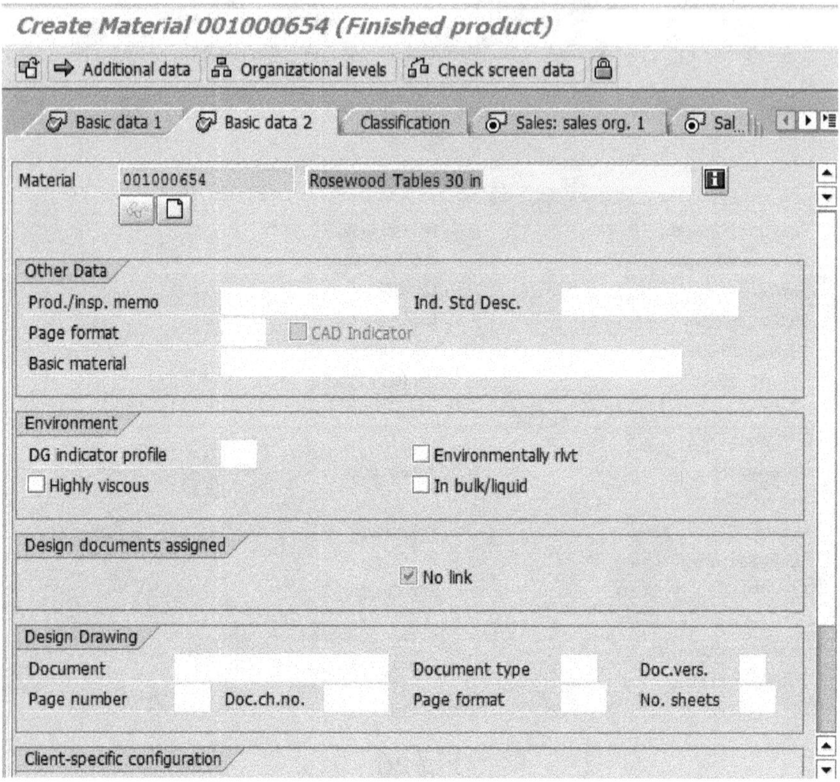

Create Material 001000654 (Finished product)

Additional data | Organizational levels | Check screen data

Basic data 1 | Basic data 2 | Classification | Sales: sales org. 1 | Sal

Material   001000654   Rosewood Tables 30 in

Other Data
Prod./insp. memo   Ind. Std Desc.
Page format   CAD Indicator
Basic material

Environment
DG indicator profile   ☐ Environmentally rlvt
☐ Highly viscous   ☐ In bulk/liquid

Design documents assigned
                   ☑ No link

Design Drawing
Document   Document type   Doc.vers.
Page number   Doc.ch.no.   Page format   No. sheets

Client-specific configuration

Fig 27

The indicator Material is configurable is an important check and used for materials that can be configured for example. computers, cars etc.

Sales Org 1

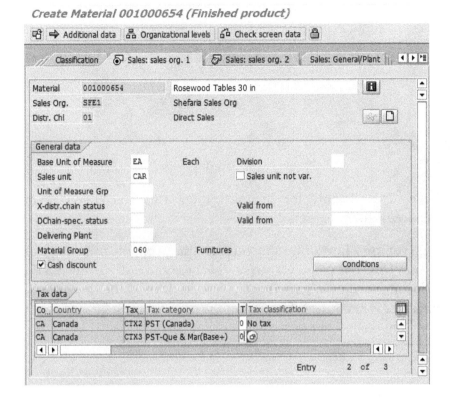

Create Material 001000654 (Finished product)

🔲 ⇒ Additional data 🔳 Organizational levels 🔲 Check screen data 🔒

| Classification | Sales: sales org. 1 | Sales: sales org. 2 | Sales: General/Plant | ◀ ▶ ⦙ |

Material   001000654   Rosewood Tables 30 in
Sales Org.   SFE1   Shefaria Sales Org
Distr. Chl   01   Direct Sales

General data

Base Unit of Measure	EA	Each	Division	
Sales unit	CAR		☐ Sales unit not var.	
Unit of Measure Grp				
X-distr.chain status		Valid from		
DChain-spec. status		Valid from		
Delivering Plant				
Material Group	060	Furnitures		

☑ Cash discount   [Conditions]

Tax data

Co.	Country	Tax	Tax category	T	Tax classification	
CA	Canada	CTX2	PST (Canada)	0	No tax	
CA	Canada	CTX3	PST-Que & Mar(Base+)	0		

                                        Entry   2 of 3

Fig 28

Important fields:

Sales unit – this may differ from the base unit. For example. a coke can may have a base unit EA, however, if it can be sold only in cartons of 12, then we would define the base unit as EA and the Sales unit as CAR. Then, in the ⇒ Additional data we would define the conversion factor/relationship between the two:

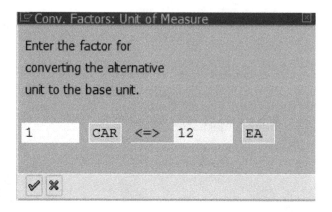

Fig 29

Note: This is only for demonstration, this conversion is not applicable to our material.

Delivering Plant: If we ship this material primarily from one plant or only from one plant, we can set that here and SAP will default that value in the sales orders. It can be over written at the time of order creation. What is necessary is that the material must be extended to the plant it is being replaced to.

Sales Org 2 data

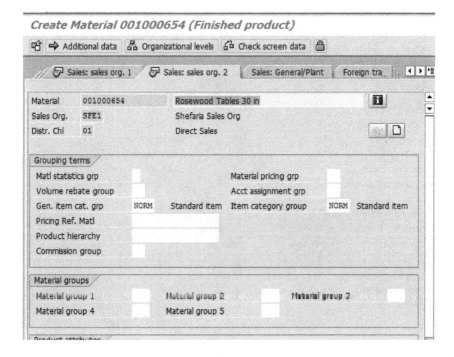

Fig 30

The most important field here it the Gen item category group and Item category group, they are used to determine how the product will be shipped, priced, copied from one SD document to another.

Acct assignment group: Is used to post the revenues of the material/service to the appropriate G/L accounts.

The other fields are informational but can be used to make the system behave in a certain way as required.

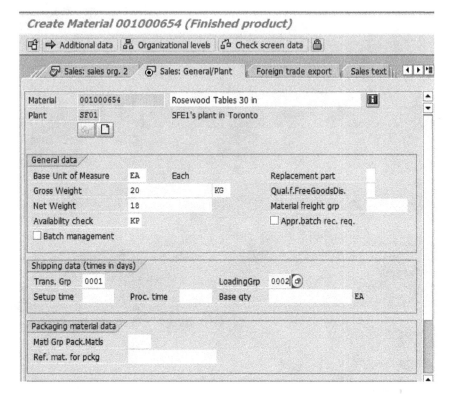

Fig 31

Availability check – with MRP (Materials resource planning) turned on, this is a key indicator to decide how procurement will take place, availability finalized and/or replenishments done. KP means no check required and we work on the premise that stocks will be available to order processing.

Transportation group – how the goods will be transported

Loading group – how they will be loaded onto the truck/ship etc. Both these groups play a pivotal role in the delivery and shipment process in our module.

Other fields as necessary. The serial number profile comes in handy for products that have serial numbering as differentiators e.g. engines, computers, machinery etc.

With the data we now need, we can save the material:

Material 001000654 created

Fig 32

Stock overview and posting

Now we have a customer and a finished product ready to be used together to create an order after we complete some other configurations relating to pricing and order management.

To use the material, we need to have sufficient quantity in stock. The stock of material can be checked using MMBE.

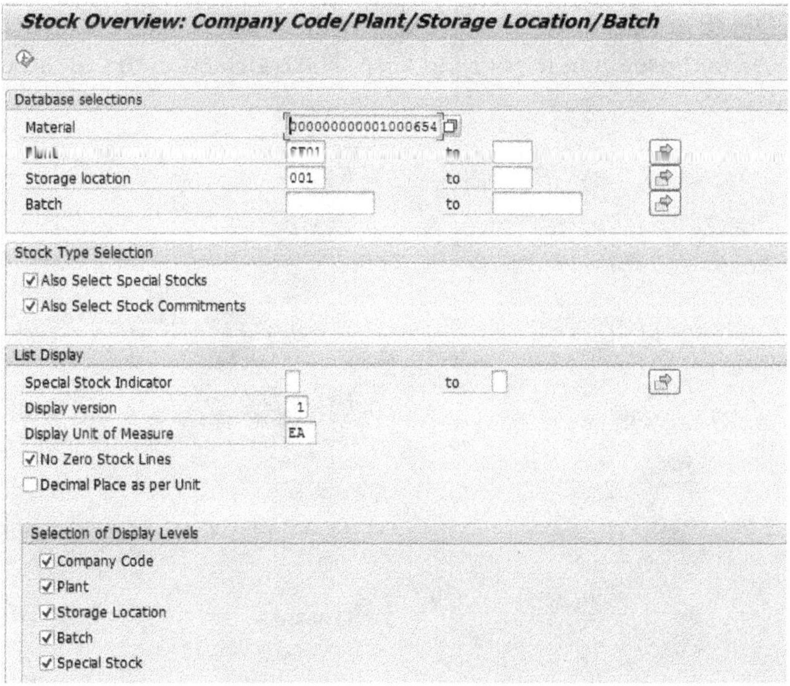

Stock Overview: Company Code/Plant/Storage Location/Batch

Database selections

Material	000000000001000654	
Plant	FT01	to
Storage location	001	to
Batch		to

Stock Type Selection

☑ Also Select Special Stocks
☑ Also Select Stock Commitments

List Display

Special Stock Indicator		to
Display version	1	
Display Unit of Measure	EA	

☑ No Zero Stock Lines
☐ Decimal Place as per Unit

Selection of Display Levels

☑ Company Code
☑ Plant
☑ Storage Location
☑ Batch
☑ Special Stock

Fig 33

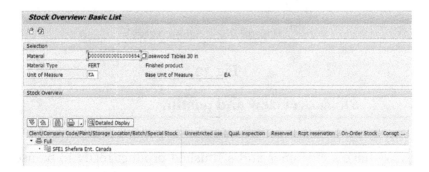

Fig 34

Since this is newly created material we do not have any stocks yet. While there are many ways of entering stocks – procurement and then a Goods receipt, production and then posting as finished goods via QM or even returns into stock, we will, in SD, post stocks directly in SAP and use them for our purpose. The transaction to post stocks is MB1C:

Enter Other Goods Receipts: Initial Screen

New Item   To Reservation...   To Order...   WM Parameters...

Document Date	12.05.2017	Posting Date	12.05.2017
Material Slip			
Doc.Header Text		GR/GI Slip No.	

Defaults for Document Items

Movement Type	561	Special Stock	
Plant	SF01	Reason for Movement	
Storage Location	0001	☐ Suggest Zero Lines	

GR/GI Slip

☐ Print

○ Individual Slip
◉ Indiv.Slip w.Inspect.Text
○ Collective Slip

Fig 35

70

The movement type 561 is a pre-requisite for this, most other movement types will not work. This mvt. Type is used for initial entries of stock for example. when a company goes live with SAP.

Hit Enter to step into the detailed screen:

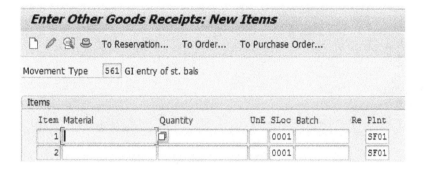

Fig 36

Enter the material and quantity you want to enter:

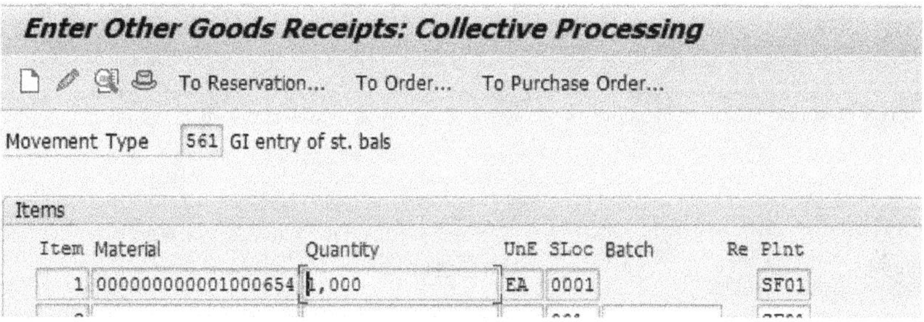

Fig 37

Hit Enter & Save:

Fig 38

One way to confirm stocks is to look in transaction MMBE. It is very useful for sales people to verify stocks and reservations before committing:

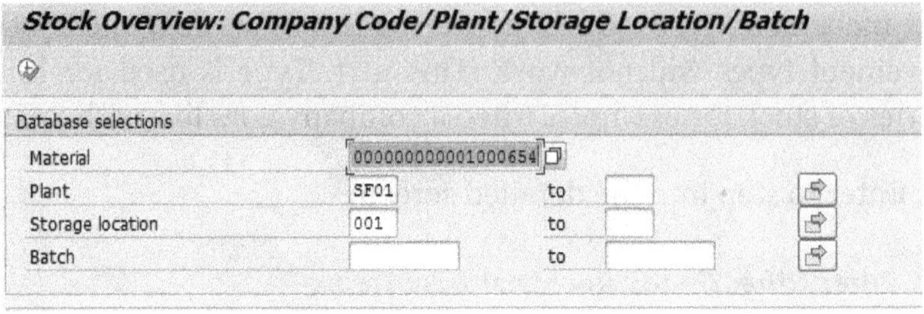
Stock Overview: Company Code/Plant/Storage Location/Batch
Database selections
Material
000000000001000654
Plant
SF01
to
Storage location
001
to
Batch
to

Fig 39

Execute:

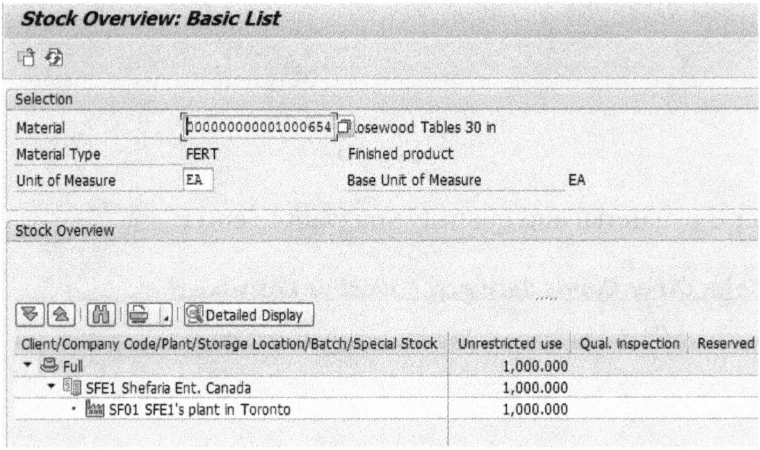
Stock Overview: Basic List
Selection
Material
000000000001000654
osewood Tables 30 in
Material Type
FERT
Finished product
Unit of Measure
EA
Base Unit of Measure
EA
Stock Overview
Detailed Display
Client/Company Code/Plant/Storage Location/Batch/Special Stock
Unrestricted use
Qual. inspection
Reserved
Full
1,000.000
SFE1 Shefaria Ent. Canada
1,000.000
SF01 SFE1's plant in Toronto
1,000.000

Fig 40

We notice our 1,000 tables stock is in unrestricted use.

The same is also visible in the material master – we can go there in MM03 or via MMBE:

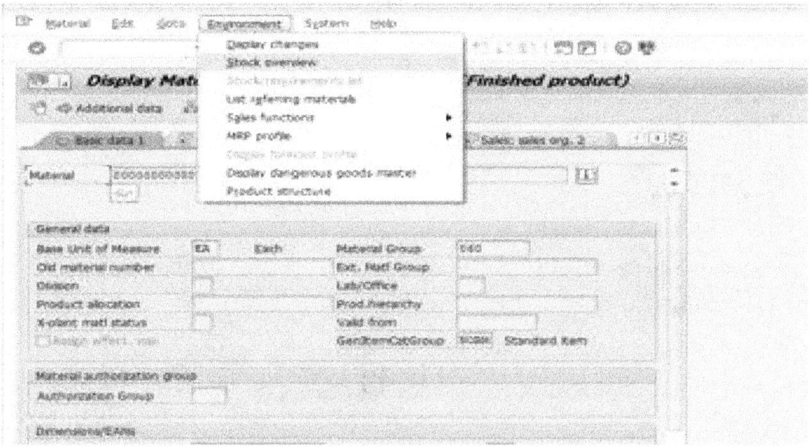

Fig 41

And then to the view:

Fig 42

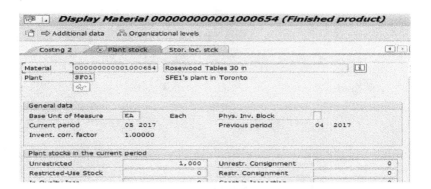

Fig 43

PRICING (U)

We now have a customer and a material. To sell it though, we need pricing. Though pricing can be entered manually in a sales order, volume of transactions often necessitate setting up of prices as master data also.

Pricing in SAP (as many other areas also) works on condition technique. We will visit this condition technique for configuration purposes in more detail later under the sub-module Pricing. For the moment, we will create a simple price in the system to create a sales order and see how all our data till now comes together.

The transaction code to create pricing is VK11 or follow the path:

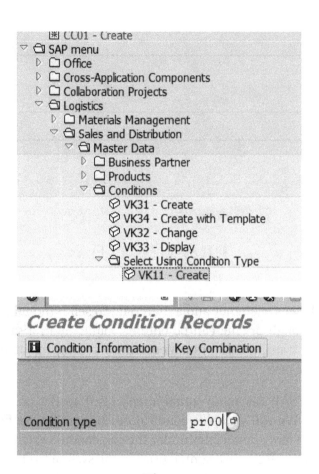

Fig 1

Hit Enter and choose the 3rd radio button:

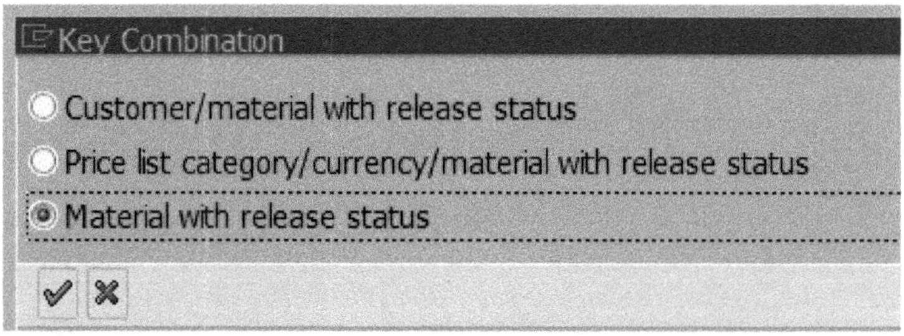

Fig 2

Enter the data as below:

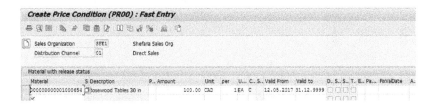

Fig 3

Just entering the SO, DC, material code (it is not necessary to enter the leading zeros) and the Amount is sufficient. The system determines the rest of the data.

Save this 'condition record':

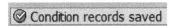

Fig 4

We now have a customer, material with stocks and the price we will sell at.

SALES ORDER PROCESSING IN SD (C/U)

This is one of the biggest sub-areas in SD and from where the SD process begins with a sales document. The order type will define, directly and indirectly, how the transaction will be handled in SD-LE from the perspective of order fulfilment, delivery and invoicing. To look at a few kinds of sales document types, in SPRO follow the path (or use t code VOV8):

1. ORDER TYPES – HEADER (C)

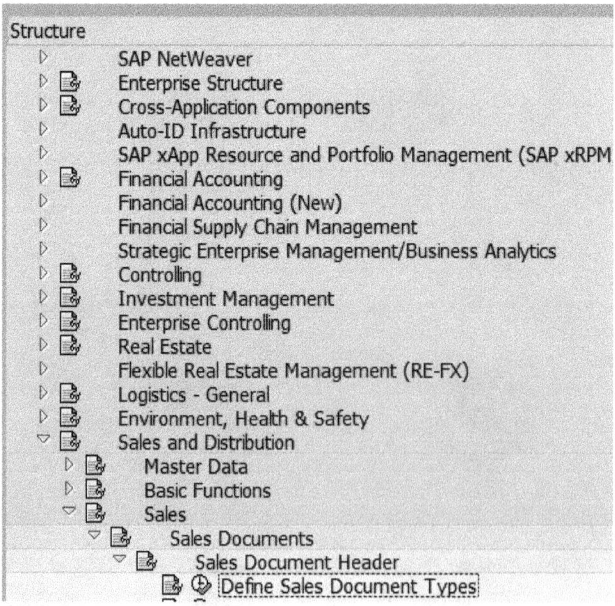

Structure
- ▷ SAP NetWeaver
- ▷ Enterprise Structure
- ▷ Cross-Application Components
- ▷ Auto-ID Infrastructure
- ▷ SAP xApp Resource and Portfolio Management (SAP xRPM
- ▷ Financial Accounting
- ▷ Financial Accounting (New)
- ▷ Financial Supply Chain Management
- ▷ Strategic Enterprise Management/Business Analytics
- ▷ Controlling
- ▷ Investment Management
- ▷ Enterprise Controlling
- ▷ Real Estate
- ▷ Flexible Real Estate Management (RE-FX)
- ▷ Logistics - General
- ▷ Environment, Health & Safety
- ▽ Sales and Distribution
  - ▷ Master Data
  - ▷ Basic Functions
  - ▽ Sales
    - ▽ Sales Documents
      - ▽ Sales Document Header
        - Define Sales Document Types

Fig 1

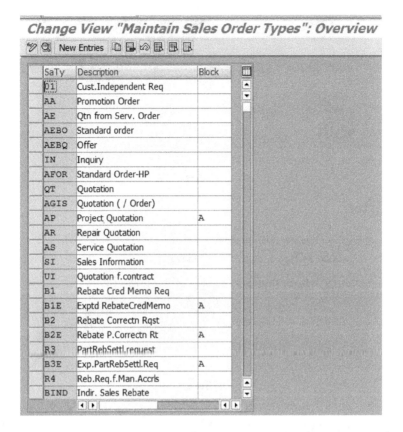

Fig 2

In detail screen of each document there is more data that will tell us about the usage and behavior of each document type.

In SAP, a standard order is abbreviated as 'OR'. Let us find it using the Position Key or scrolling down to it:

Fig 3

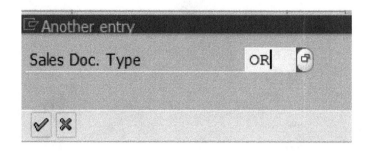

Fig 4

Hit Enter:

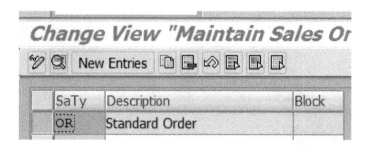

Fig 5

Highlight the line and click on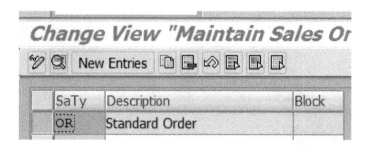

Change View "Maintain Sales Order Types": Details

New Entries

Sales Document Type	OR	Standard Order			
SD document categ.	C		Sales document block		
Indicator					

Number systems

No.range int.assgt.	01		Item no.increment	10
No. range ext. assg.	02		Sub-item increment	10

General control

Reference mandatory			Material entry type	
Check division			☑ Item division	
Probability	100		☑ Read info record	
Check credit limit	D		Check purch.order no	
Credit group	01		☐ Enter PO number	
Output application	V1		Commitment date	

Transaction flow

Screen sequence grp.	AU	Sales Order	Display Range	UALL
Incompl.proced.	11	Sales Order	FCode for overv.scr.	UER1
Transaction group	0	Sales order	Quotation messages	B
Doc. pric. procedure	A		Outline agrmt mess.	B
Status profile			Message: Mast.contr.	
Alt.sales doc. type1			ProdAttr.messages	
Alt.sales doc. type2			☐ Incomplet.messages	
Variant				

Fig 6

Scheduling agreement

Corr.delivery type			Delivery block	
Usage				
MRP for DlvSchType				

Shipping

Delivery type	LF	Delivery	Immediate delivery	
Delivery block				
Shipping conditions				
ShipCostInfoProfile	STANDARD	Standard freight information		

Billing

Dlv-rel.billing type	F2	Invoice (F2)	CndType line items	EK02
Order-rel.bil.type	F2	Invoice (F2)	Billing plan type	
Intercomp.bil.type	IV	Intercompany billing	Paymt guarant. proc.	01
Billing block			Paymt card plan type	03
			Checking group	01

Requested delivery date/pricing date/purchase order date

Lead time in days			☑ Propose deliv.date
Date type			☐ Propose PO date
Prop.f.pricing date			
Prop.valid-from date			

Fig 7

81

Contract			
PricProcCondHeadr		Contract data allwd.	🔄
PricProcCondItem		FollUpActivityType	
Contract profile		Subseq.order type	
Billing request	DR	Check partner auth.	A
Group Ref. Procedure		☐ Update low.lev.cont.	

Availability check		
Business transaction	OR	Sales Order

Fig 8

A typical configuration screen of a sales document type has many fields as we notice above. Many of them are self-explanatory and for those that require more explanation, position the cursor in the field and click on F1 to display a Help window.

For the most part, standard SAP will be able to meet the requirements but if we desire to have our own order type, we can do so, with the only restrictions being that the code should begin with a 9, Y or Z otherwise it may get overwritten when we upgrade to a different version of SAP.

The different document types exist for different purposes:

- A standard order for a typical and most common sales order from the customers, and would typically have a value
- A Rush order which will 'shortcut' the delivery process and pick up the product without extra/manual intervention
- A quotation which can be given to the customers if they desire so
- A debit memo request or a credit memo request which are created to provide the customers with the credit or debits for price differences, quantity differences etc. This request is converted into actual credit and debit in the billing process of SD.
- Scheduling agreement which is an arrangement or a forecast of the shipping of goods or provision of services that will take place for agreed quantities at pre-agreed times

- Some special purpose ones like inquiries, consignment orders and fulfilments, replenishments and pick-ups.

2. NUMBERING OF SD DOCUMENTS (C)

Driven by the field Number range assignments, these codes (here, 01 and 02) are given an actual series of numbers they would follow when an order type OR is created as an example below.

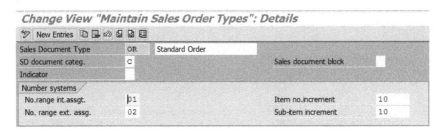

Fig 9

This numbering is done in transaction VN01 or by following the path:

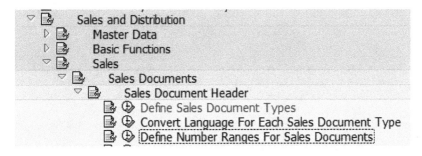

Fig 10

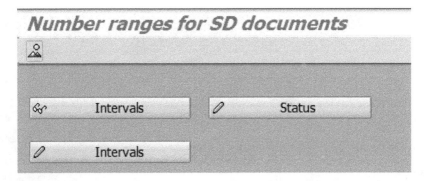

Fig 11

One is a display interval, other to change the intervals and the 3rd to merely view the status. Click on Change interval

Fig 12

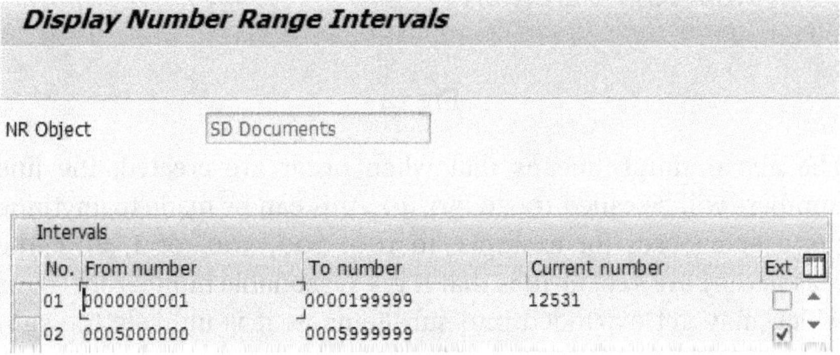

Display Number Range Intervals

NR Object   SD Documents

Intervals

No.	From number	To number	Current number	Ext
01	0000000001	0000199999	12531	☐
02	0005000000	0005999999		☑

Fig 13

Thus, we notice that for internal number range (numbering being done within SAP), the latest order # was 12531. Thus, the next will be 12532. The check box Ext means the numbering is not being done within SAP but external data is flowing into SAP and SAP is 'accepting' whatever is coming in. This is useful when an order taking software is outside of SAP but its processing will be done within SAP. In such cases, the order # is created elsewhere and fed into SAP with the same number tor better tracking.

The numbering sequences can be modified or new ones added via the button ⊞ Interval. Any sequence will work so long as:

1. It is within the min and max # of digits allowed

2. It is not repeated as 2 different sequences can't have an overlap to avoid redundancy

85

The numbering defined above applies to the order number i.e. the header of the order. In an order, in standard SAP, there can be up to 999 lines. Each of those lines also need to be separated from each other. That is done by giving them numbers. The increments these numbers will take are decided by

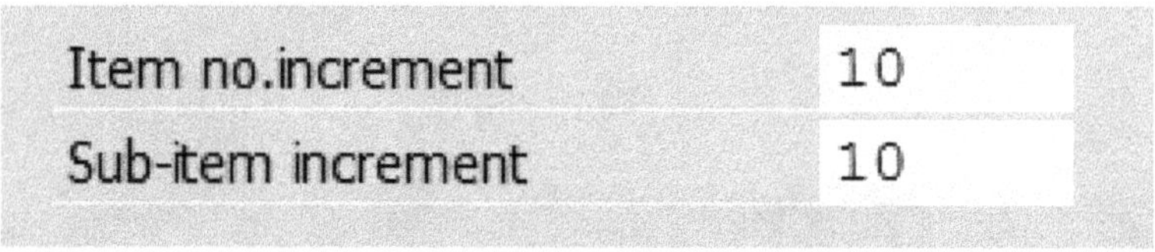

Item no.increment	10
Sub-item increment	10

Fig 14

The above simply means that when order are created, the line numbers will be called 10, 20, 30, 40...this can be made to anything the user chooses for example. to 100, 200, 300...or 1, 2, 3...the reason they are kept at 10 is that it is a reasonable number for items which may get expanded into sub-items as it is unlikely the sub-items would be more than 10. However, it is need based and can be increased or decreased as necessary.

3. PURCHASE ORDER TYPES (C)

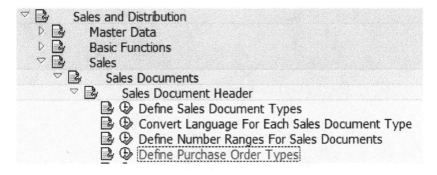

Fig 15

These are the ways the customers will place their purchase orders on the sales department. A few standard SAP types are provided. More can be created:

Pur. ord. type	Description
DFUE	Data Transfer
MUEN	Orally
SCHR	Written
TELE	By telephone

Fig 16

4. ORDER REASONS (C)

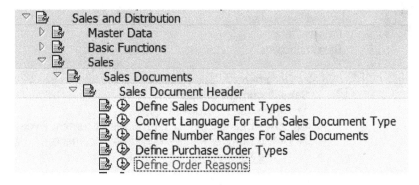

Fig 17

Often, companies will make this a mandatory field to fill in the order when a user requests a credit. These reasons are defined in the above configuration path and SAP provides a few standard ones:

Change View "Sales Documents: Order Reasons": Overvie

New Entries

Order reason	R	Description
000		Internet OK
001		Sales call
002		Trade fair sales activity
003		Television commercial
004		Customer recommendation
005		Newspaper advertisement
006		Excellent price
007		Fast delivery
008		Good service
100		Price discrepancy: price was too high
101		Poor quality
102		Damaged in transit
103		Quantity discrepancy
104		Material ruined
105		Free of charge sample

Fig 18

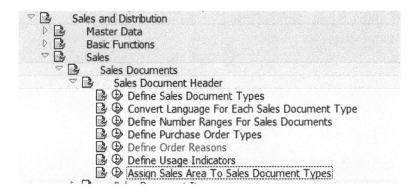

Fig 19

Unless this assignment is done, a sales area can't use the order type. Thus, for our sales area to be able to create a standard order, the order type OR must be attached to it in this configuration:

Choose Activity	
Activities	
Perfo	Name of Activity
	Combine sales organizations
	Combine distribution channels
	Combine divisions
	Assign sales order types permitted for sales areas

Fig 20

In the first activity, we assign our sales org to a reference sales org which is usually itself. The idea of this is to use this same setting for any more sales orgs that we may set up in the future. This the reference SO will become the 'parent' SO of the subsequent SOs thereby preventing unnecessary configs. Find the SO we are using in this training:

Change View "Sales Organizations - Assign Order Type": Overview

SOrg.	Name	Ref. SOrg	Name	
SFE1	Shefaria Sales Org	1000	Shefaria Sales Org	
SL31	USA Los Angeles	SL31	USA Los Angeles	

89

Fig 21

It currently shows 1000 as the Ref SOrg because we copied 1000 into SFE1 at the latter's time of creation. Now, we will replace 1000 with SFE1 and save:

SOrg.	Name	Ref. SOrg	Name
SFE1	Shefaria Sales Org	SFE1	Shefaria Sales Org

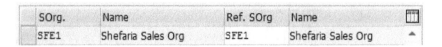

Fig 22

A message at the bottom may indicate:

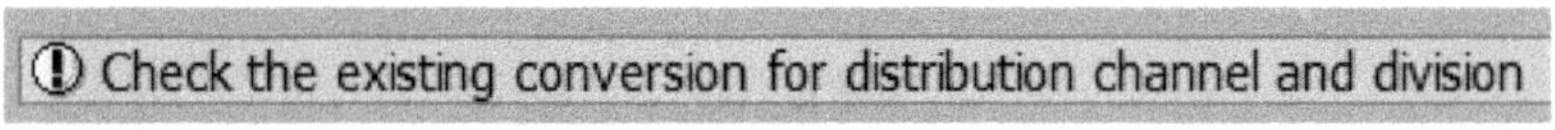

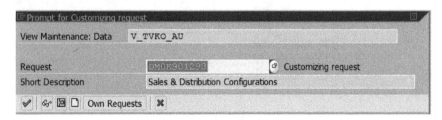

Fig 23

We will do these configs in the next 2 activities.

Save the change from 1000 to SFE1.

Fig 24

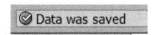

Fig 25

Let us repeat the same steps for the DC and Div also:

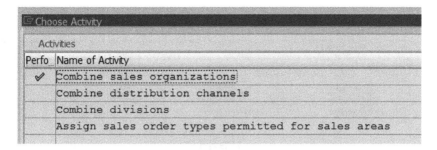

Fig 26

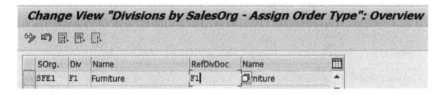

Fig 27

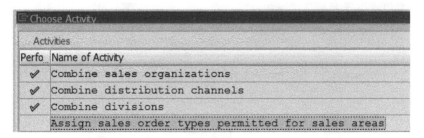

Fig 28

Lastly, we attach the sales area to the order types we will be using:

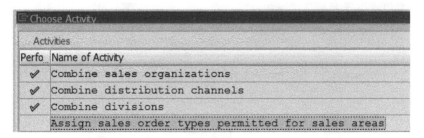

Fig 29

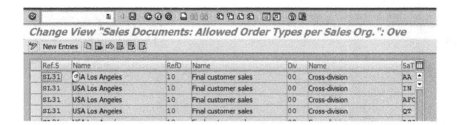

Fig 30

Click on ![New Entries] and make the entries we need, for the moment, let's say to order types IN, QT, OR, CR, DR, RE, RO.

New Entries: Overview of Added Entries

	Ref.S	RefD	Name	Div	Name	SaTy	Description	
	SFE1	01	Direct Sales	F1	Furniture	IN	Inquiry	
	SFE1	16	Factory sales	F1	Furniture	IN	Inquiry	
	SFE1	01	Direct Sales	F1	Furniture	QT	Quotation	
	SFE1	16	Factory sales	F1	Furniture	QT	Quotation	
	SFE1	01	Direct Sales	F1	Furniture	CR	Credit Memo Reques	
	SFE1	16	Factory sales	F1	Furniture	CR	Credit Memo Reques	
	SFE1	01	Direct Sales	F1	Furniture	DR	Debit Memo Request	
	SFE1	16	Factory sales	F1	Furniture	DR	Debit Memo Request	
	SFE1	01	Direct Sales	F1	Furniture	RE	Returns	
	SFE1	16	Factory sales	F1	Furniture	RE	Returns	
	SFE1	01	Direct Sales	F1	Furniture	RO	Rush Order	
	SFE1		Factory sales	F1	Furniture	RO	Rush Order	

Fig 31

Prompt for Customizing request

View Maintenance: D...	V_TVAKZ	
Request	DM0K901433	Customizing request
Short Description	Nkowa & Son's finished material	

Fig 32

6. PRICING PROCEDURE DETERMINATION (C)

Before we can get into a position to use these order types so configured in our sales areas SFE1/01/F1 and SFC2/16/F1 we must make one last bit of configuration. While pricing itself will be discussed in greater detail later in this course, at this point we merely allow our sales area to use a process of pricing, called 'pricing procedure' in SAP.

This step is in the path:

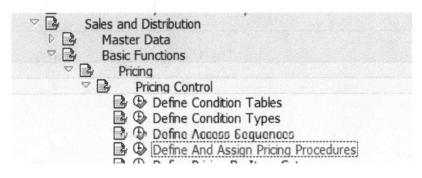

Fig 33

```
Choose Activity

  Activities

Perfo  Name of Activity
       Maintain pricing procedures
       Define customer pricing procedure
       Define document pricing procedure
       Assign document pricing procedures to order types
       Assign document pricing procedures to billing types
       Define Pricing Procedure Determination
       Check Settings for Pricing Procedures
```

Fig 34

SOrg.	DChl	Dv	DoPr	CuPP	PriPr.	Pricing procedure	CTyp	Condition type
SFE1	01	F1	A	1	ZRVA01	PP for Direct & Factor	ZPR1	Base Price

Fig 35

Save.

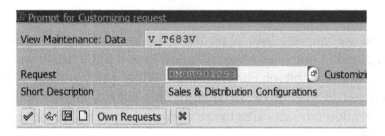

Fig 36

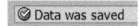

Fig 37

SALES ORDER (U)

1. SALES ORDER CREATION

We are now ready to create our first sales order in SAP. To do this, use transaction code VA01 or follow the path:

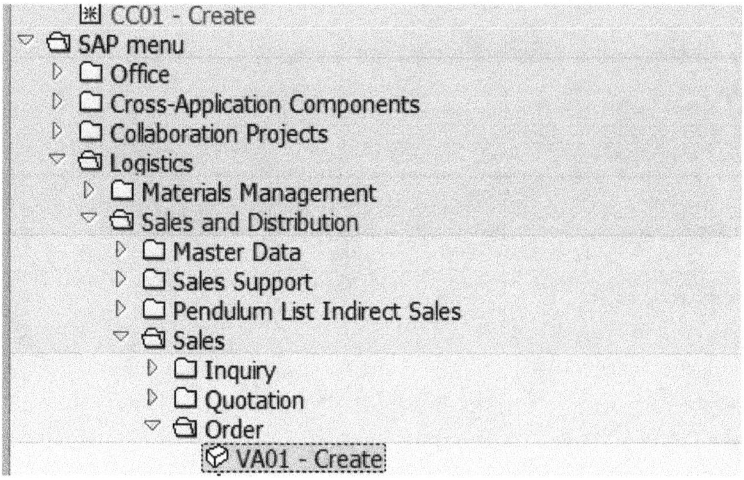

```
      ⊞ CC01 - Create
  ▽ 🗁 SAP menu
      ▷ 🗀 Office
      ▷ 🗀 Cross-Application Components
      ▷ 🗀 Collaboration Projects
      ▽ 🗁 Logistics
          ▷ 🗀 Materials Management
          ▽ 🗁 Sales and Distribution
              ▷ 🗀 Master Data
              ▷ 🗀 Sales Support
              ▷ 🗀 Pendulum List Indirect Sales
              ▽ 🗁 Sales
                  ▷ 🗀 Inquiry
                  ▷ 🗀 Quotation
                  ▽ 🗁 Order
                      ⊘ VA01 - Create
```

Fig 1

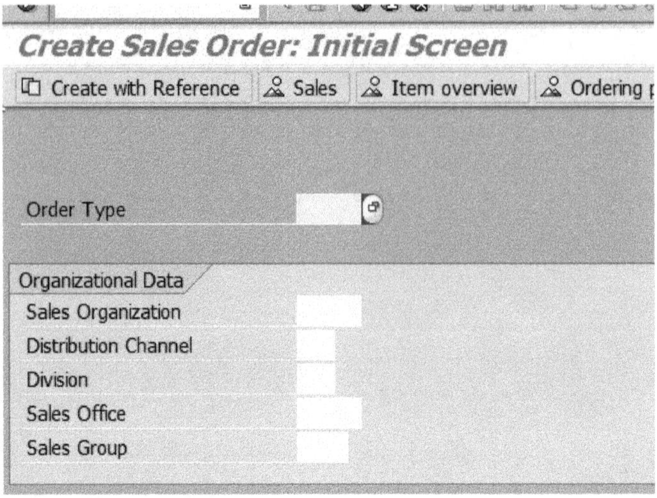

Create Sales Order: Initial Screen

Create with Reference   Sales   Item overview   Ordering

Order Type

Organizational Data
- Sales Organization
- Distribution Channel
- Division
- Sales Office
- Sales Group

Fig 2

The order type is a mandatory field as we see and if we recall, we are currently limited to a few order types we configured with our sales areas. Here, we will use one of them, standard order, OR to create a sales order. Enter the order type and/or the sales area on this screen:

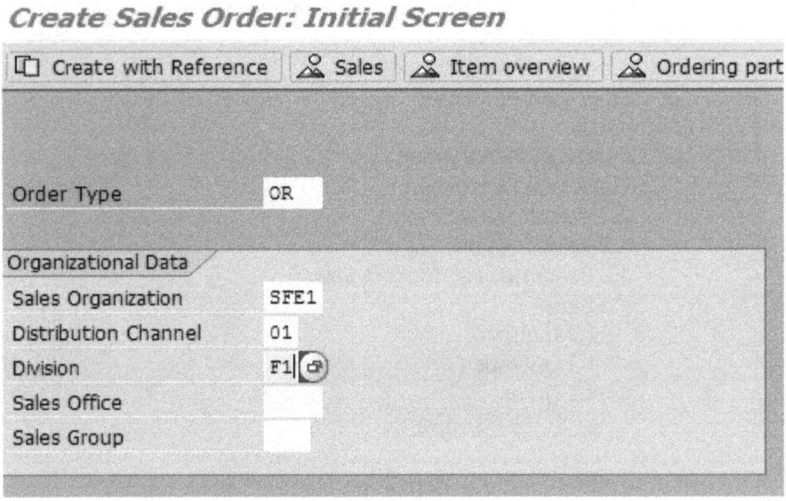

Create Sales Order: Initial Screen

Create with Reference   Sales   Item overview   Ordering part

Order Type   OR

Organizational Data
- Sales Organization   SFE1
- Distribution Channel   01
- Division   F1
- Sales Office
- Sales Group

Fig 3

Hit Enter.

A blank screen opens:

Create Standard Order: Overview

Standard Order				Net value		0.00	
Sold-to party							
Ship-to party							
PO Number				PO date			

| Sales | Item overview | Item detail | Ordering party | Procurement | Shipping | Reason for rejection |

Req. deliv.date	D	15.05.2017		Deliver.Plant	
☐ Complete dlv.				Total Weight	0.000
Delivery block				Volume	0.000
Billing block				Pricing date	15.05.2017
Payment card				Exp.date	
Payment terms				Incoterms	
Order reason					
Sales area	SFE1 / 01 / F1	Shefaria Sales Org, Direct Sales, Furniture			

All items

Item	Material	Order Quantity	SU	Description	S	Customer Material Numb	ItCa

Fig 4

To create an order, SAP needs a lot of data, most of which will default from the customer and material masters, the rest from the configurations. At the minimum, depending on how this data is organized, SAP requires us to enter the sold to party, the material # and quantity as these are the real variables that can change from order to order. All the rest of the data is linked to the sold to and material in some way or the other. Let us then enter our sold to, material # and the order quantity in the respective fields:

Create Standard Order: Overview

Standard Order			Net value		0.00	
Sold-to party	601361					
Ship-to party						
PO Number			PO date			

| Sales | Item overview | Item detail | Ordering party | Procurement | Shipping | Reason for rejection |

Req. deliv.date	D	15.05.2017		Deliver.Plant	
☐ Complete dlv.				Total Weight	0.000
Delivery block				Volume	0.000
Billing block				Pricing date	15.05.2017
Payment card				Exp.date	
Payment terms				Incoterms	
Order reason					
Sales area	SFE1 / 01 / F1	Shefaria Sales Org, Direct Sales, Furniture			

All items

Item	Material	Order Quantity	SU	Description	S	Customer Material Numb	ItCa
	1000654	10					

Fig 5

Hit Enter.

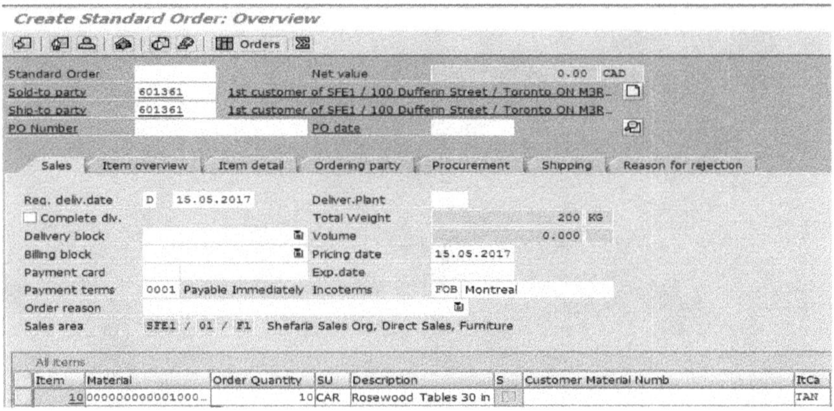

Fig 6

Notice how SAP got the rest of the information on its own:

a) it defaulted the payment terms 0002 and the Incoterms FOB from the customer master at the header level

b) It got the plant SFC2 at the line item level from the customer master. To default a plant, SAP considers 3 data records – the CMIR, customer material info record (we will look at this functionality later), the customer master and finally the material master. A Plant is a necessary field to create deliveries so the order will not go beyond if it is missing. Since we have not set up the CMIR, it must have got this from the customer master as we had set it there in the shipping tab area.

c) Price – since we had set the price PR00 @ 100/EA, it also got the CAR from the material master as that is what we said is the sales unit. Using the multiplier 3 CAR (=36 EA), it made the sales order of a value of $3,600 based on the conversion in the material master:

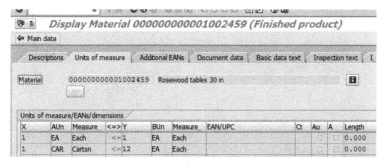

Fig 7

Save the order.

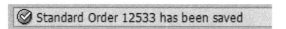

Fig 8

CONFIGURATION OF SALES DOCUMENT TYPE (C)

Instructions: Follow Menu Path: SPRO→IMG → Sales and Distribution → Sales → Sales Documents → Sales Document Header → Define Sales Document Type.

Click ⊕

'OR' is SAP provided standard sales document type as it is existing Sales document type the same can be modified or copied, choose the document type from list and click on ⌕ to get into details

Change View "Maintain Sales Order Types": Details

New Entries

Sales Document Type	OR	Standard Order
SD document categ.	C	Sales document block
Indicator		

Number systems

No.range int.assgt.	01		Item no.increment	10
No. range ext. assg.	02		Sub-item increment	10

General control

Reference mandatory			Material entry type	
Check division			☑ Item division	
Probability	100		☑ Read info record	
Check credit limit	D		Check purch.order no	
Credit group	01		☐ Enter PO number	
Output application	V1		Commitment date	

Transaction flow

Screen sequence grp.	AU	Sales Order	Display Range	UALL
Incompl.proced.	11	Sales Order	FCode for overv.scr.	UER1
Transaction group	0	Sales order	Quotation message	R
Doc. pric. procedure	A		Outline agrmt mess.	B
Status profile			Message: Mast.contr.	
Alt.sales doc. type1			ProdAttr.messages	
Alt.sales doc. type2			☐ Incomplet.messages	
Variant				

Fig 1

The controls are grouped in various blocks like Number Systems, General Control, Transaction flow etc. which can be configured as per design document.

Go to Transaction VA01
Pass the values as below and press enter

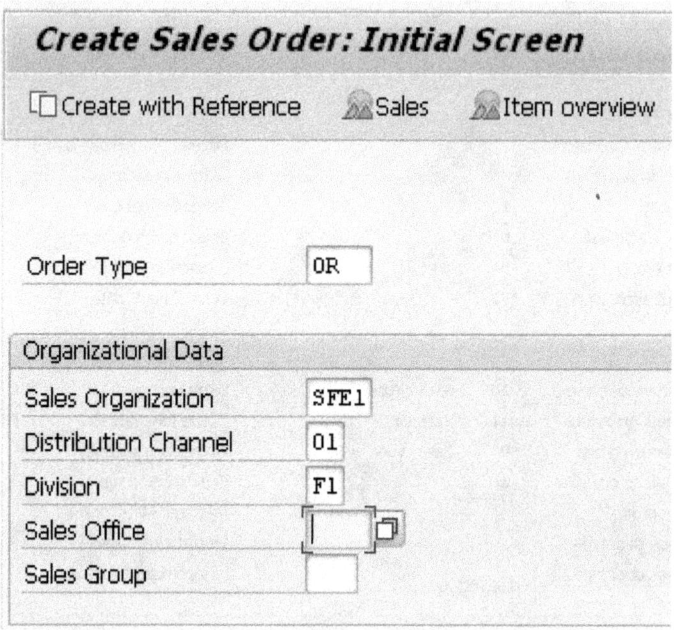

Create Sales Order: Initial Screen

☐ Create with Reference   ▨ Sales   ▨ Item overview

Order Type	OR

Organizational Data

Sales Organization	SFE1
Distribution Channel	01
Division	F1
Sales Office	
Sales Group	

Fig 2

Pass Sold-to party, Ship-to party, P.O number, Material & Order quantity and Press enter

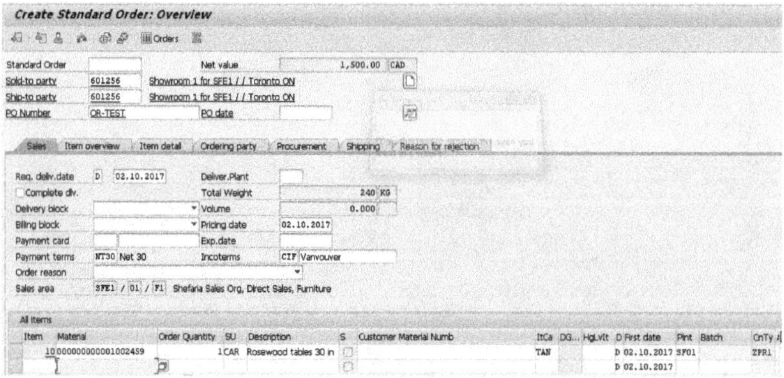

102

Fig 3

Go-to Edit→ Incompletion Log and check whether document is complete.

Save 🖫 to generate the Order Number – 12599.

Go-to VL01N (delivery creation-Fig 3)

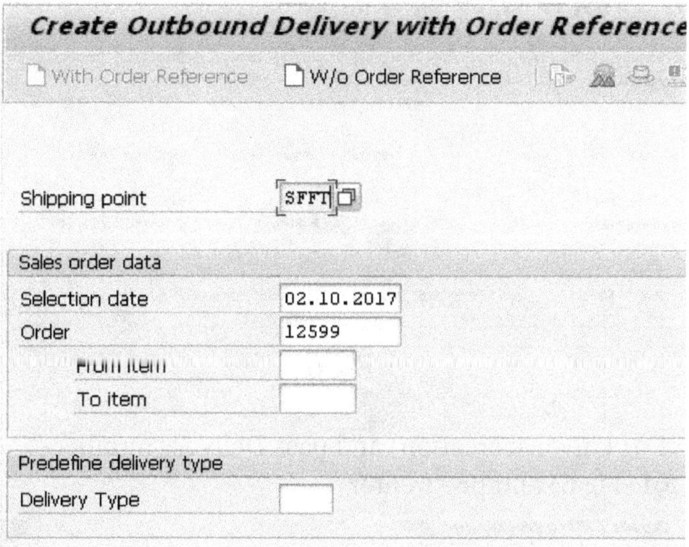

Create Outbound Delivery with Order Reference

☐ With Order Reference   ☐ W/o Order Reference   🗋 📉 🖨 ▪

Shipping point   `SFFT` 🗗

Sales order data

Selection date	02.10.2017
Order	12599
From item	
To item	

Predefine delivery type

| Delivery Type | |

Fig 4

And pass Order number-12599 and Shipping Point (Fig 4) and press enter

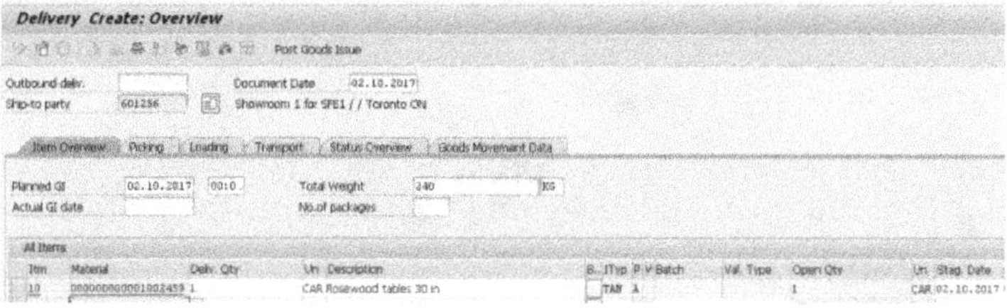

Delivery Create: Overview

Fig 5

Check incompletion log and Save 🖫

Delivery Document 80015491 Generated.

Go-to VL02N (Delivery Change) and pass Delivery number-80015491, press enter

Complete Picking & Press on Post Goods Issue to complete goods issue (Fig 6).

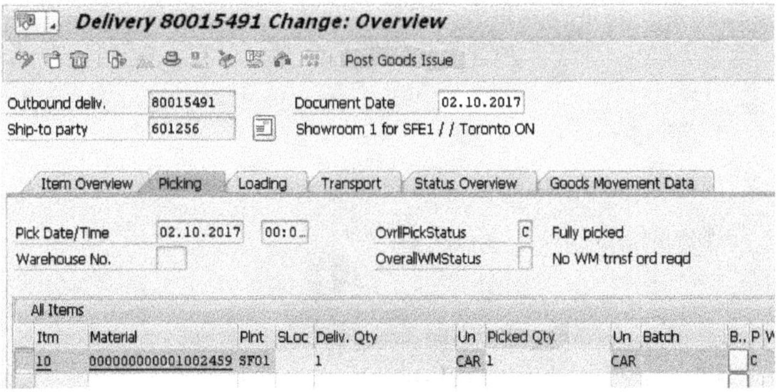

Fig 6

Go-to VF01 (Invoice creation) and pass Delivery number-80015491 (Fig 6) and press enter

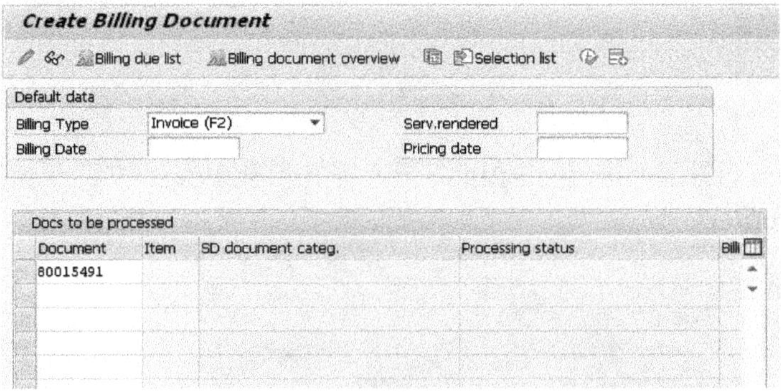

Fig 7

Press 💾 Save

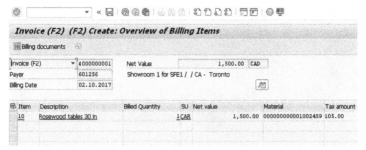

Fig 8

Upon saving, Billing Document-90036895 is generated. Below Figure 9 explains the flow of document

Fig 9

CONFIGURATION OF SALES DOCUMENT TYPE FOR RUSH ORDER (C)

Instructions: Follow Menu Path: SPRO→IMG → Sales and Distribution → Sales → Sales Documents → Sales Document Header → Define Sales Document Type.

Click 🌐

'RO is SAP provided standard sales document type - As it is existing Sales document type the same can be modified or copied, choose the document type from list and click on 🔍 to get into details (Fig 9)

The controls are grouped in various blocks like Number Systems, General Control, Transaction flow etc. which can be configured as per design document.

106

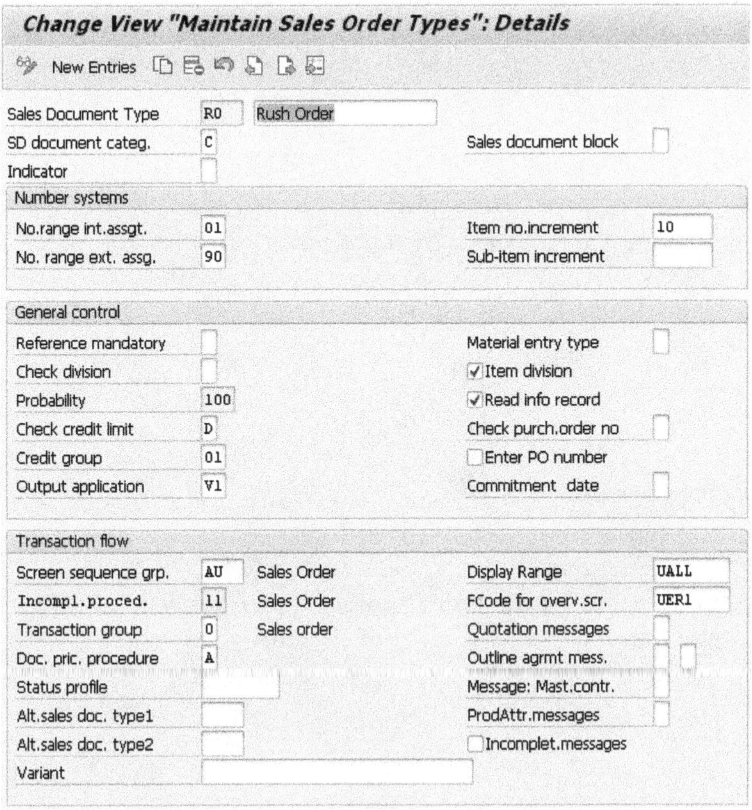

Change View "Maintain Sales Order Types": Details

New Entries

Sales Document Type	RO	Rush Order		
SD document categ.	C		Sales document block	
Indicator				

Number systems

No.range int.assgt.	01		Item no.increment	10
No. range ext. assg.	90		Sub-item increment	

General control

Reference mandatory			Material entry type	
Check division			☑ Item division	
Probability	100		☑ Read info record	
Check credit limit	D		Check purch.order no	
Credit group	01		☐ Enter PO number	
Output application	V1		Commitment date	

Transaction flow

Screen sequence grp.	AU	Sales Order	Display Range	UALL
Incompl.proced.	11	Sales Order	FCode for overv.scr.	UER1
Transaction group	0	Sales order	Quotation messages	
Doc. pric. procedure	A		Outline agrmt mess.	
Status profile			Message: Mast.contr.	
Alt.sales doc. type1			ProdAttr.messages	
Alt.sales doc. type2			☐ Incomplet.messages	
Variant				

Fig 1

RUNNING SALES CYCLE FROM ORDER TO BILLING WITH SALES DOCUMENT TYPE – RO (U)

Go to Transaction VA01:

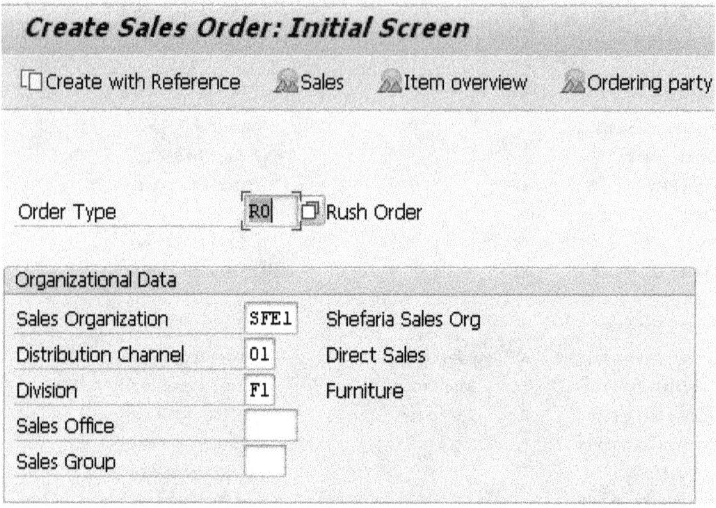

Create Sales Order: Initial Screen

☐ Create with Reference   Sales   Item overview   Ordering party

| Order Type | RO| ☐ Rush Order |

Organizational Data

Sales Organization	SFE1	Shefaria Sales Org
Distribution Channel	01	Direct Sales
Division	F1	Furniture
Sales Office		
Sales Group		

Fig 2

Enter the values as above and press enter sold-to party, Ship-to party, P.O number, Material & Order quantity as below hit enter

Fig 3

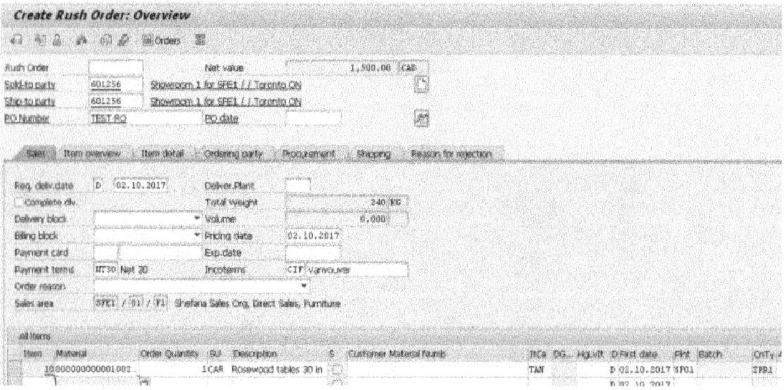

Fig 4

Go-to Edit→ Incompletion Log and check whether document is complete.

Once Saved 🖫 we can see Order Number 12600 has been saved and delivery 80015492 also created automatically (Fig 5).

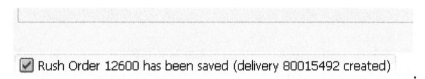

☑ Rush Order 12600 has been saved (delivery 80015492 created)

Fig 5

Go-to VL02N (Delivery Change) and enter the Delivery number-80015492, press enter Complete Picking & click on

Post Goods Issue to complete goods issue (Fig 6).

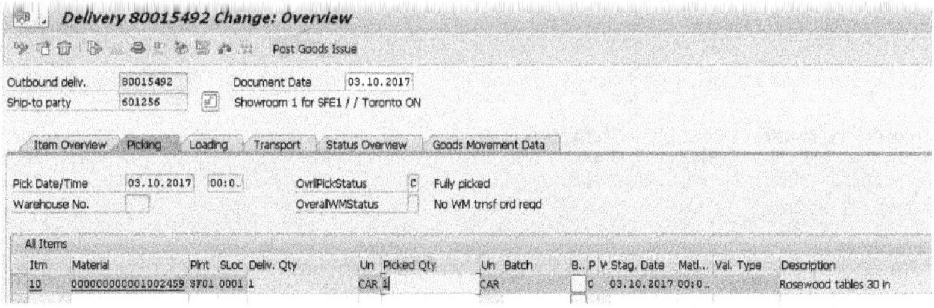

Delivery 80015492 Change: Overview

Post Goods Issue

| Outbound deliv. | 80015492 | Document Date | 03.10.2017 |
| Ship-to party | 601256 | Showroom 1 for SFE1 / / Toronto ON |

Item Overview | Picking | Loading | Transport | Status Overview | Goods Movement Data

| Pick Date/Time | 03.10.2017 | 00:0.. | OvrlPickStatus | C | Fully picked |
| Warehouse No. | | | OverallWMStatus | | No WM trnsf ord reqd |

All Items

| Itm | Material | Plnt Sloc Delv. Qty | Un Picked Qty | Un Batch | B.. P V Stag. Date Matl.. Val. Type Description |
| 10 | 00000000001002459 | 3701 0001 1 | CAR 1 | CAR | C 03.10.2017 00:0.. Rosewood tables 30 in |

Fig 6

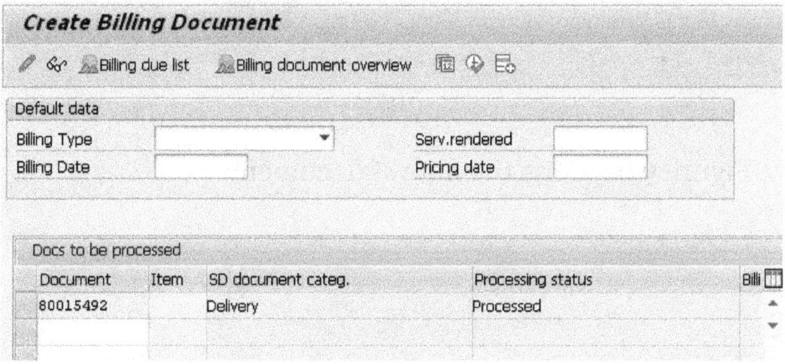

Create Billing Document

🖉 ⟨⟩ Billing due list Billing document overview 🖳 ⊕ 🖺

Default data

| Billing Type | ▼ | Serv.rendered | |
| Billing Date | | Pricing date | |

Docs to be processed

| Document | Item | SD document categ. | Processing status | Billi |
| 80015492 | | Delivery | Processed | |

Fig 7

Go-to VF01 (Invoice creation) and pass Delivery number-80015492 and press enter

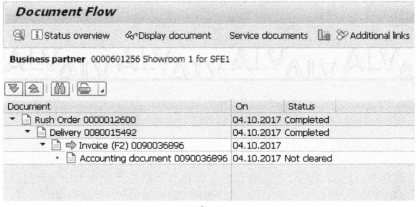

Fig 8

Press ⊟ , upon saving, Billing Document- 90036896 is generated.

Document Flow

Status overview &Display document Service documents Additional links

Business partner 0000601256 Showroom 1 for SFE1

Document	On	Status
▼ Rush Order 0000012600	04.10.2017	Completed
▼ Delivery 0080015492	04.10.2017	Completed
▼ ⇨ Invoice (F2) 0090036896	04.10.2017	
• Accounting document 0090036896	04.10.2017	Not cleared

Fig 9

Above Figure 9 explains the flow of document.

Since SAP is such an integrated system, on the order to cash cycle, most of the data is determined at the order stage itself and flows from one document to the next. On the SD side, this could mean the sales data transfers the data into the delivery > shipment > cost document > invoice > accounting. Thus, it is imperative we understand where this data originates from and what effects it can have as we process the transaction down the line. There are 3 levels in which the data is stored in a sales order:

1. Header – most of this data originates directly or indirectly from the customer related data and will remain same for the entire document

2. Line item – most of this originates directly or indirectly relating to the material and/or in combination with the customer. It can, for the most part, be different for each line

3. Schedule lines – relevant only if physical goods are being shipped. This data is really a part of the line item but important enough to be understood and listed on its own.

i)   Header Data

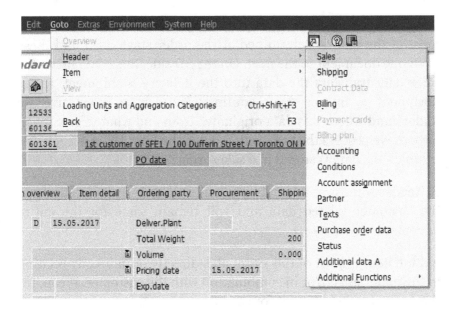

Fig 10

Header data is split into many different screens as above and reached either from the above path, or by clicking on the button

on the screen which will lead to the same header tabs:

Fig 11

One should go through all these tabs individually and verify the data is what is needed. At most places, we can change it to anything else that may be available. In all cases, the tabs are self-explanatory as to what kind of data they contain.

ii)   Item Data

We can view this data by selecting the relevant line (highlighting) and Goto>Item as below:

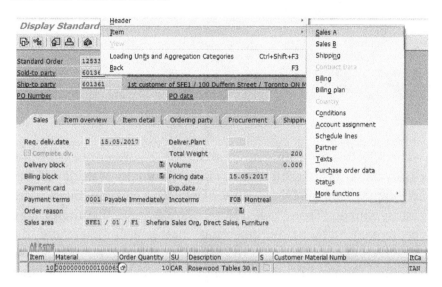

Fig 12

Or simply double click the line in the middle and see the same tabs:

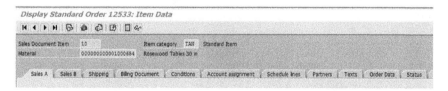

Fig 13

In many cases, they seem same/like the header tabs but they are not and can have their own data different from the header data. For instance, at the header level, we may have a credit terms of 30 days but for a special item, we may decide to extend them to 60. In that case, for that line item, we can change it to 60 if the order has defaulted to 30 (which it will if the customer master has 30 in it).

iii)   Schedule Line data

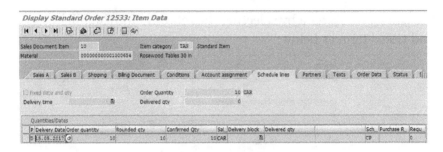

Fig 14

A schedule line is a unique combination of order quantity and delivery date. It is a result of many inputs from the Material master and shipping configurations, some of which we will understand later in this course. The MRP (Materials resource Planning) and Procurement data of the material master will determine the availability of the material, the shipping points and plants will determine the time it takes to deliver the goods to the customer. This, an order of 3 can potentially have 3 schedules lines, depending on the product availability.

More individual details about each schedule line are available in the 3 tabs:

Fig 15

Each schedule line will become a separate delivery to the customer because the delivery date is at the header level in a delivery. One delivery can't have multiple delivery dates, this, since each schedule line would have its own delivery date, the 2 can't get combined.

We will come to these different screens of a sales order again later when we see the effects of our configurations esp. of pricing, material availability and shipping. At this point, a good

114

understanding of these fields will help so the student is encouraged to read their definitions and usage by clicking on F1 in the important fields.

PRICING IN SALES DOCUMENTS (C)

Short cut to Pricing Area Menu – VOKo.

The pricing sub-module in SAP is to be found under the section Basic Functions:

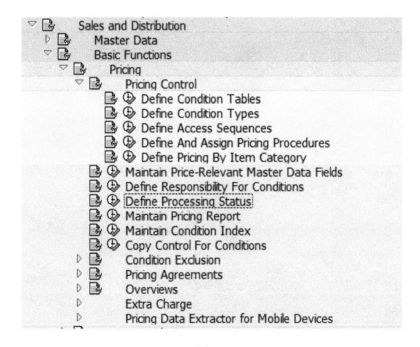

Fig 1

The documentation icon ⬚ right before the execute node carries a wealth of information and the student is advised to read through it for better grasp.

Pricing in SD (as are many other areas also) are based on a condition technique. Simply stated, a condition technique is a combination of 'IF' statements with the components acting as 'place holders' in the equations. This concept will become clearer as we look at the first element in pricing – condition tables.

1. CONDITION TABLE

Click on   🖹 ⊕ Define Condition Tables

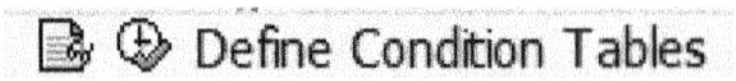

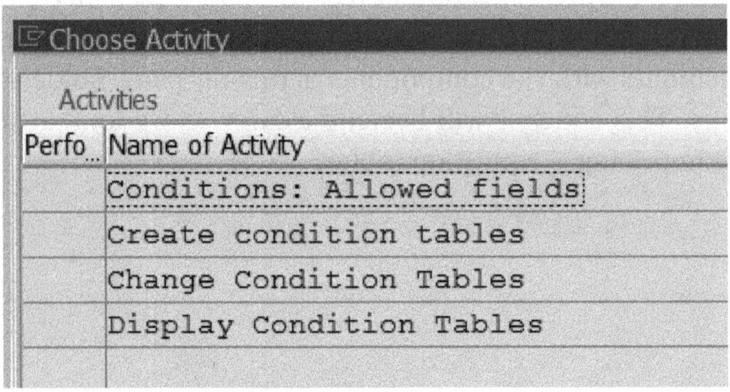

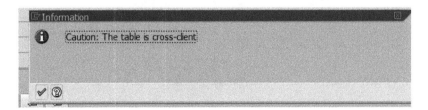

Fig 2

Click on Create Allowed fields:

Fig 3

The above message is common in SAP. Often, in real time SAP setups, there are multiple clients – a client merely means one 'setup' of SAP which will be connected to the other setups. Different clients are used for different types of work, most common being one for configuration, another for programming (also called development) and one for testing the changes made in the either two. The above message means any change made in this Condition table will get done in all the clients that may have been set up.

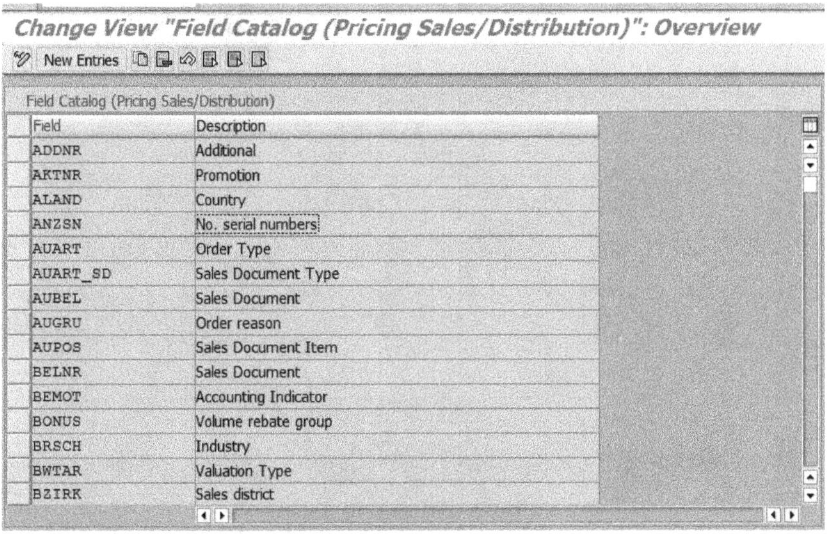

New Entries

Field Catalog (Pricing Sales/Distribution)	
Field	Description
ADDNR	Additional
AKTNR	Promotion
ALAND	Country
ANZSN	No. serial numbers
AUART	Order Type
AUART_SD	Sales Document Type
AUBEL	Sales Document
AUGRU	Order reason
AUPOS	Sales Document Item
BELNR	Sales Document
BEMOT	Accounting Indicator
BONUS	Volume rebate group
BRSCH	Industry
BWTAR	Valuation Type
BZIRK	Sales district

Fig 4

The above is the list of fields available to use as of the time of this screen shot. 178 fields from various tables can be brought together to create a 'condition' table. The others can be seen by scrolling on the right scroll bar. More can be added if this list does not have the field/s we need.

Let us assume we will use 3 fields to create a condition table – material, price list and plant.

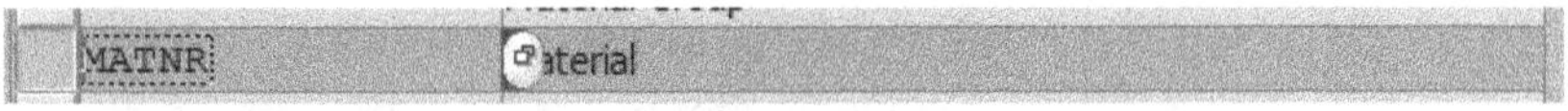

MATNR	Material

Fig 5

PLTYP	Price List

Fig 6

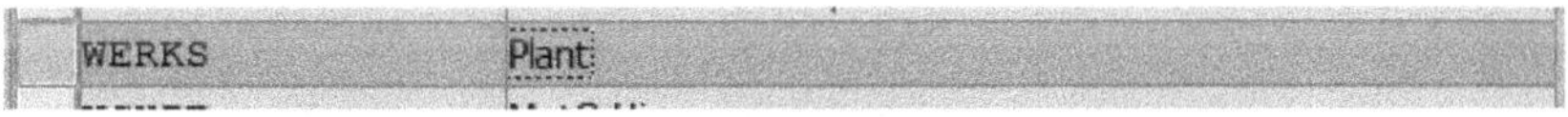

WERKS	Plant

Fig 7

Step back and click on Create Condition table:

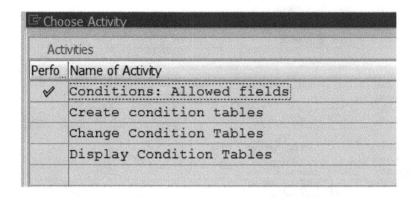

Fig 8

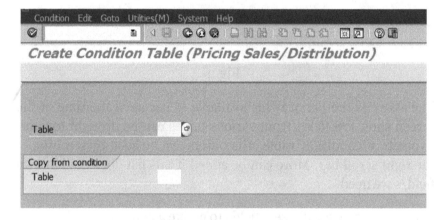

Fig 9

We can copy from an existing one and then to modify it in Change Condition table option. However, we will create a new one here.

Do a dropdown (F4) in the field Table and you will see 234 tables already exist. Normally, these pre-existing tables are good enough for most requirements. However, we find there is no table with Material/Price List/ Plant as the fields in it. So, we proceed to create it.

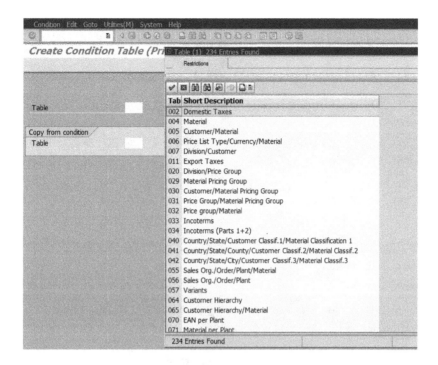

Fig 10

Sap has reserved the numbers from 001 to 500 for itself in condition tables for pricing. We are required to create one only with 501 to 999 (the maximum possible)

From the drop down, see the first number available after 500:

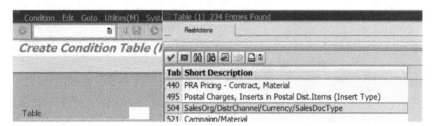

Fig 11

We find 504 is taken but 501/502/503 are still available. We will create a 501 table with the above 3 fields in it.

Enter 501 and Hit Enter:

121

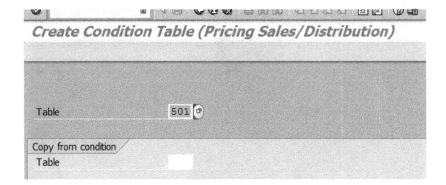

Table   501

Copy from condition
Table

Fig 12

Create Condition Table (Pricing Sales/Distribution): Field Overview

Select field | Technical view | Other description | Field attributes...

Table   501

☑ With validity period
☑ with release status

Selected fields	FieldCatlg
Long Key Word	Long Key Word
	Accounting Indicator
	Activity Code GI Tax
	Agreement
	Base Unit of Measure
	Batch
	Bill-to party
	CAP prod. group
	Campaign ID
	Catalog
	City code
	City of deliv.plant
	Commission group
	Condition Contract
	Conditn pricing date
	Control code
	Country
	Country
	County code

Fig 13

Use the scrolling keys at the top to find the fields Material/Price List/ Plant that we need and double click on them to bring them to the left side screen:

Fig 14

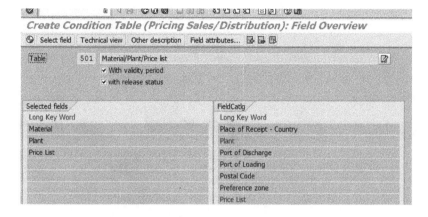

Fig 15

Click on the generate button 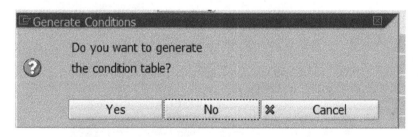 to generate the table:

Say Yes to this popup:

Fig 16

A message at bottom right of the screen will appear:

Fig 17

123

And then an info message:

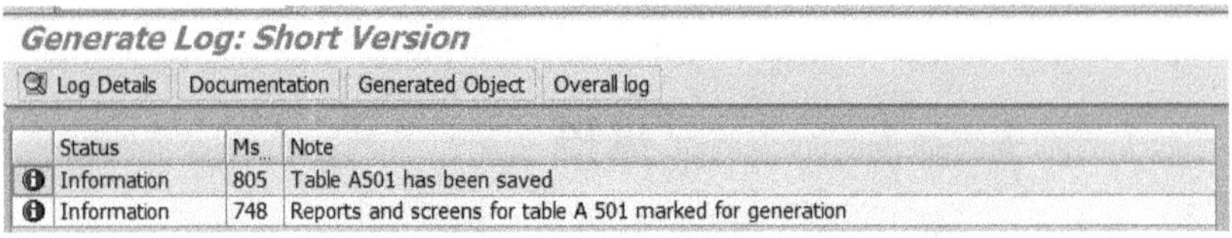

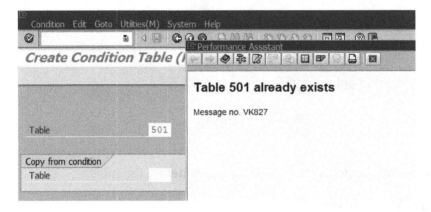

Fig 18

Step out of the screen and if you try to create it again, we get the message:

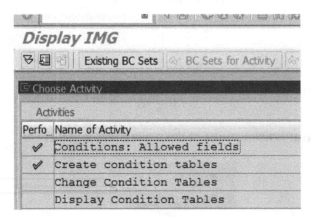

Fig 19

Step back to display what we just created:

Fig 20

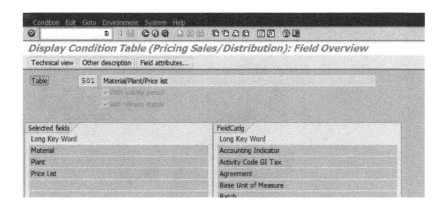

Fig 21

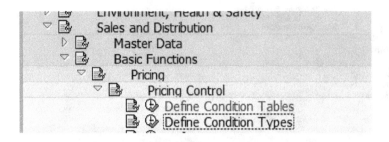

Fig 22

This is the most commonly used element in pricing on a day to day basis and has a lot of meaning and configuration behind it.

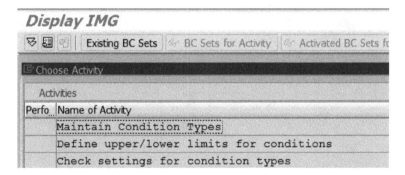

Fig 23

A condition type can be of many kinds to represent different areas in pricing:

- The price itself which could be by customer or material or price list or any other relevant data or a combination thereof like the table we created in the previous section
- Relating to discounts and/or surcharges
- Relating to freight which may not be a part of the revenue but we would still to charge to the customer or accrue the value of it
- Taxes that need to be charges for the product and/or services

- To represent special requirements of clients from time to time

Let us create one of our own and see the details behind it:

Change View "Conditions: Condition Types": Overview

New Entries

CTyp	Condition Type	Condition class	Calculation type
AMIW	Minimum SalesOrdrVal	Discount or surcharge	Fixed amount
AMIZ	Minimum ValueSurchrg	Discount or surcharge	Fixed amount
ATX1	G.S.T.	Taxes	Percentage
AUFS	VKP Calcultn Surchrg	Discount or surcharge	Percentage
AUFX	VKP Calcultn Surchrg	Discount or surcharge	Percentage
A2WR	Down Pay./Settlement	Discount or surcharge	Fixed amount
BAS2	Brazil Tax base ICMS	Discount or surcharge	Percentage
BASI	Brazil Expenses	Discount or surcharge	Percentage
BCO1	COFINS Rate	Taxes	Percentage
BCO2	COFINS Base	Taxes	Percentage
BCOP	COFINS Pauta Amount	Taxes	Quantity
BCOZ		Taxes	Percentage
BCSZ		Taxes	Percentage
BGEZ		Taxes	Percentage
BI00	Dummy for Tax	Taxes	Percentage
BIRZ		Taxes	Percentage
BO01	Group Rebate	Expense reimbursement	Percentage
BO02	Material Rebate	Expense reimbursement	Quantity
BO03	Customer Rebate	Expense reimbursement	Percentage
BO04	Hierarchy Rebate	Expense reimbursement	Percentage
BO05	Hierarchy rebate/mat	Expense reimbursement	Percentage
BO06	Sales Indpndt Rebate	Expense reimbursement	Fixed amount

Fig 24

If we scroll down or use the Position key to find, we will see PR00, the one condition type we used earlier in this course to set up the price for our order. Let us copy it to a new condition type which we will call ZPR1.

Highlight PR00 and click on the copy icon:

New Entries

CTyp	Condition Type	Condition class	Calculation type
PR00	Price	Prices	Quantity

Fig 25

127

Replace PR00 with ZPR1 and give your own description to it though you can retain the same too:

Before:

Fig 26

After:

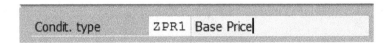

Fig 27

Hit Enter:

ZPR1 comes to the top on the previous screen:

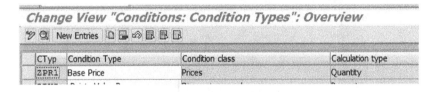

Fig 28

You can also give the minimum or maximum values that this condition can take i.e. the minimum or maximum base price that can be charged when using this condition:

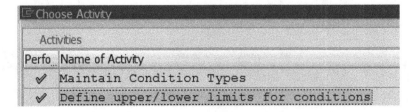

Fig 29

128

It is not usually used via configuration by most companies and handled via master data of pricing conditions though SAP gives the ability to do at condition type level also as above.

3. Access Sequence

Our next configuration relates to access sequence which is where the condition technique comes into play.

Define Access Sequences

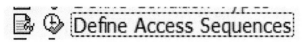

Fig 30

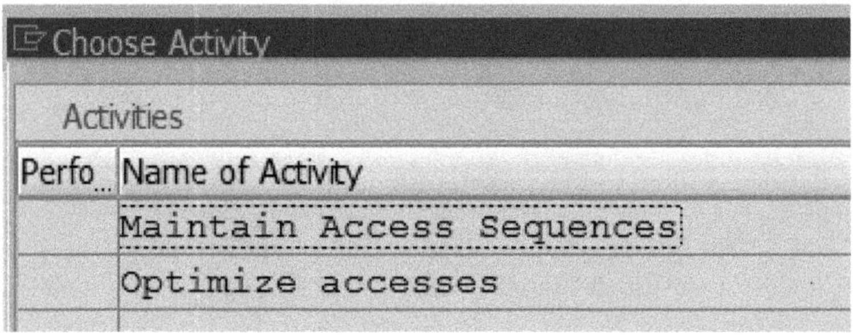

Choose Activity
Activities
Perfo...
Name of Activity
Maintain Access Sequences
Optimize accesses

Fig 31

An access sequence is the order in which the system searches for prices. Generally, it will go from most specific to most generic. The more the fields in the table (qualifying data that needs to come together), the more specific the sequence.

Thus, our table 501 which will look for Material/PL/Plant is more 'specific' than 406:

406
Plant/material

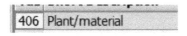

Fig 32

Which looks for the combination of plant AND material and 406 is more specific than 404:

004
Material

Fig 33

Which is prices only for the material and does not care about any other data. Thus, when we create sequence of accesses, we should create them in the order 510, 406, 004 so that the system first searched for the most specific and not finding it, moves to the next but lesser specific one.

This is called condition technique with plant, material and price list being 'place holders' – when different conditions are met, different results get applied. In this case, the result is the determination of the price to be applied. On other cases in SAP, this result may be a determination of batch for the product or determination of a shipping point for the delivery etc.

Click on the activity Maintain Access sequence:

Fig 34

Hit Enter.

Fig 35

Again, we find every access has a 4-digit code like the pricing conditions. Let us create our own access beginning with a Z – again, we can use ZPR1 as this is an independent object than the pricing condition ZPR1.

Click on New Entries

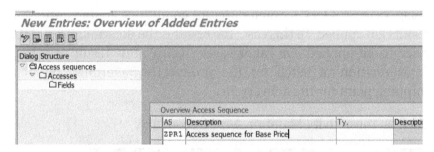

Fig 36

Leave the field Ty. Blank (unless this will be used for rebates, in which case populate it with 1)

Hit Enter:

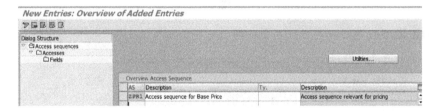

Fig 37

Highlight the line and double click on Accesses on the left:

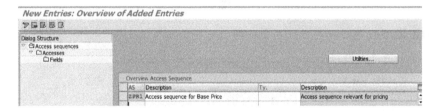

Fig 38

To enter the accesses, click on New Entries

All the fields open for entry:

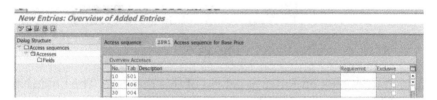

New Entries: Overview of Added Entries

Dialog Structure						

Access sequence   ZPR1 Access sequence for Base Price

Fig 39

Our next task is to populate this sequence with the accesses it will have. These will be represented by the fields No. and the Table (501, 406 and 004 in order) This is to be done carefully – the standard SAP functionality is to go in sequence so there is a tendency to give the numbering at 1, 2, 3 etc. However, bear in mind, there may be a requirement down the road to have an even more specific sequence and if the number 1 is taken, it can't be inserted before 501. So, a prudent methodology is to number them as 10, 20, 30 thereby leaving gaps for others that may need to get inserted. Enter the details as below:

New Entries: Overview of Added Entries

Access sequence   ZPR1 Access sequence for Base Price

Overview Accesses

No.	Tab	Description	Requiremnt	Exclusive
10	501			
20	406			
30	004			

Fig 40

Hit Enter and ignore the message that comes below:

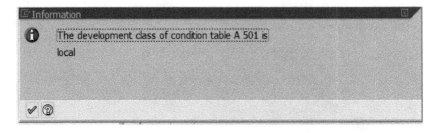

Fig 41

Check the Indicator – Exclusive for all of them:

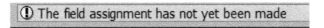

Fig 42

Check each line and click on Fields on the left side window – we may get a message:

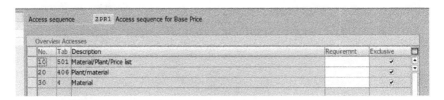

Fig 43

At each line, click on Enter to get rid of this message. The fields No. and Table will get greyed out telling you the fields have been 'assigned':

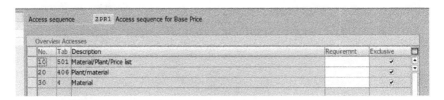

Fig 44

Click on "Save" and it will prompt you for a new transport:

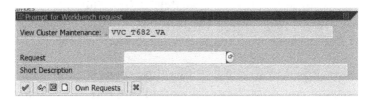

Fig 45

Click on  and get a new number as we did for the configurations:

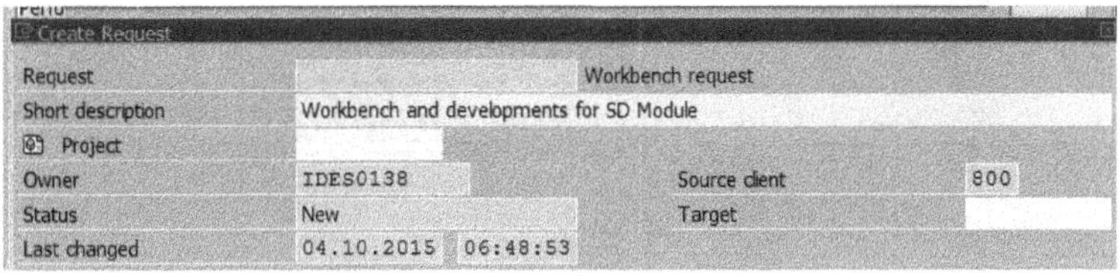

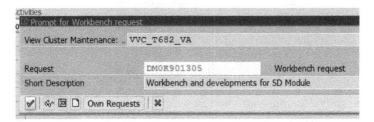

Fig 46

Save

Fig 47

Our new access sequence ZPR1 is now ready for us to use:

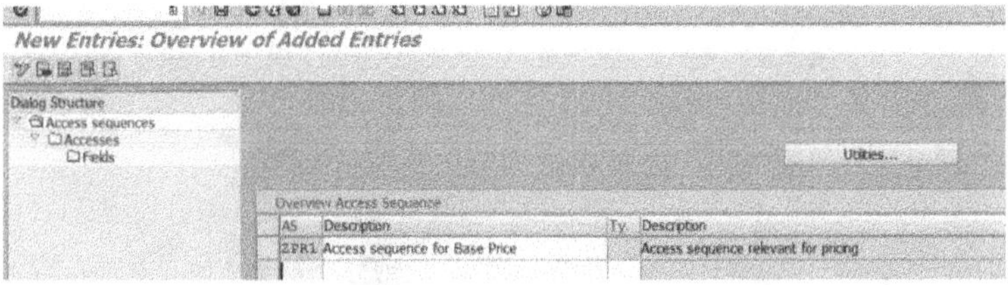

Fig 48

This access will now go to tables 501, 406 and 004 to find pricing condition records (like we set earlier in the transaction VK11 for condition PR00). On finding the first one it will stop searching for the next one because we have set the 'exclusive' indicator.

Our next task is how to use it. Since the access sequences are used by the pricing condition types, they must be linked to them. To do that, we go back to the pricing condition ZPR1:

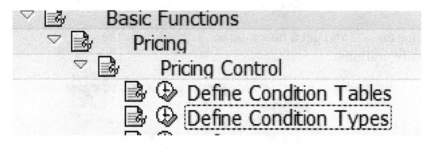

Fig 49

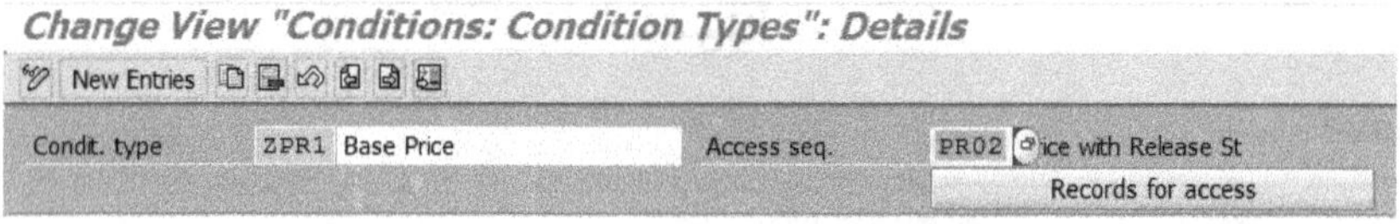

Change View "Conditions: Condition Types": Details

New Entries

| Condt. type | ZPR1 Base Price | Access seq. | PR02 ice with Release St |
| | | | Records for access |

Fig 50

Replace Access seq. PR02 with ZPR1 and save.

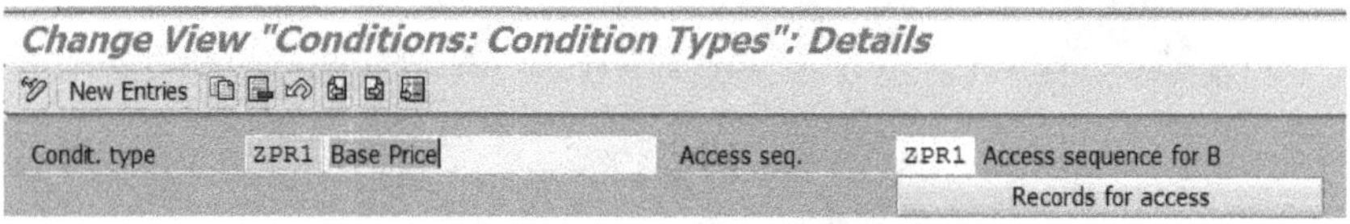

Change View "Conditions: Condition Types": Details

New Entries

| Condt. type | ZPR1 Base Price | Access seq. | ZPR1 Access sequence for B |
| | | | Records for access |

Fig 51

4. PRICING PROCEDURE

Pricing Procedure is where it all comes together – the condition types that use the access sequences that are comprised of condition tables.

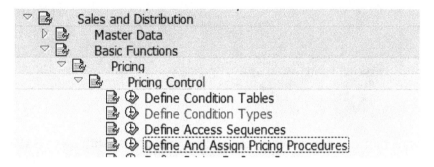

Fig 52

A pricing procedure is set up in steps where the latter step gets applied on the previous ones automatically unless specified differently. To understand this, let us select Maintain Pricing Procedure from the choices below:

Choose Activity
Activities
Perfo.. Name of Activity
Maintain pricing procedures
Define customer pricing procedure
Define document pricing procedure
Assign document pricing procedures to order types
Assign document pricing procedures to billing types
Define Pricing Procedure Determination
Check Settings for Pricing Procedures

Fig 53

Again, we find many standard SAP ones already set up which can be used easily unless there are any compelling requirements not to use them. It is not uncommon though, for companies to set up their own because overwriting or modifying standard SAP PP for anything specific is not advisable as it would get over written at the time of an upgrade.

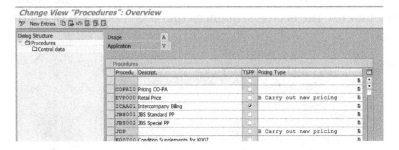

Fig 54

Let us then copy an existing one and set up our own with a Z* - SAP's most standard procedure is RVAA01:

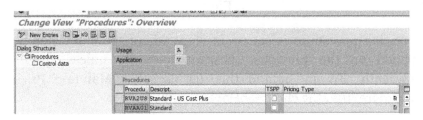

Fig 55

Select it and using the Copy button, set up another one, calling it ZRVAA01:

Say Copy All to the window:

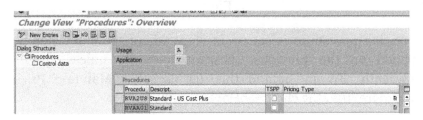

Fig 56

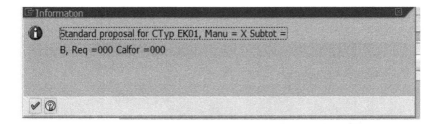

Fig 57

Hit Enter and a few times again if this message comes:

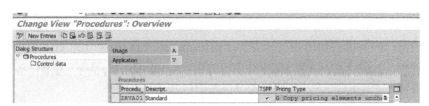

Fig 58

Fig 59

Check the box TSPP – this check is required so that the shipment costs can be transferred (we will see this in the LE course). Also select G from the options under column Pricing Type. This G ensures all pricing is copied from a sales order into the delivery and/or invoices. There is no form of re-determination. This may not be true for all companies but is generally the norm. Exceptions may be that companies require re-determination of pricing based on the concept of selling at special prices 'till stocks last'

We can also give it our own name in Description:

Fig 60

139

Save.

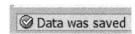

Fig 61

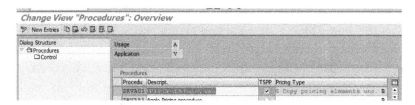

Fig 62

While we will retain all the other pricing and tax/discount condition types in ZRVA01 (as copied from the standard RVAA01), we will replace the price condition PR00 with our own ZPR1.

Select ZRVA01 and click on Control Data:

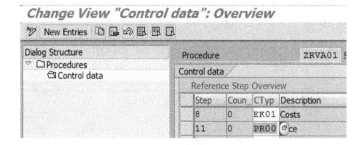

Fig 63

Fig 64

Replace PR00 with ZPR1 and save:

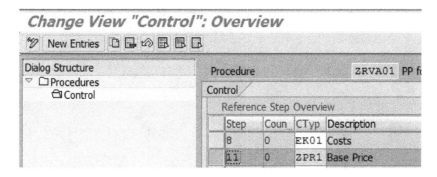

Fig 65

Step	Coun	CTyp	Description	Fro	To	Man	Req	Stats	P	SuTot	Reqt	CalType	BasType	AccKey	Accruals
8	0	EK01	Costs			✓								ERL	
11	0	ZPR1	Base Price								2			ERL	
13	0	PB00	Price (Gross)			✓					2			ERL	
14	0	PR02	Price Increased								2			ERL	
15	0	ZK01	Variant Costs						X		2			ERL	
20	0	VA00	Variants						X		2			ERL	
21	0	ZA00	General variants						X		2			ERL	
100	0		Gross Value						X	1		2			
101	0	KA00	Sales Promotion						X		2			ERS	
102	0	K032	Price Group/Material						X		2			ERS	
103	0	K005	Customer/Material						X		2			ERS	

Fig 66

Procedure ZRVA01 PP for Direct & Factory sales
Control — Reference Step Overview

Step	Coun	CTyp	Description	Fro	To	Man	Req	Stats	P	SuTot	Reqt	CalType	BasType	AccKey	Accruals
104	0	K007	Customer Discount						X		2			ERS	
105	0	K004	Material						X		2			ERS	
106	0	K020	Price Group						X		2			ERS	
107	0	K029	Mat.Pricing Group						X		2			ERS	
108	0	K030	Customer/Mat.Pr.Grp						X		2			ERS	
109	0	K031	Price Grp/Mat.Pr.Grp						X		2			ERS	
110	1	RA01	% Disc.from Gross	100		✓			X		2			ERS	
110	2	RA00	% Discount from Net			✓			X		2			ERS	
110	3	RC00	Quantity Discount			✓			X		2			ERS	
110	4	RB00	Discount (Value)			✓			X		2			ERS	
110	5	RD00	Weight Discount			✓			X		2			ERS	

Fig 67

Control — Reference Step Overview

Step	Coun	CTyp	Description	Fro	To	Man	Req	Stats	P	SuTot	Reqt	CalType	BasType	AccKey	Accruals
111	0	HI01	Hierarchy						X		2			ERS	
112	0	HI02	Hierarchy/Material						X		2			ERS	
115	0	K148	Product Hierarchy						X		2			ERS	
120	0	VA01	Variants %						X		2			ERS	
121	0	ZVC0	Discount contract	100					X		2			ERS	
300	0		Discount Amount	101	299										
302	0	NETP	Price			✓					2	6	3	ERL	
310	0	PN00	Net Price			✓					2	6		ERL	
320	0	PMIN	Minimum Price						X		2	15		ERL	
399	0	R100	100% discount						X		55		28	ERS	
400	0		Rebate Basis						7						

Fig 68

A typical PP in SD has the following fields/columns:

a) Step # - this is the step in which the prices, discounts, taxes etc. will be applied. They can be used as 'from/to' steps for the subsequent pricing conditions to get applied upon as in the above screen shot.

b) Counter – this is a sub-step of the step – if there are multiple condition types used to represent the same pricing, this counter can be used. It will allow SAP to 'search' for the pricing based on the first condition type that has been set up with a price

c) Condition type – we saw the use of this earlier. Again, the reader is advised to understand the detailed screen of a condition type as it will come in use time to time.

d) From and To fields – these are defined to enable the calculation of the corresponding condition type or sub-totals to derive their values. For example. in the above screen shot 3:

| 300 | 0 | | Discount Amount | | 101 | 299 | | | | | | | |

Fig 69

The total discount will be the total of steps 101 to 299.

e) Man – Means manual pricing condition. This will be entered manually by the user in the sales order rather than being determined via pricing condition records (master data). Examples like this will be ad hoc pricing, or a specially agreed discount etc.

f) Req – Required condition type. Mandatory. If this is not present with a value, SAP will keep the order as incomplete and not process it any further.

g) Statis – Statistical condition types do have a value but they do not post to accounting. They are used for calculation purposes only for example. costing of products – the profitability of a transaction may be calculated by net value less material cost. The material cost then, represented in out PP by EK02, one statistical condition, amongst others:

Procedure		ZRVA01	PP for Direct & Factory sales										
Control													
Reference Step Overview													
Step	Coun	CTyp	Description	Fro	To	Man	Req	Stats	Print	SuTot	Reqt	CalType	BasType	AccKey	Accruals
935	0	GRWR	Statistical Value					✓		C	B		2		
941	0	EK02	Calculated costs			✓		✓		B					

Fig 70

143

h) Print: Only if this box is checked will the SAP programs pass this value to print on invoices or other documents. Later, it can be masked not to print if necessary however this setting must be present to pass on this value for printing

i) SuTot – Different values are passed to different sub totals so that reporting can take place appropriately for example. gross amounts may go to one bucket, all discounts to another and all taxes to yet another. These different sub-totals define these buckets

j) Reqt. – This is a place to do coding to make any special treatment to the condition type for example. one may want a price to get applied only if the material is being shipped from a certain plant. Then that plant will become a part of the code requiring the price to be applied only if the plant in the line item of the sales order is that one.

k) Cal Type – If the user needs to have a different way of calculating the condition type's value, that code will be set here

l) Base type – again, if the basis of calculation needs to be different than from what is being proposed in the PP then we set that basis here and it will override the normal base

m) Acct Key – drives the G/L account in FI where this value will post to.

n) Accruals – while the acct key is for actual numbers, this field is for posting the accruals of the same numbers if they are to be accrued and not posted right away

6. CUSTOMER AND DOCUMENT PRICING PROCEDURES (C)

Again, these are 'place holder's that are used to determine which pricing procedure will be used.

i) Customer Pricing Procedure

It is used in the customer master>sales area data>Sales tab:

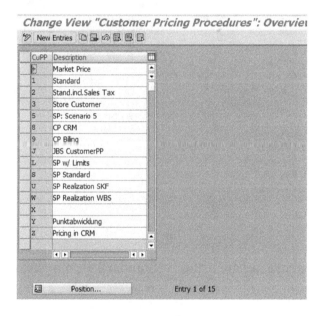

Fig 71

Customer master (U)

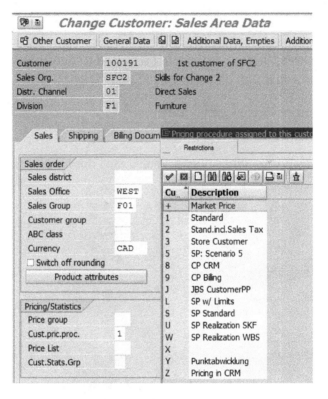

Fig 72

As noticed above, we are using 1 – Standard for our customer.

Document Pricing Procedure (C)

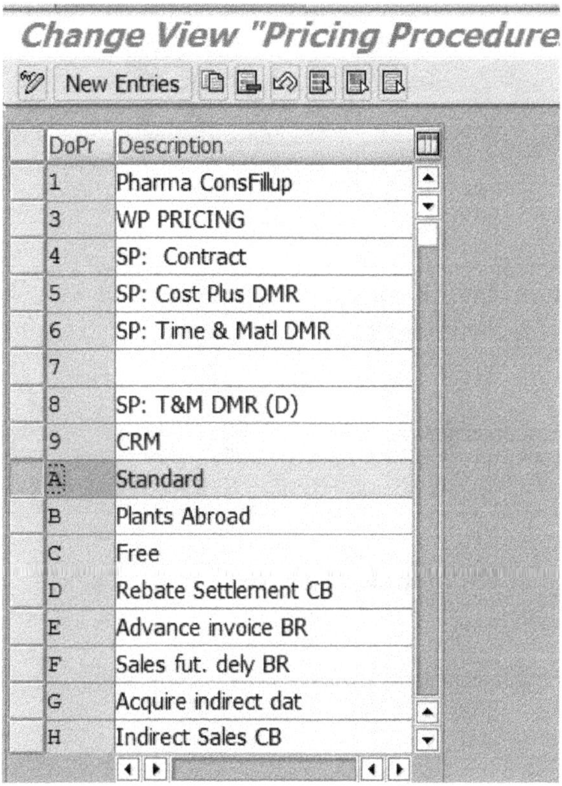

Change View "Pricing Procedure

New Entries

DoPr	Description
1	Pharma ConsFillup
3	WP PRICING
4	SP: Contract
5	SP: Cost Plus DMR
6	SP: Time & Matl DMR
7	
8	SP: T&M DMR (D)
9	CRM
A	Standard
B	Plants Abroad
C	Free
D	Rebate Settlement CB
E	Advance invoice BR
F	Sales fut. dely BR
G	Acquire indirect dat
H	Indirect Sales CB

Fig 73

We recall we have configured 6 order types to be used, the primary of them being OR. In the next step, we assign this A to OR (if not already assigned):

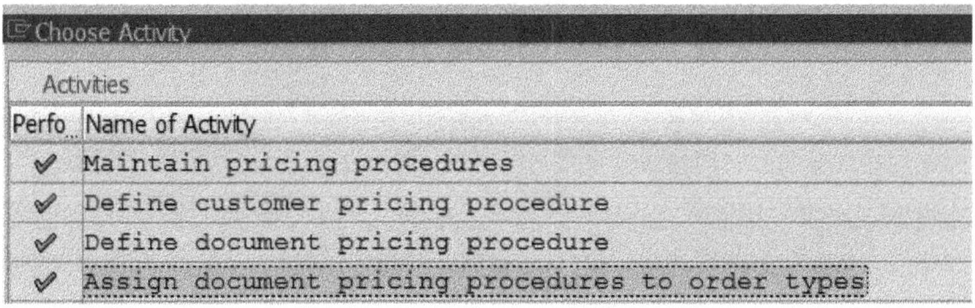

Choose Activity

Activities

Perfo	Name of Activity
✔	Maintain pricing procedures
✔	Define customer pricing procedure
✔	Define document pricing procedure
✔	Assign document pricing procedures to order types

Fig 74

147

We find it already exists:

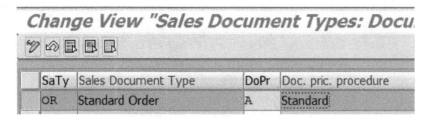

Fig 75

Since we said in the PP configuration set up that we will be copying from the sales document to the next, we don't have to assign this with the Billing types:

Fig 76

The billing will automatically get the same pricing from the sales order or delivery.

7. PRICING PROCEDURE DETERMINATION (C)

The final step it to make SAP recognize which PP to call upon in the document based on all the configurations we did and will be using.

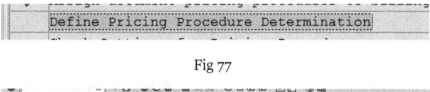

Define Pricing Procedure Determination

Fig 77

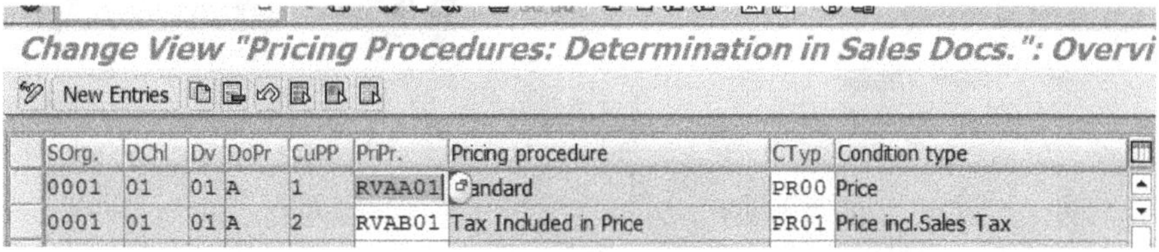

Change View "Pricing Procedures: Determination in Sales Docs.": Overvi

New Entries

SOrg.	DChl	Dv	DoPr	CuPP	PriPr.	Pricing procedure	CTyp	Condition type	
0001	01	01	A	1	RVAA01	Standard	PR00	Price	
0001	01	01	A	2	RVAB01	Tax Included in Price	PR01	Price incl.Sales Tax	

Fig 78

In the above we see how the place holders are used. The above line states that for sales area 0001/01/01, when the document pricing procedure is A and the customer pricing procedure is 1, then call for the Pricing procedure RVAA01. We need to do a similar association for our PP and our sales area. We already have an entry for our sales area because we created an order based on PR00. We will thus replace that PP with our ZRVA01. Had we not had any existing entry, we would use the button  New Entries to create them.

Using the position key, search for SFE1/01/F1 and SFE1/16/F1:

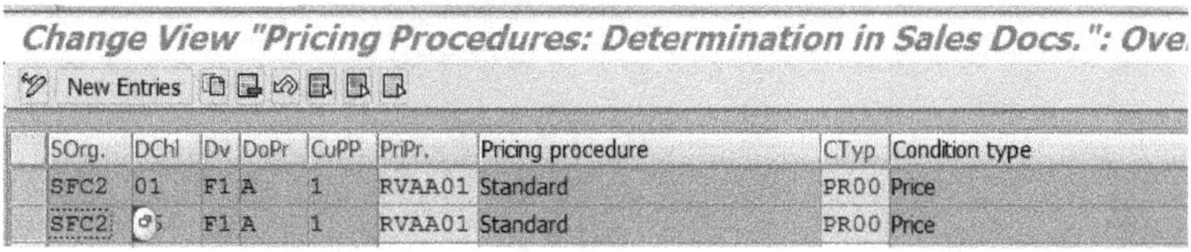

Change View "Pricing Procedures: Determination in Sales Docs.": Ove

New Entries

SOrg.	DChl	Dv	DoPr	CuPP	PriPr.	Pricing procedure	CTyp	Condition type
SFC2	01	F1	A	1	RVAA01	Standard	PR00	Price
SFC2	05	F1	A	1	RVAA01	Standard	PR00	Price

Fig 79

Replace the PP and the CTyp with our own and save:

149

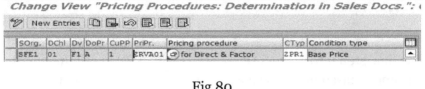

Fig 80

Fig 81

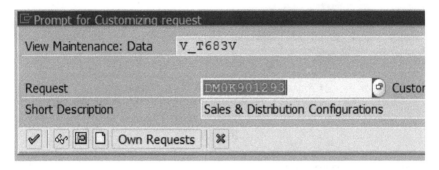

Fig 82

We are now ready to use our pricing procedure but before we do that, let us set up a pricing condition record for our material. We know from our set up that out pricing condition type ZPR1 uses the access ZPR1 which has the most specific access comprising of material, Price list and Plant.

In the customer master, set the PL = 2 (Retail) and save:

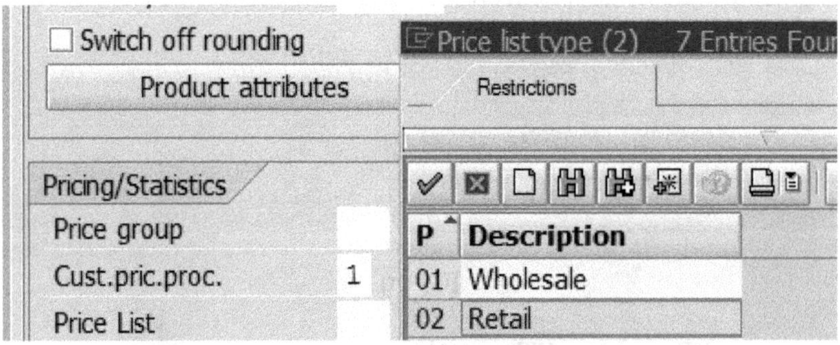

☐ Switch off rounding	⊡ Price list type (2) 7 Entries Foun	
Product attributes	Restrictions	

Pricing/Statistics	✓ ☒ ☐ 🕮 🕮 ⬚	🖵 🗎
Price group		P Description
Cust.pric.proc.	1	01 Wholesale
Price List		02 Retail

Fig 83

We know our material to be 1000654 and the plant SF01. Using these 3 data elements, let's set up a pricing condition in VK11 for ZPR1:

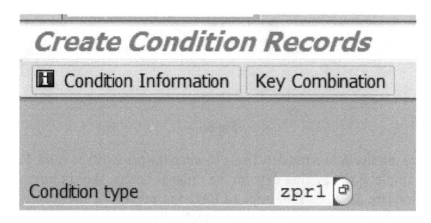

Fig 84

Hit Enter and the system will display the 3 accesses we saw earlier:

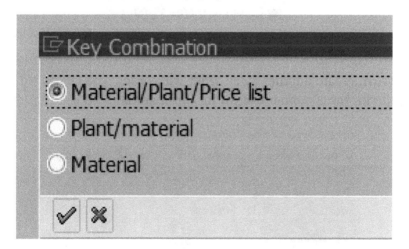

Fig 85

These 3 are tables 501, 406 and 004 respectively – from most specific to most generic.

Select the first one and click on Enter:

Enter the data:

Fig 86

The validity date is the date from/to when the price will be valid. For example. if the pricing date on the order is before May 15 2017 or after Dec 31 2017, this price of CAD 135 per EA of the material 1000654 will not apply to that automatically.

Save the data.

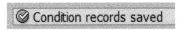

Fig 87

In VA01, create another sales order with order type OR as we did earlier for the customer 601361 for this material.

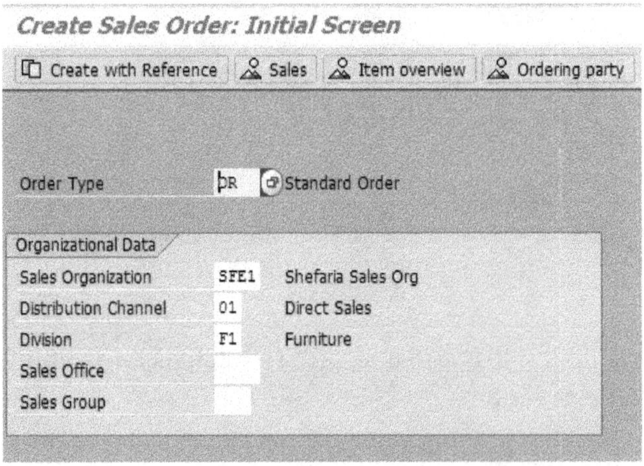

Fig 88

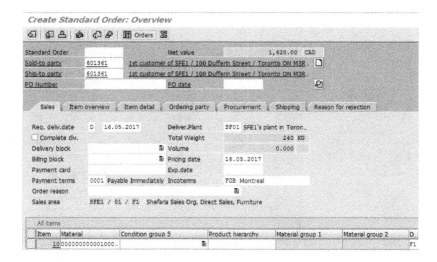

Fig 89

Note how our new price got applied.

1 CAR = 12 EA = 12* CAD 135 = CAD 1,620.

To see that process in more detail, let us go to Item>Pricing:

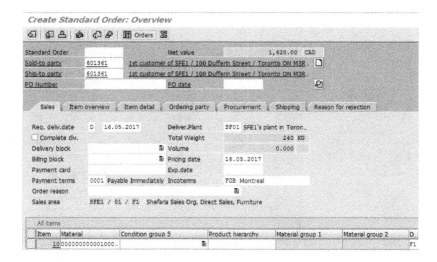

Fig 90

Click on

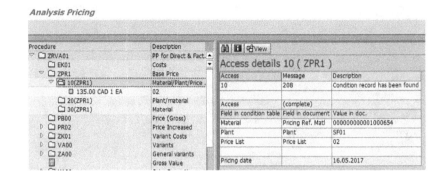

Fig 91

The screen on the right tells us the data that SAP found in the order – 1000654/SF01/02 based on that it found the pricing condition record of CAD 135/EA. Since it found this, it did not go to the next sequence of Plant/Material as we see below:

Fig 92

This is the result of checking the 'Exclusive' indicator in the access sequence of ZPR1 in configuration. Save this order

Fig 93

TAXES IN SAP (C/U)

Though taxes in SAP are a function of 3 modules - FI, SD and MM, the main structure and configurations are set up in FI and it is worthwhile to look at the user/functional aspect of this set up. The tax procedure in SAP is set up for each country; it is independent of the company code i.e. all company codes in any certain country can have only one tax procedure.

While not going into the details of the configurations because they are not company code specific, it is important to understand what these tax procedures are and how they are implemented in SAP.

Taxes in North America and Europe are calculated in different ways. We will concentrate on the Canadian taxes here which, though calculated the same way as US ones, are far less complex than US taxation because of 2 reasons:

1. In Canada, it is a 2-tiered structure of Federal and Provincial taxes only
2. In the US, it is 4 tiered depending on industry, though generally most will fall under 3 tiers. The 4 tiers are state, city, county and district. Very few industries will get the district tax applied.

For this complex taxation and rates, corporations in the US also depend on external services, the 2 most popular being Vertex and Thomson Reuters (also called Sabrix). Often these external systems also keep track of the taxes applied and prepare reports for audits and compliance as well as for filing with the appropriate authorities.

There are 2 primary kinds of taxes in SAP:

- Input tax, used for purchases
- Output tax, used for sales

Depending on the complexity of the company's taxation i.e. based on the customer base and product offering, it may decide to:

- Follow a simple tax procedure whereby all calculations in SAP are done in a standard fashion, not dependent on the exact location of the customer. In Canada, this would typically apply to companies which do business only in the same one province.
- May use the location of the customer if the business is done across provincially as the federal tax also will now come into play. This procedure uses Jurisdiction codes which are provided by the govt. or can be created in SAP and are based on exact locations since taxes are always applied based on the place of consumption. However, the calculation of them still, would take place within SAP.
- If the requirement is complex in terms of product and service offerings which may be subject to different rates of taxation, the company may decide to connect to an external system like Vertex as noted above. The taxes here too, are calculated based on the jurisdiction code however the calculation does not take place within SAP. Instead, the required data is sent out to the external system via a transmission and the taxation numbers are returned by that system and applied in SAP. This is usually real time.

Within SAP, the process is driven by tax procedures, tax codes and tax classifications. The mechanism is as follows:

WHO: Ship to customer in output or purchasing plant in input in SAP. Taxes are generally applied based on the place of consumption/use.

IF: If tax will be applied. Tax classifications are master data and the customers are given the appropriate tax class in their customer master. Alike, vendors in the vendor master. The tax classifications are usually simple – 0 means customer is non-taxable and 1 means taxable. Occasionally we may have something additional also, like partial taxation. A similar indicator exists in the material master which decides if the product or service is taxable or not. Only when both, customer and material are set as taxable, does the tax get applied.

HOW: The tax procedure decides this. How will the tax be applied i.e. directly intra provincial, via jurisdiction codes internally or from an external system? As we know, we can configure only one tax procedure per country so before SAP is implemented this choice is generally made.

HOW MUCH: This is decided by the tax codes or external systems. In a typical taxation setup, the Finance or accounting department sets up these tax codes in a transaction FTXP which replicates the tax procedure being used and sets up the correct tax rates. The same are replicated by SD for sales and MM for purchases in their respective tax pricing conditions.

1. TAX CODE DEFINITION (U)

To set up taxes in a tax code. Go to transaction FTXP, in the pop up window, say CA (for Canada):

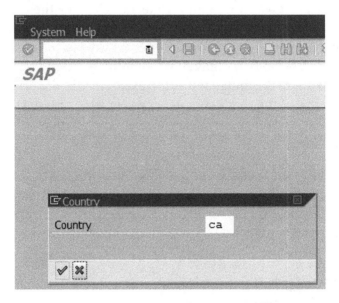

Fig 1

In the window that comes up:

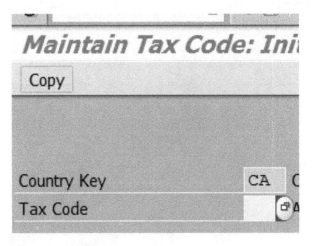

Fig 2

Place the cursor in the Tax code field and hit F4 or ask for the drop down:

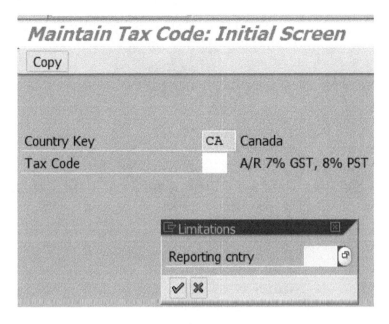

Fig 3

Hit Enter again without entering CA and all the tax codes set up for Canada will come up:

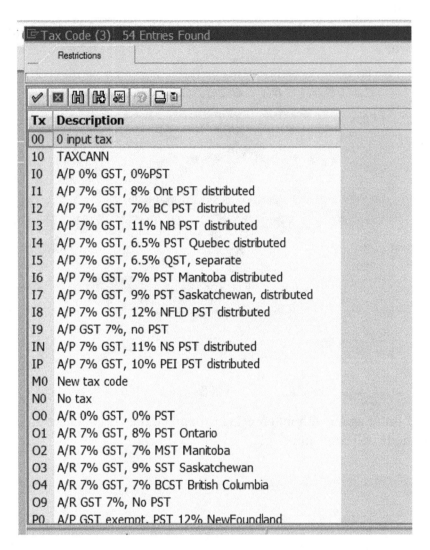

Tx	Description
00	0 input tax
10	TAXCANN
I0	A/P 0% GST, 0%PST
I1	A/P 7% GST, 8% Ont PST distributed
I2	A/P 7% GST, 7% BC PST distributed
I3	A/P 7% GST, 11% NB PST distributed
I4	A/P 7% GST, 6.5% PST Quebec distributed
I5	A/P 7% GST, 6.5% QST, separate
I6	A/P 7% GST, 7% PST Manitoba distributed
I7	A/P 7% GST, 9% PST Saskatchewan, distributed
I8	A/P 7% GST, 12% NFLD PST distributed
I9	A/P GST 7%, no PST
IN	A/P 7% GST, 11% NS PST distributed
IP	A/P 7% GST, 10% PEI PST distributed
M0	New tax code
N0	No tax
O0	A/R 0% GST, 0% PST
O1	A/R 7% GST, 8% PST Ontario
O2	A/R 7% GST, 7% MST Manitoba
O3	A/R 7% GST, 9% SST Saskatchewan
O4	A/R 7% GST, 7% BCST British Columbia
O9	A/R GST 7%, No PST
P0	A/P GST exempt, PST 12% NewFoundland

Fig 4

Let us choose O9 as the one we will set up taxation in. Double click on it and Hit Enter:

Maintain Tax Code: Tax Rates

Properties	Tax accounts	Deactivate line

Country Key	CA	Canada
Tax Code	O9	A/R GST 7%, No PST
Procedure	TAXCA	
Tax type	A	Output tax

Percentage rates

Tax Type	Acct Key	Tax Percent. Rate	Level	From Lvl	Cond. Type
*			0	0	
Base Amount			100	0	BASB
***********			105	0	
A/P and MM			106	0	
Federal Taxes (US):			107	0	
*	VSC		110	100	GTI1
*	TR1		112	100	TRA1
A/P Sales Tax 1 Inv.	NVV		115	100	AP1I
*	NVV		120	100	GTI2
Subtotal			199	0	
Subtotal			200	0	
Provincial Taxes (Ca			210	0	
*	NVV		220	100	PTI1
*	VST		230	100	PTI2

Fig 5

Percentage rates

Tax Type	Acct Key	Tax Percent. Rate	Level	From Lvl	Cond. Type
*	TR2		232	100	TRA2
*			250	0	
Separate G/L posting			251	0	
*	NVV		260	199	PTI3
*	VST		270	199	PTI4
*	TR3		272	199	TRA3
Subtotal			298	0	
*			299	0	
Self assessed:			300	0	
*	VSC		310	100	GTI3
*	VST		320	100	PTI5
*	VST		330	199	PTI6
*************			399	0	
Self assess Prov.			410	0	

Fig 6

Percentage rates						
Tax Type	Acct Key	Tax Percent. Rate	Level	From Lvl	Cond. Type
*	MW1		420	100	PTU1
*	MW2		430	200	PTU2
*			498	0	
*********			499	0	
A/R and SD			600	0	
*	MWS		610	100	GTO0
*			698	0	
Subtotal			700	0	
*	MWS		710	100	GTO1
*	MW1		720	700	GTO2
Subtotal			750	0	
*	MWZ		830	100	PST1
*	MWZ		840	750	PST2

Fig 7

The above is the tax procedure TAXCA being used in our system in Canada. Thus, all company codes in Canada are using this. The main columns denote:

-   Tax type – input, output. Though we have called for tax code O9, the procedure is common to both, input and output.
-   Account key. This key is a determining factor of how the tax values are going to post
-   Tax percent rate. This is the field you would be most concerned about. This is where the actual numbers relating to tax percentages will be entered.

Click on the tax

Here we can alter/enter the description of what this tax code represents. Let's say we retain this and our customers are charged 7% GST when we sell them the products. Just having 7% in the description does not mean it will get charged. We now need to enter this 7% in the field relating to MWS as the account key.

162

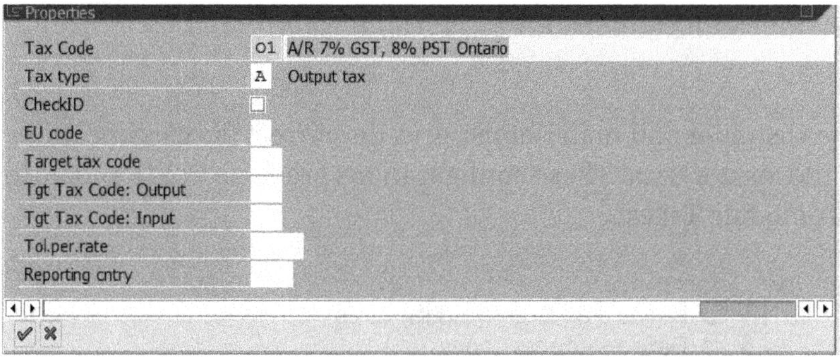

Fig 8

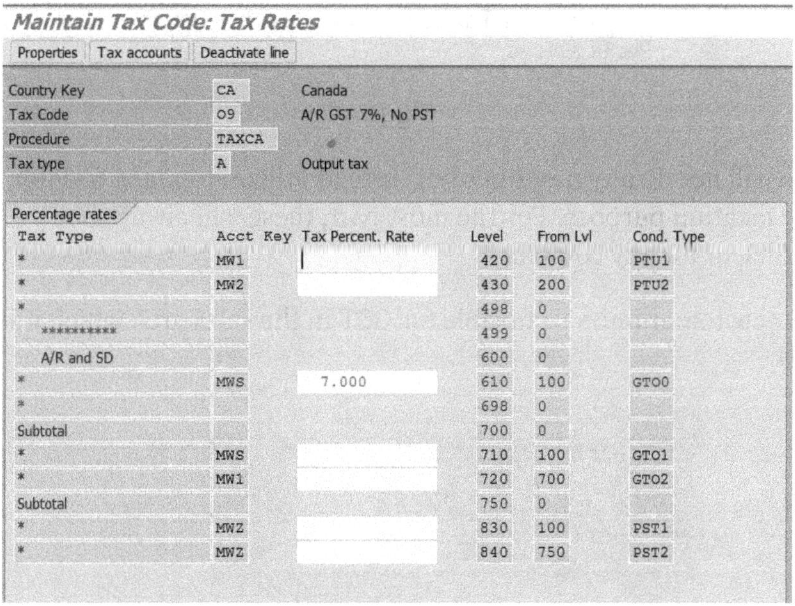

Fig 9

In our case, we are not using the jurisdiction based tax procedure so configurations are missing and we don't want to alter that because it will affect all company codes of others also that have been created in Canada. However, the above must be maintained if we use a JC based procedure. Currently, because the tax procedure being used is not based off the JCs, it will not allow us to save.

2. TAX RELEVANCY OF MASTER RECORDS (C)

The customer and material requires the correct tax classifications in the master data. These configurations are done in SD under the sub-module Taxes:

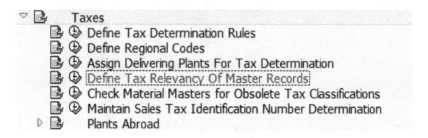

Fig 10

We will not do any new ones but instead utilize standard SAP for the taxation purpose. For the most part, these will always be sufficient for any company.

Our customer must be taxable for GST in the sales area which it is (U)

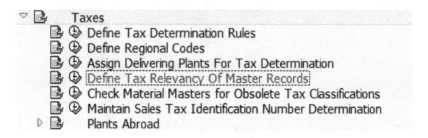

Fig 11

Our material also to taxable as we know taxes get applied only when both are set to taxable:

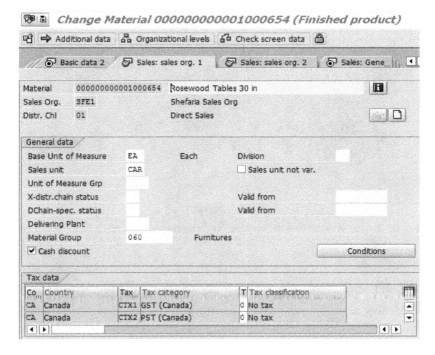

Fig 12

So, we make it taxable:

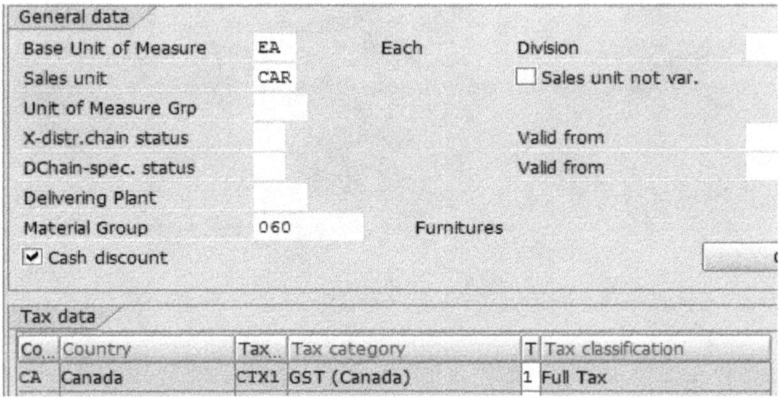

Co.	Country	Tax.	Tax category	T	Tax classification
CA	Canada	CTX1	GST (Canada)	1	Full Tax

Fig 13

3. MAINTAIN TAX CONDITION RECORD (U)

Next, we set a tax pricing condition only on the SD side. This is done in transaction VK11:

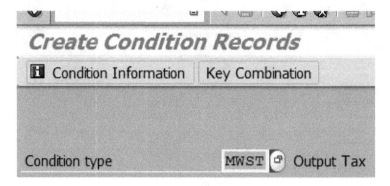

Fig 14

Hit Enter and choose the 2nd sequence as we are doing domestic sales here:

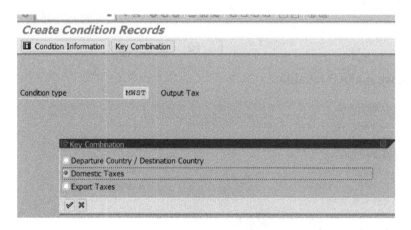

Fig 15

Enter data as below:

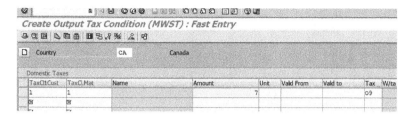

Fig 16

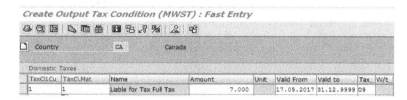

Fig 17

Save. We said in above, that when the material and customer, both are taxable i.e. the tax class is 1 for both, then apply a domestic tax of 7% based on the tax code O9 (only GST).

Let us create a sales order and see the effect:

We see on the pricing screen that the system has now applied the 7% tax we set up:

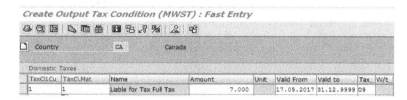

Fig 18

ACCOUNT ASSIGNMENT/COSTING (C)

REVENUE ACCOUNT DETERMINATION

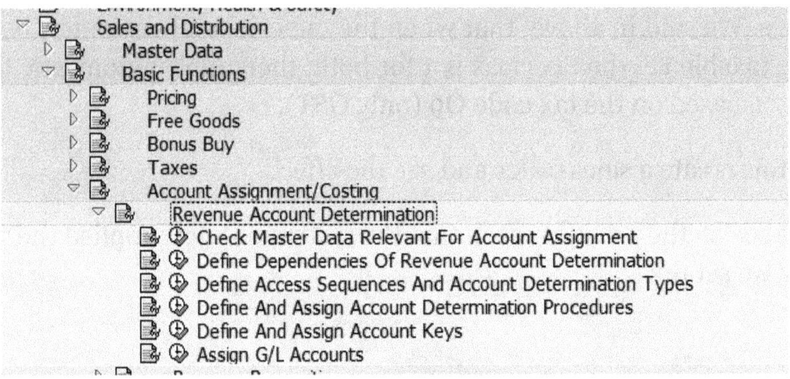

Fig 1

Revenue Account determination is the cusp between SD and FI. With the revenues, taxes, discounts etc. finding their way into the G/L accounts, the data is handed over from SD to Finance. Though the G/L accounts themselves will be decided and set up by FI, the G/L account determination takes place in SD. This determination comes into play when the invoice is created and released to accounting. We will see the effects of this determination when we do billing. Now, we will understand how this is set up in SD. Again, like at many places, condition technique comes into play here where certain master data will act as 'place holder' to get to the desired result.

Fig 2

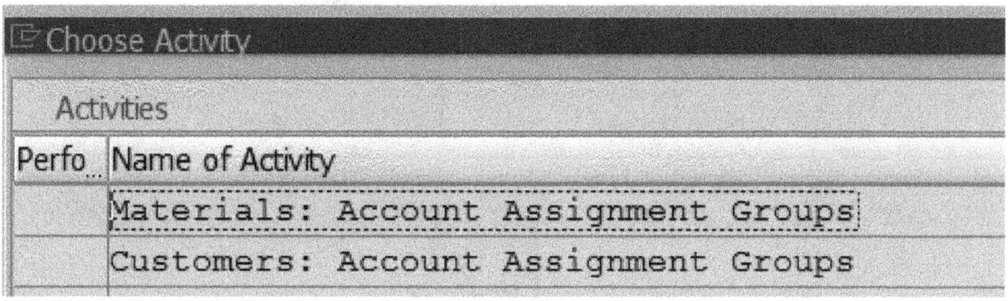

Fig 3

Account assignment groups 'group' the materials and customers into required buckets. For example. we may want all the domestic customers to belong to one group when it comes to posting revenues. Similarly, we may want a certain category/group of materials to belong to the same group for this reason. We set up these groups in the above configuration. SAP provides some groups as standard, new ones can be set up with 2 digit alpha numeric codes.

i)   Material AAG

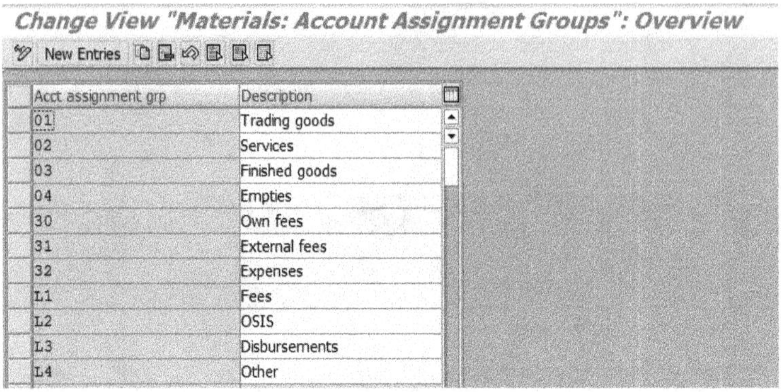

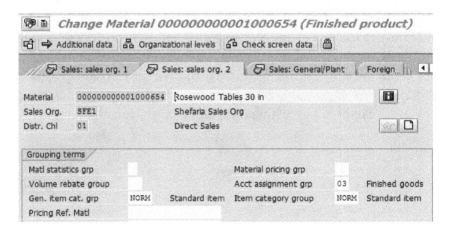

Fig 4

In the material master these groups are assigned in the Sales area data:

Fig 5

Thus, it is possible to make a material belong to different AAGs in different sales areas. This may come in handy in a backward integrated company which may use the same material as a RM for another group company while also selling it outside to external customers. In that case, it can have a RM AAG and a FG AAG in the

170

2 areas. It can also be used like a kind of product or service rather than just a FG/RM/WIP etc.

ii)   Customer AAG

Works exactly like the material AAG:

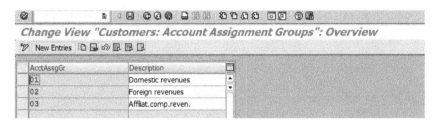

Fig 6

In the customer master, it is found in the billing tab in the sales area data:

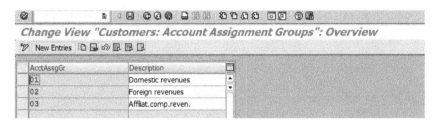

Fig 7

Again, it can be different in different sales areas. A customer in Germany may be domestic for the sales area of Germany and export/foreign for the sales area of Canada. So, it can have a different AAG in different areas.

The next 2 steps are like the condition tables, access sequences and the PP so we will skip it:

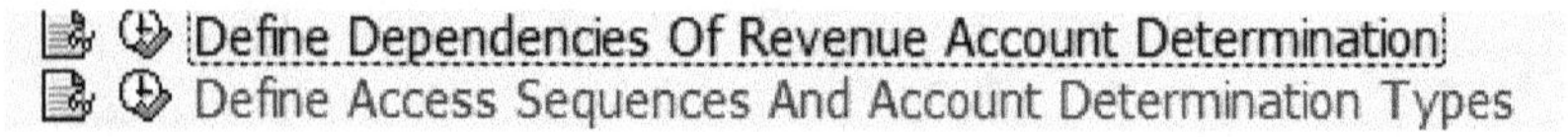

📑 ⊕ Define Dependencies Of Revenue Account Determination
📑 ⊕ Define Access Sequences And Account Determination Types

Fig 8

The standard account determination procedure in SAP is called KOFI:

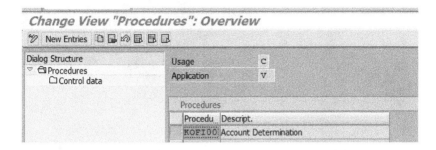

Fig 9

Click on the Control data for KOFI:

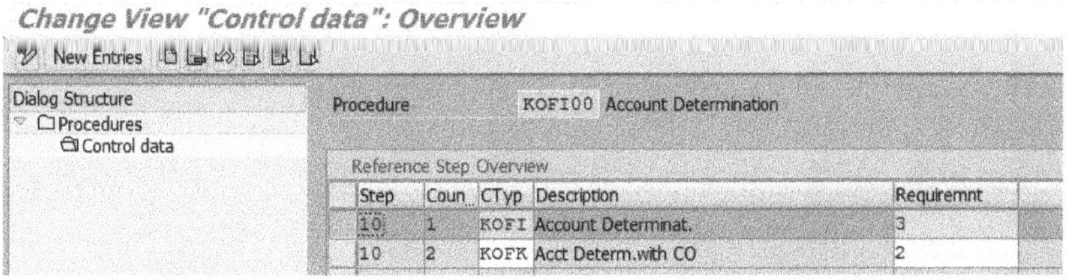

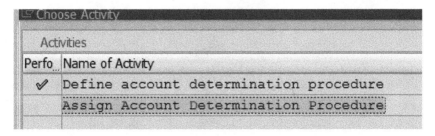

Fig 10

The 2nd one, KOFK is used by FI in conjunction with controlling module (CO) and we will limit our training to the 1st one as that is what SD utilizes and we look at its assignment:

Fig 11

SAP has already provided all the configuration needed for it to be used with the existing Billing types:

BillT	Description	ActDPr	Description	CaAc	Name	
CB2	Rebate Correction CB	KOFI00				
CB3E	ExpRebPartSettlm CB	KOFI00				
CB4	RebManual Accrls CB	KOFI00				
CB5E	ExpRebCreMemoInd CB	KOFI00				
CB7E	ExpRebPartSettInd CB	KOFI00				
CBCI	Ind Cancellation	KOFI00				
CBF2	BEV Invoice	KOFI00				
CBG2	BEV Credit Memo	KOFI00				
CBID	Ind Invoice Reb CB	KOFI00				
CBS1	Cancel CreditMemo CB	KOFI00				
CHFK	Bil.Ext.CH Trans. D	KOFI00				
CHFX	Bil.Ext.CH Trans. C	KOFI00				
F1	Invoice (F1)	KOFI00				
F2	Invoice (F2)	KOFI00				
F2B	Nota fiscal	KOFI00				
F5	Pro Forma for Order					

Title: Change View "Billing: Document Types - Account Determination": Overvie

Fig 12

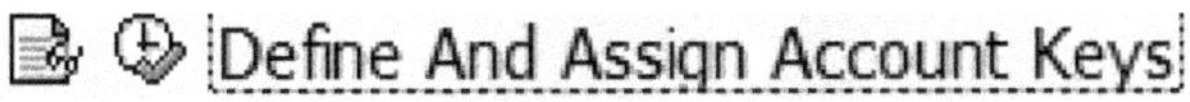

Fig 13

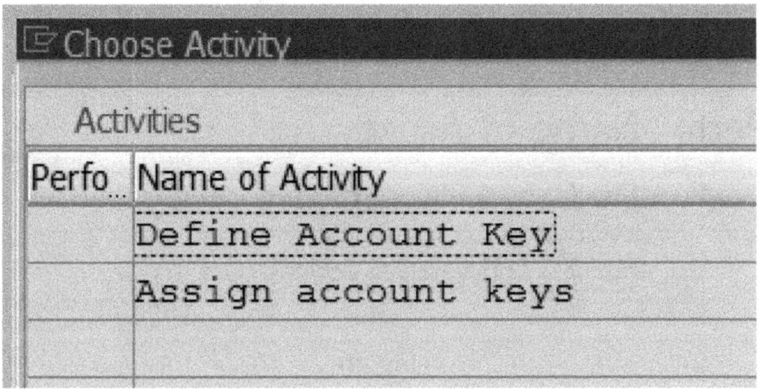

Fig 14

We saw the use of the account keys in the Pricing Procedure earlier. This is the place where we define them:

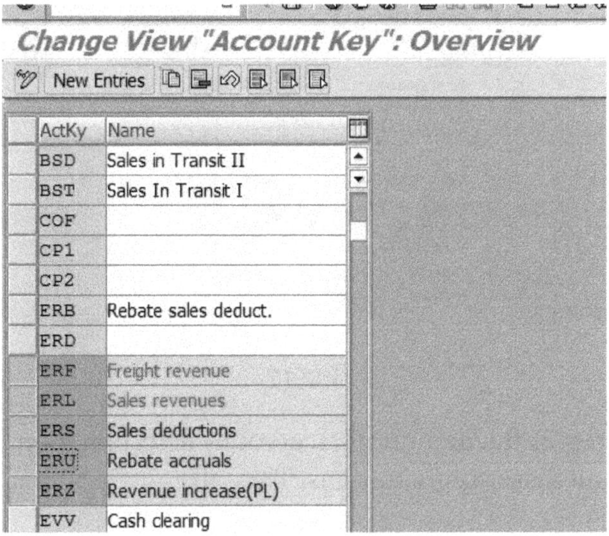

ActKy	Name
BSD	Sales in Transit II
BST	Sales In Transit I
COF	
CP1	
CP2	
ERB	Rebate sales deduct.
ERD	
ERF	Freight revenue
ERL	Sales revenues
ERS	Sales deductions
ERU	Rebate accruals
ERZ	Revenue increase(PL)
EVV	Cash clearing

Fig 15

More can be defined freely as required using the letter Z.

Next, we assign them here or this step can be done directly in the PP also.

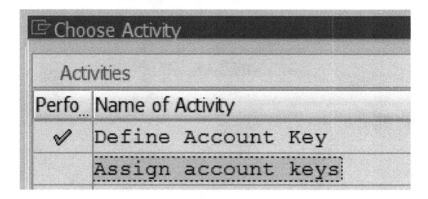

Fig 16

Proc.	Step	Cntr	CTyp	Name	ActKy	Name	Accrls	Name
ZRVA01	8	0	EK01	Costs	ERL	Sales revenues		Sales
	11	0	ZPR1	Base Price	ERL	Sales revenues		
	13	0	PB00	Price (Gross)	ERL	Sales revenues		
	14	0	PR02	Price Increased	ERL	Sales revenues		
	15	0	ZK01	Variant Costs	ERL	Sales revenues		
	20	0	VA00	Variants	ERL	Sales revenues		
	21	0	ZA00	General variants	ERL	Sales revenues		
	101	0	KA00	Sales Promotion	ERS	Sales deductions		
	102	0	K032	Price Group/Material	ERS	Sales deductions		
	103	0	K005	Customer/Material	ERS	Sales deductions		
	104	0	K007	Customer Discount	ERS	Sales deductions		
	105	0	K004	Material	ERS	Sales deductions		
	106	0	K020	Price Group	ERS	Sales deductions		
	107	0	K029	Mat.Pricing Group	ERS	Sales deductions		
	108	0	K030	Customer/Mat.Pr.Grp	ERS	Sales deductions		
	109	0	K031	Price Grp/Mat.Pr.Grp	ERS	Sales deductions		

Change View "Pricing Procedures: Revenue Account Determination": Overv

Fig 17

The last step in the account G/L account determination process is the use of all these configurations. They all come together in:

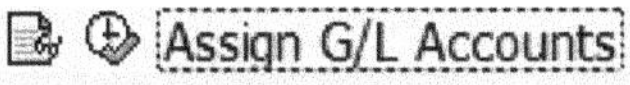

⤷ ⊕ Assign G/L Accounts

Fig 18

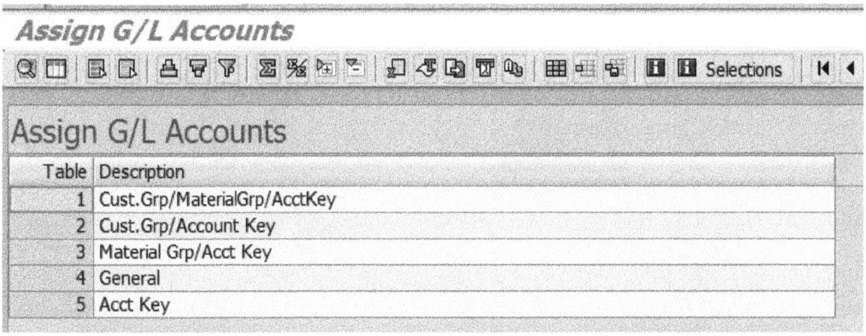

Assign G/L Accounts

Q □ | 🖹 🗋 | ⚍ 🖤 🖤 | 🖩 ％ 🔢 🖹 | 🗓 ⚍ 🗗 🖤 🕲 | 🖩 ⬛ 🖥 | ▤ ▤ Selections | I◀ ◀

Assign G/L Accounts

Table	Description
1	Cust.Grp/MaterialGrp/AcctKey
2	Cust.Grp/Account Key
3	Material Grp/Acct Key
4	General
5	Acct Key

Fig 19

The above are the standard SAP provided accesses, like in Pricing, these are actual tables we saw earlier and they work their way down from the most specific to the most generic.

Thus, in our case, if we were to post the revenue of from the sale of this material 1000654 (AAG =3) and customer 601361 (AAG = 1) then for the account key ERL (Revenue) then we could set it up in the 1st sequence:

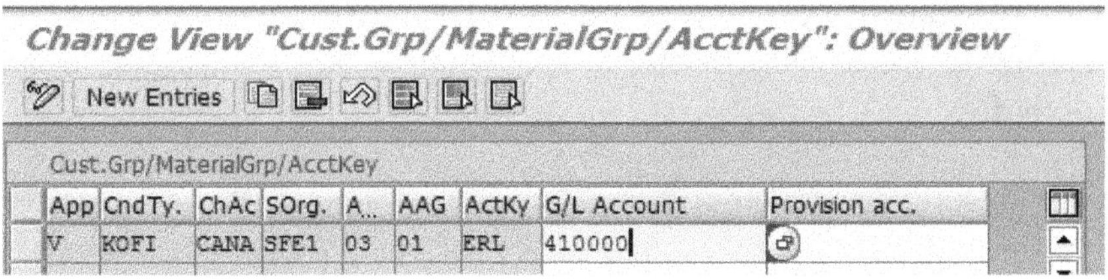

Change View "Cust.Grp/MaterialGrp/AcctKey": Overview

🖉 New Entries 🗋 🖳 🐼 🖳 🖳 🖳

Cust.Grp/MaterialGrp/AcctKey

App	CndTy.	ChAc	SOrg.	A..	AAG	ActKy	G/L Account	Provision acc.	
V	KOFI	CANA	SFE1	03	01	ERL	410000	⊡	

Fig 20

And save it. Now any revenue coming from any customer that has AAG 01 and Material having AAG of 03 would go to G/L account 410000.

OUTPUT DETERMINATION (C/U)

In SAP, every document and its details that print, either on paper or in electronic form, is called an Output. The more common and generally preferred method of creating Outputs on the SD side is doing it via the condition technique. In principle, it behaves very similar to Pricing technique except it is less complex and more flexible because it is not as sensitive as pricing is.

Different Output determination procedures exist for different activities and all work in the same way. Here, we will discuss the one relating to the sales order as that is what we are working through currently:

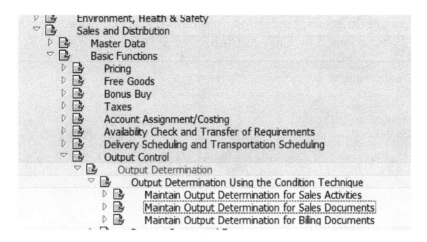

Fig 1

The area Menu for Output control is NACE and can be very useful in finding everything at one place.

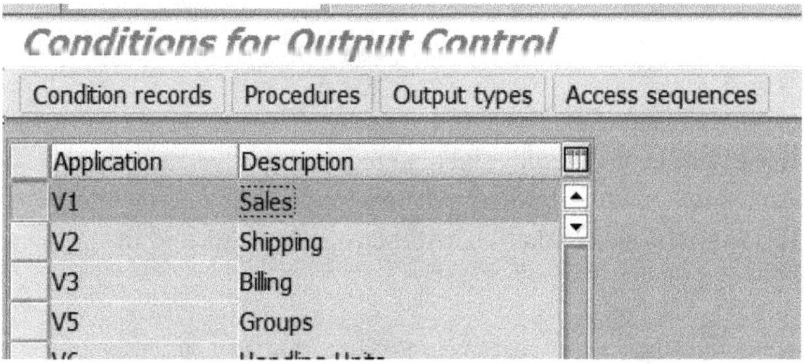

Conditions for Output Control

Condition records	Procedures	Output types	Access sequences

Application	Description	
V1	Sales	
V2	Shipping	
V3	Billing	
V5	Groups	

Fig 2

Highlight the application we are working on, Sales, and then on Procedures:

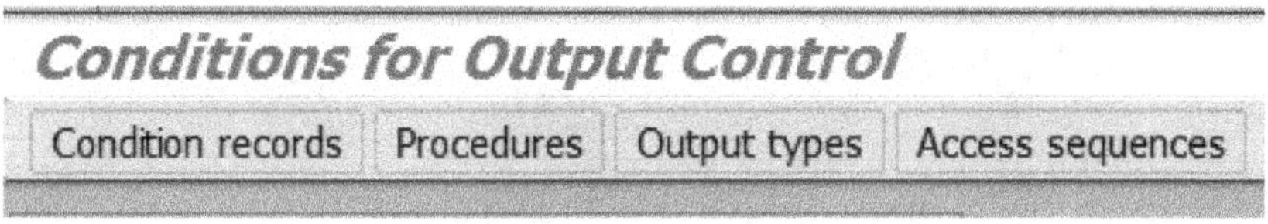

Conditions for Output Control

Condition records	Procedures	Output types	Access sequences

Fig 3

There are different standard Output determination procedures that SAP has provided for different sub areas of Order processing:

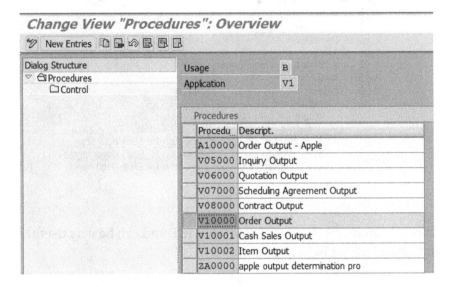

Change View "Procedures": Overview

New Entries

Dialog Structure		
▽ ⊟ Procedures		
☐ Control		

Usage   B
Application   V1

Procedures

Procedu	Descript.
A10000	Order Output - Apple
V05000	Inquiry Output
V06000	Quotation Output
V07000	Scheduling Agreement Output
V08000	Contract Output
V10000	Order Output
V10001	Cash Sales Output
V10002	Item Output
ZA0000	apple output determination pro

Fig 4

VIoooo is the standard for Order header. VIooo2 would work where we need details of the material also to print on the document – often information relating to Dangerous goods, Shelf lives etc. can be important on documents like order confirmations and in those cases this procedure would be used.

Double clicking on Control gives us the details of this procedure:

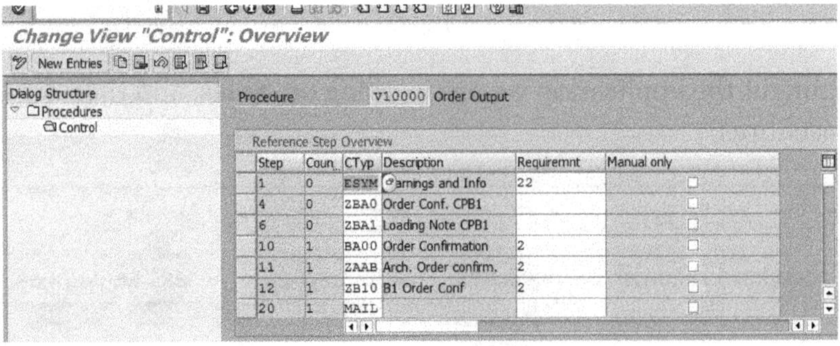

Change View "Control": Overview

New Entries

Dialog Structure		
▽ ☐ Procedures		
⊟ Control		

Procedure   V10000   Order Output

Reference Step Overview

Step	Coun.	CTyp	Description	Requiremnt	Manual only	
1	0	ESYM	�▢arnings and Info	22	☐	
4	0	ZBA0	Order Conf. CPB1		☐	
6	0	ZBA1	Loading Note CPB1		☐	
10	1	BA00	Order Confirmation	2	☐	
11	1	ZAAB	Arch. Order confirm.	2	☐	
12	1	ZB10	B1 Order Conf	2	☐	
20	1	MAIL			☐	

Fig 5

Similarly, clicking on Output types will tell us all the outputs being used in the area of Sales:

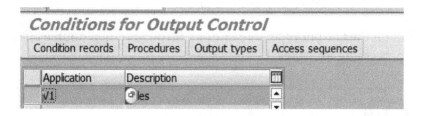

Fig 6

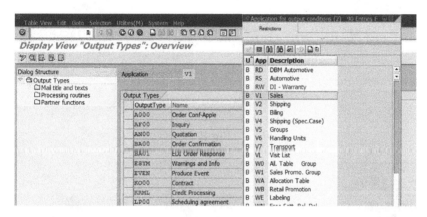

Fig 7

Each Output type requires its own set up for its application:

i.   HOW: This is a result of a print program which will decide how the output will create

ii. WHAT: Most popular way of doing this is called smart form which takes all the data and 'lays it out' as/on the form. Both these are part of ABAP/4 programming and out of scope of this course

iii. WHEN: Exactly as in the pricing condition technique, the output will get triggered when certain qualifying data is found in the document

iv. WHERE: Usually a part of output conditions but can be entered manually. A user can direct the printing of the output to any pre-configured printers in SAP. The user may also direct it electronically to any external email address or device/platform which may further convert this into a finished product.

Click on the Output type for example. BA00 and then double click on processing Routines:

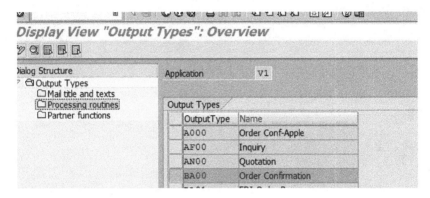

Fig 8

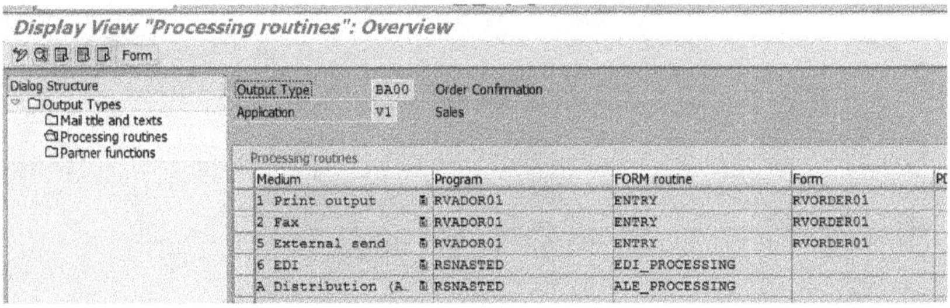

Fig 9

The above configuration tells is that program RVADOR01 is the HOW and Form RVORDER01 is the WHAT.
Now click on an output type BA00 again and then on the detail

button :

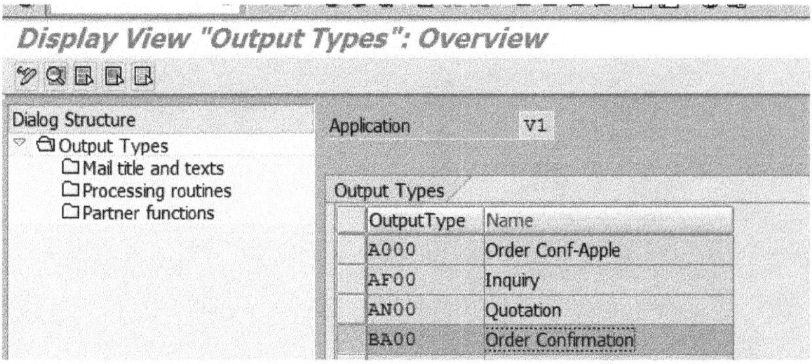

Fig 10

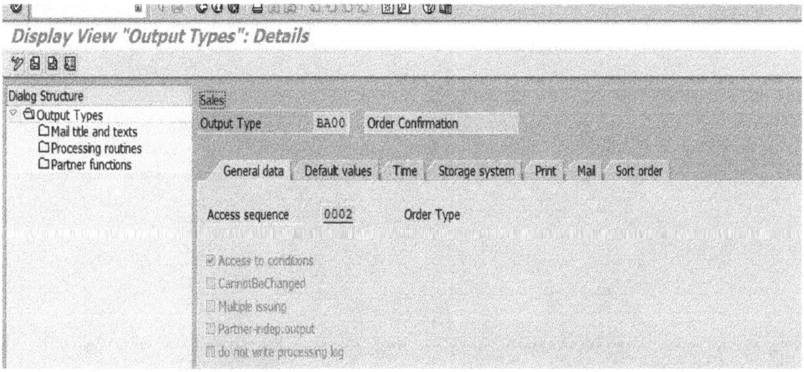

Fig 11

As always, we see an access sequence associated with an output, here 0002 will be used by the Output condition BA00 to find the required condition records. This is the WHEN. The above is the default data (i.e. the data that will get proposed in the output condition record but can for the most part, be replaced if the configuration allows).

Let us set up an Output condition record for BA00 to understand the WHERE. The transaction code to set up an output condition for sales orders is VV11 or follow the path:

CC01 - Create
SAP menu
Office
Cross-Application Components
Collaboration Projects
Logistics
Materials Management
Sales and Distribution
Master Data
Business Partner
Products
Conditions
Output
Sales Document
VV11 - Create
VV12 - Change
VV13 - Display

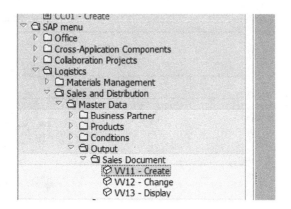

Fig 12

Enter BA00 and Hit enter:

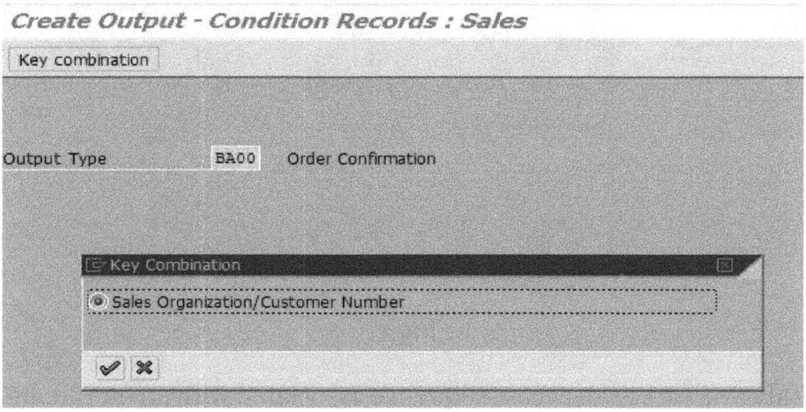

Create Output - Condition Records : Sales
Key combination
Output Type
BA00
Order Confirmation
Key Combination
Sales Organization/Customer Number

Fig 13

As we see, access sequence 0002 is a very simple access sequence which looks at a simple access which in turn needs only the Order type as its qualifying data. In the familiar screen that follows, enter the data:

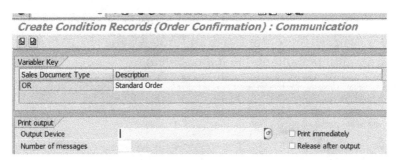

Create Condition Records (Order Confirmation): Fast Entry

| Communication 🔍 🗑 | | | | | | | | |

| Sales Organization | SFE1 | | Shefaria Sales Org | | | | |

Condition Recs.

Customer	Name	Funct	Partner	M..	Dat..	Lang..
601361		SP		1	3	☝

Fig 14

- 601361 is the customer when this output will get triggered as it comes across this customer order.
- 1 (Print) is the medium of transmission
- 3 is the timing i.e. when would the output print. 3 means a job will print it, for the time being it will only create. 4 would mean it will print right away.

Highlight the line and click on Communication tab:

Create Condition Records (Order Confirmation) : Communication

Variabler Key	
Sales Document Type	Description
OR	Standard Order

Print output
| Output Device | | ☐ Print immediately |
| Number of messages | | ☐ Release after output |

Fig 15

185

Output device is the WHERE. Do a drop down to select or enter PDF1 in this system:

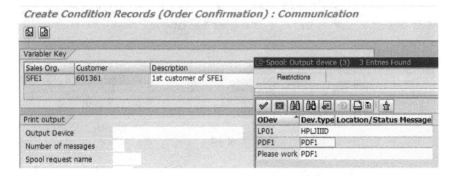

Fig 16

Save:

Fig 17

Let us now go back to the order we had created earlier, 11920 and see if we can see this output in it. In VA02, Change Sales order enter the order number and on the main screen:

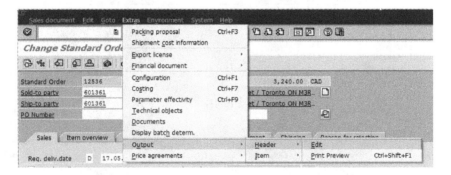

Fig 18

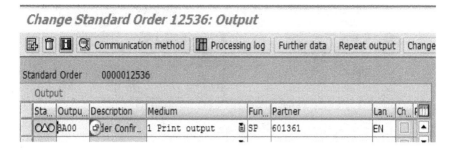

Fig 19

In the same way as we analyze pricing, Outputs can also be analyzed. The only difference is, Outputs can be analyzed only in the Change mode in the document, while pricing can be analyzed in change and in display mode.

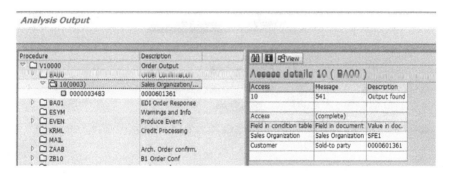

Fig 20

We find the output triggered because it found the sales organization SFE1 and customer 601361.

We can preview an output from the same spot:

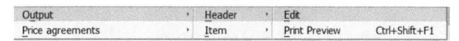

Fig 21

Alternatively, the more preferred method is to do it directly from the VA02/VA03 screen:

187

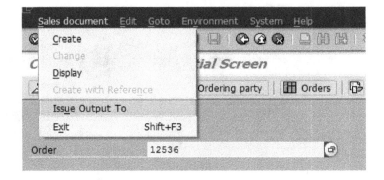

Fig 22

Highlight the output you want to preview and select the preview button 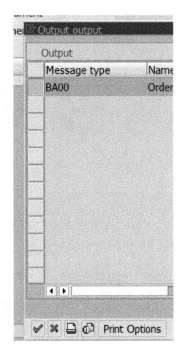:

Fig 23

IOBE US Inc. 1230 Lincoln Avenue 10019 New York

1st customer of SFE1	**Order confirmation**
100 Dufferin Street	Number/Date
Toronto ON M3R 4W2	12536 / 2017.05.17
	Reference no./Date
	Delivery date
	Day 2017.05.17
	Cust. no.
	601361

We deliver according to the following conditions: Currency CAD
Terms of payment Within 14 days 3.000 % cash discount
                 Within 30 days 2.000 % cash discount
                 Within 45 days without deduction
Terms of delivery   FOB Montreal

Weights (gross/net) - Volume - Mark
Gross weight   480 KG Net weight   432 KG

Fig 24

The above is the 'form' which we referred to as WHAT. We can also change the printer to any other pre-configured on in SAP using the

button **Print Options**

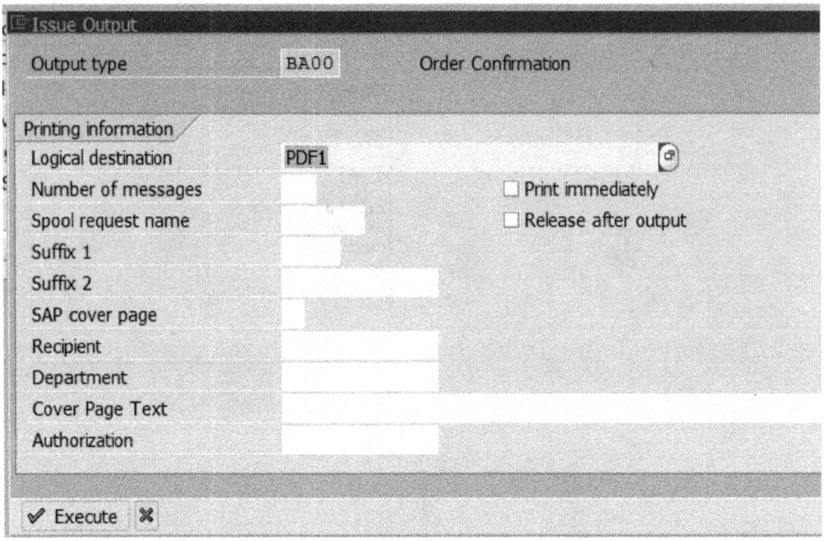

Fig 25

TEXT CONTROL (C/U)

Yet another application of SAP's condition technique:

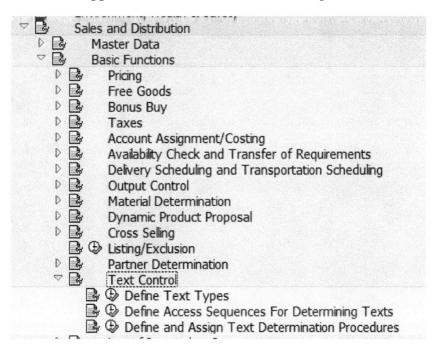

Fig 1

Texts are used to add data to the document that may be:

- Ad hoc or temporary and relating to a document only
- To print notes on certain documents that are not required to be seen by the external parties (like customers) but are necessary in execution of the order.
- Data that is unable to flow from master data or the previous transaction because it was not available

The process again is exactly like the one for pricing and outputs when it comes to determining the texts. What is different is where these texts are placed in SAP and how they are transferred from the customer master to documents.

TEXT TYPES (C)

Text Control
Define Text Types
Define Access Sequences For Determining Texts
Define and Assign Text Determination Procedures

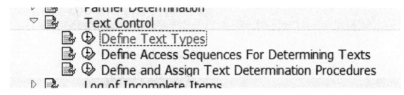

Fig 2

Click on Define text types:

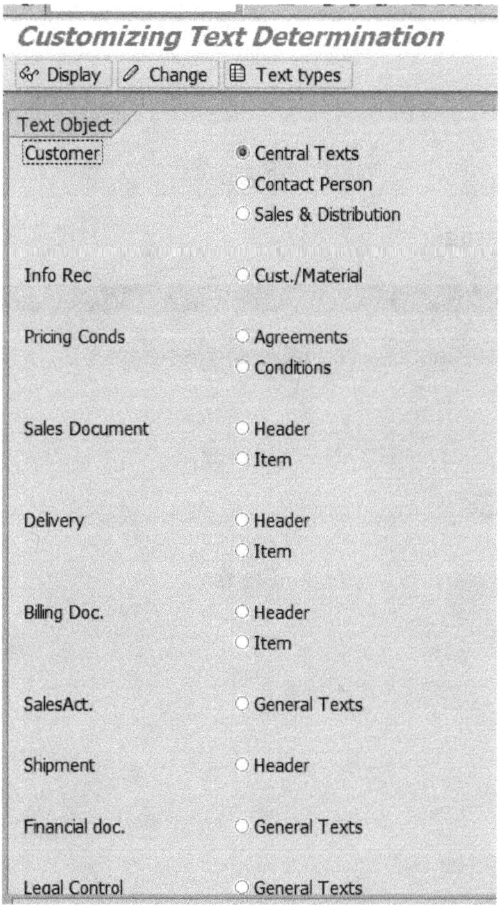
Customizing Text Determination
Display
Change
Text types
Text Object
Customer
Central Texts
Contact Person
Sales & Distribution
Info Rec
Cust./Material
Pricing Conds
Agreements
Conditions
Sales Document
Header
Item
Delivery
Header
Item
Billing Doc.
Header
Item
SalesAct.
General Texts
Shipment
Header
Financial doc.
General Texts
Legal Control
General Texts

Fig 3

Number of different kinds of texts exist in different areas:

Let us see the customer master texts and where they can be found:

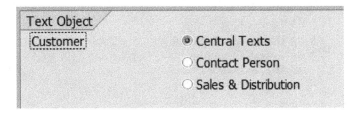

Fig 4

Click on Text types:

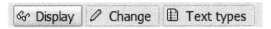

Fig 5

Ignore the message:

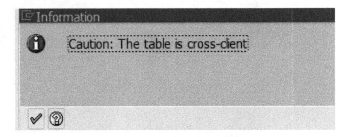

Fig 6

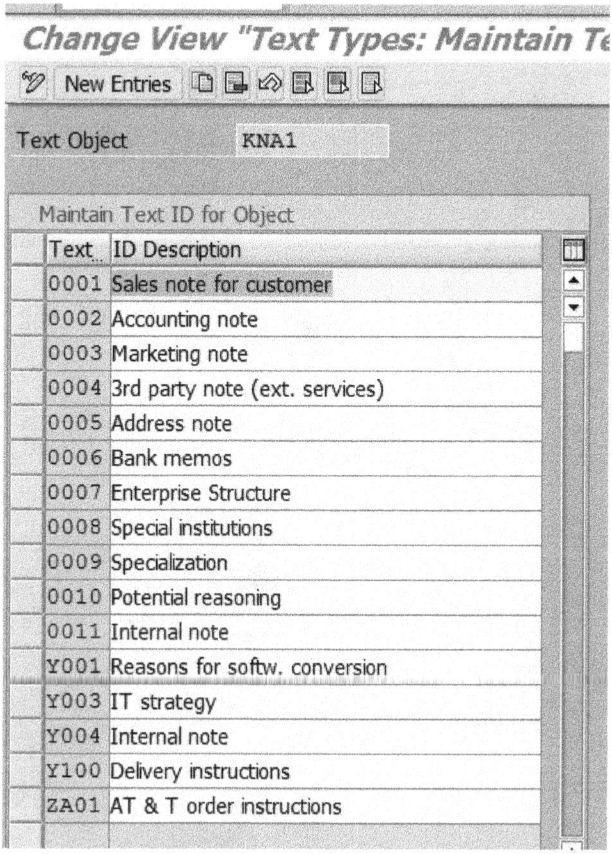

Change View "Text Types: Maintain T~~e~~

New Entries ☐ ☐ ◈ ☐ ☐ ☐

Text Object   KNA1

Maintain Text ID for Object

Text	ID Description
0001	Sales note for customer
0002	Accounting note
0003	Marketing note
0004	3rd party note (ext. services)
0005	Address note
0006	Bank memos
0007	Enterprise Structure
0008	Special institutions
0009	Specialization
0010	Potential reasoning
0011	Internal note
Y001	Reasons for softw. conversion
Y003	IT strategy
Y004	Internal note
Y100	Delivery instructions
ZA01	AT & T order instructions

Fig 7

As we see there are several texts provided by SAP and we also can define our own (the ones beginning with Y or Z). The text object KNA1 refers to the customer master table where the general data is stored (hence these are called central texts i.e. they will apply regardless of which sales area the customer is in).

In the customer master, we will find them in the General area. Let us see our customer 601361:

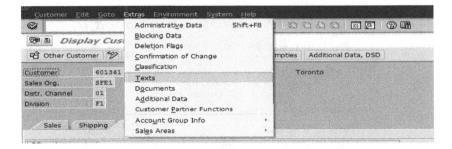

Fig 8

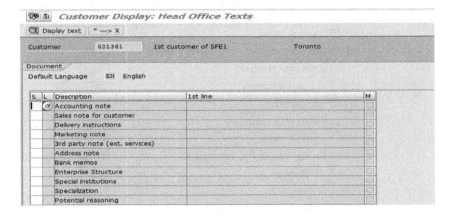

Fig 9

We can enter infinite amount of text in the space provided under 1st line by double clicking on the required text line:

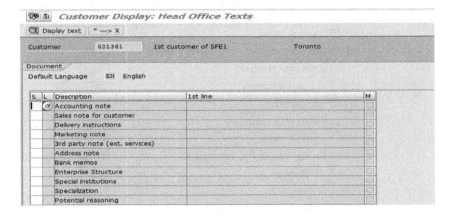

Fig 10

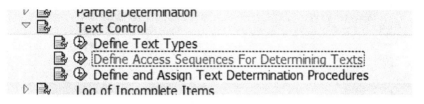

Fig 11

Access sequences come into play when a document needs to pick up a certain text from the customer master but we may want to define the process of picking it. As we know there can be 4 major (amongst more) partners on a document – the sold to, the ship to, the bill to and the payer. Often the sold to have multiple ship to's and different ship to's may have different texts. We may be required to first look up the ship to for a text and not finding anything, may have to look at the sold to. It will be best shown with an example. Let's say we need to look up the text 0001 (Sales note for customer) from SH first and then from the SP. In the text determination configuration for the sales order Header texts:

Customizing Text Determination

&° Display   ∅ Change   ▣ Text types

Text Object

Customer	○ Central Texts
	○ Contact Person
	○ Sales & Distribution
Info Rec	○ Cust./Material
Pricing Conds	○ Agreements
	○ Conditions
Sales Document	◉ Header
	○ Item

Fig 12

197

Click on Change

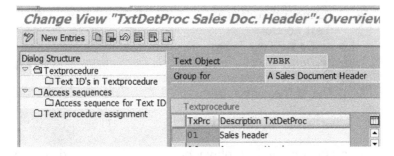

Fig 13

Highlight the 01 Procedure and double click on Text ID's in procedure:

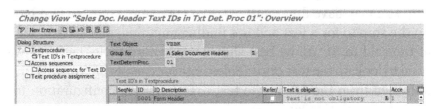

Fig 14

The above screen tells us that:

In the sales order> Header texts (text object VBBK) the ID 0001 – form header is not a mandatory text and it will be determined by the Access sequence 1. To see this sequence, double click on Access sequences after highlighting as above to display all the sequences:

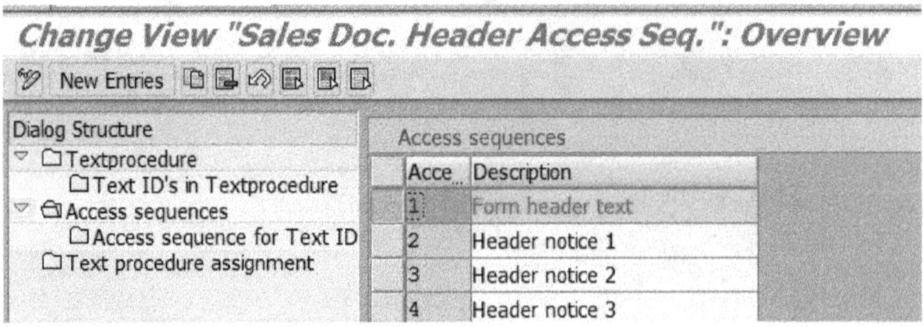

Change View "Sales Doc. Header Access Seq.": Overview

Fig 15

198

Highlight as above and now double click on Access Sequence for Test ID:

Re-align the columns in the screen that comes by pulling them to the left:

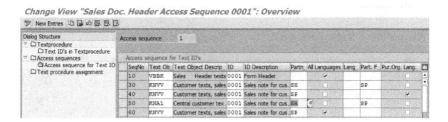

Fig 16

The above screen tells us that the access sequence 1 will search for the sales notes in the above order i.e. for sales area specific text (KNVV) first for ship to, then sold to and then in the central texts (KNA1) for first ship to and then sold to again. It will pick up the first one it finds while following this sequence. Since the text is non-mandatory, if it does not find any of these 4, it will allow the user to save the order without any errors.

TEXT PROCEDURE ASSIGNMENT (C)

The last configuration in determining the texts is to assign the document types to the text procedure we want to us. It is self-explanatory:

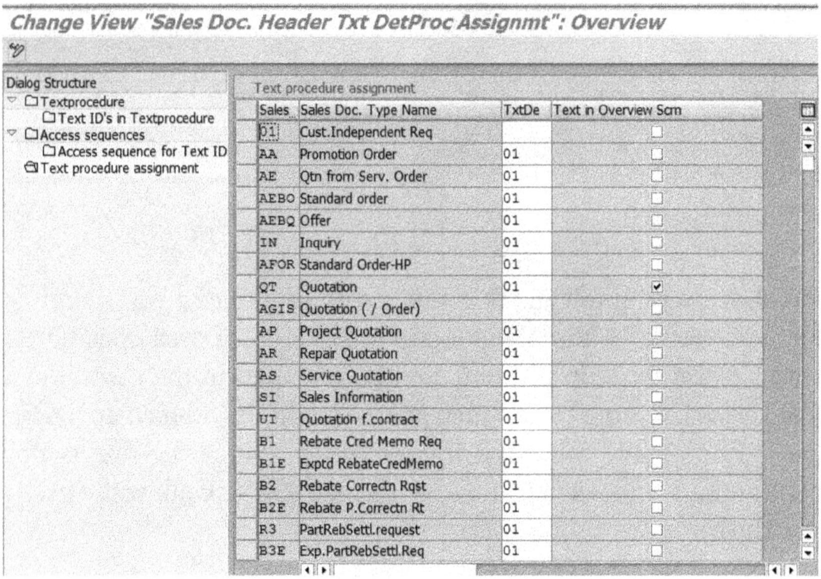

Fig 17

We find that our order type OR is using the custom text determination procedure ZA:

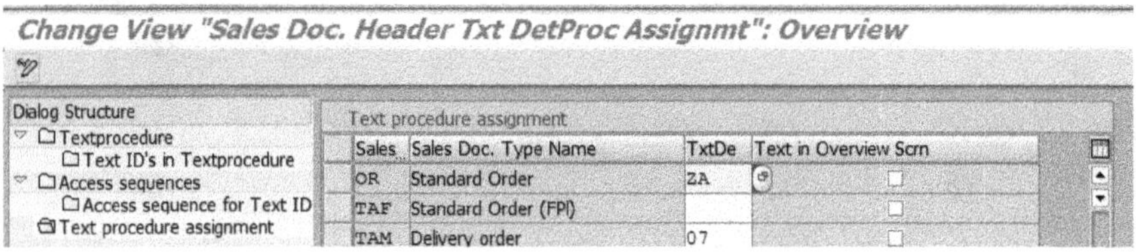

Fig 18

ZA's texts are:

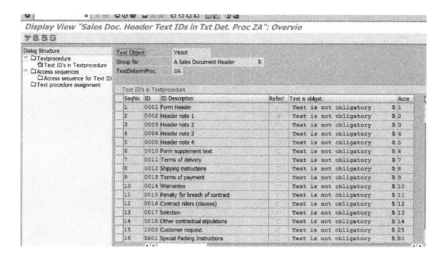

Fig 19

Which can be seen in the sales order > Header > texts:

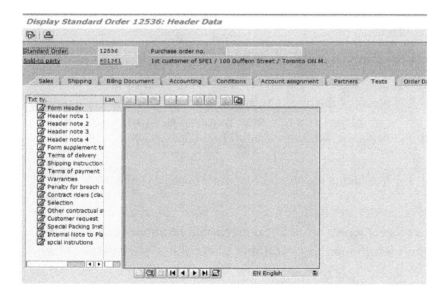

Fig 20

MATERIAL DETERMINATION (C/U)

Often materials can be substituted by other materials under certain conditions:

- They indeed are inter-changeable, only for branding reasons they have keep kept separate from each other
- Stock of the one required is over and the delivery needs to be completed and the other material will work just as well
- It makes no difference to the customer if an alternative one is supplied instead
- Replacing an obsolete material with a new one

Material determination makes this possible by swapping one with the other. Again, the condition technique comes of use as we require it for identifying the 'conditions' under this swap will take place.

The path for configuration:

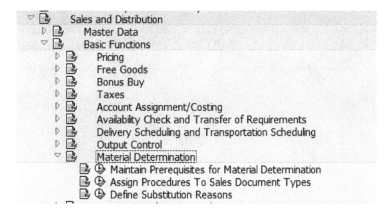

Fig 1

MAINTAIN PREREQUISITES - MATERIAL DETERMINATION (C)

Click on maintain Prerequisites for Material Determination:

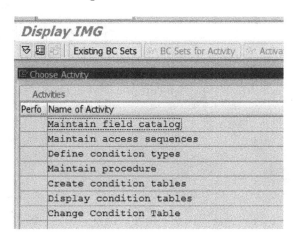

Fig 2

The procedure is the same as for condition technique in pricing or Outputs:

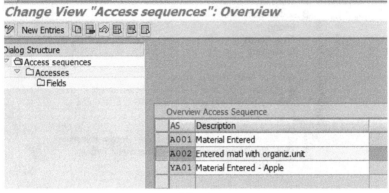

Fig 3

The access sequence decides which tables the system will look at in which order to get the required data.

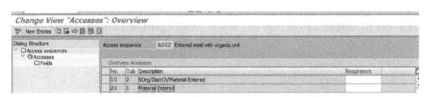

Fig 4

Then, in the condition type, we can use that access:

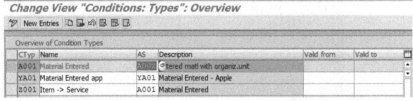

Fig 5

In maintain Procedure we use the condition types we would like to:

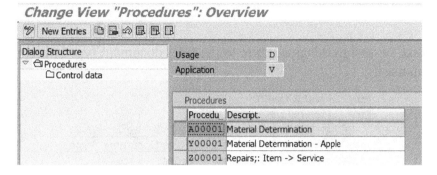

Fig 6

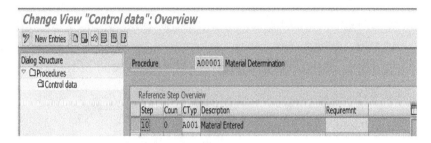

Fig 7

ASSIGNMENT OF PROCEDURES TO SALES DOCUMENT TYPES

Next, we assign this procedure to the sales document types which can use it:

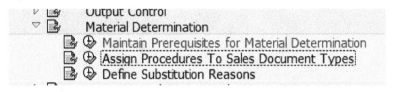

Fig 8

Like order type OR is linked to this procedure A00001:

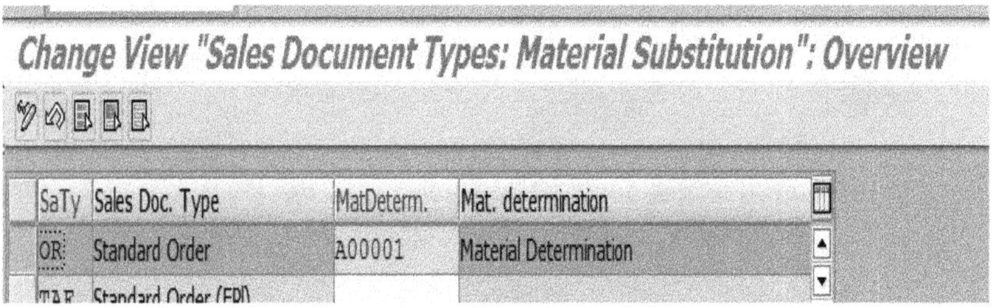

Fig 9

MATERIAL DETERMINATION REASONS

Fig 10

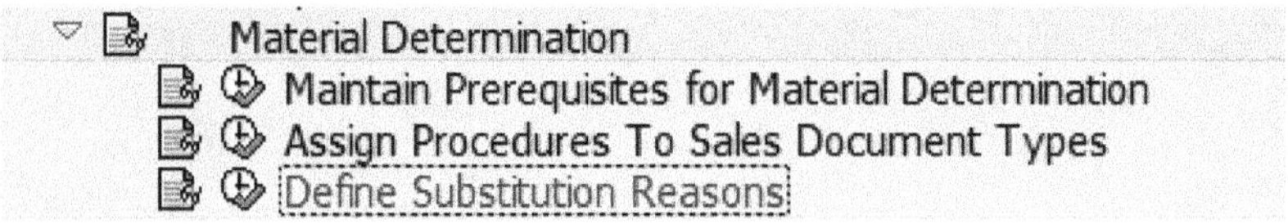

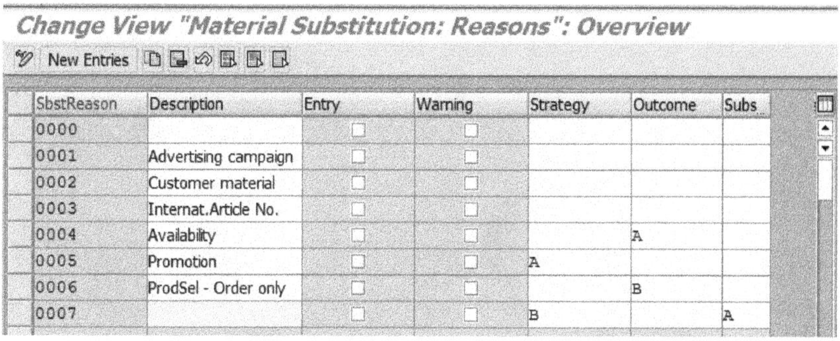

New Entries

SbstReason	Description	Entry	Warning	Strategy	Outcome	Subs	
0000		☐	☐				
0001	Advertising campaign	☐	☐				
0002	Customer material	☐	☐				
0003	Internat.Article No.	☐	☐				
0004	Availability	☐	☐		A		
0005	Promotion	☐	☐	A			
0006	ProdSel - Order only	☐	☐		B		
0007		☐	☐	B		A	

Fig 11

The above screen defines how the process of material determination will be controlled when invoked. There are a few choices:

i. Entry – It controls whether you would like the system to print the name or number of the original material on the order confirmation

ii. Warning – if set, this will give a warning message to the user that a material determination will be taking place for the material entered

iii. Strategy – Used to promote if the substitution should be automatic or if the proposed material determination items should be displayed through a selection box.

iv. Outcome – automatic replacement or to display the substitution as a sub-item

The condition records for material determination are set up in VB11 or follow the path:

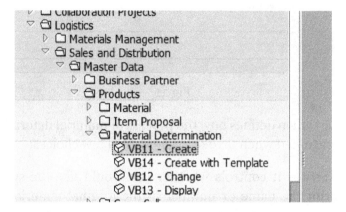

Fig 12

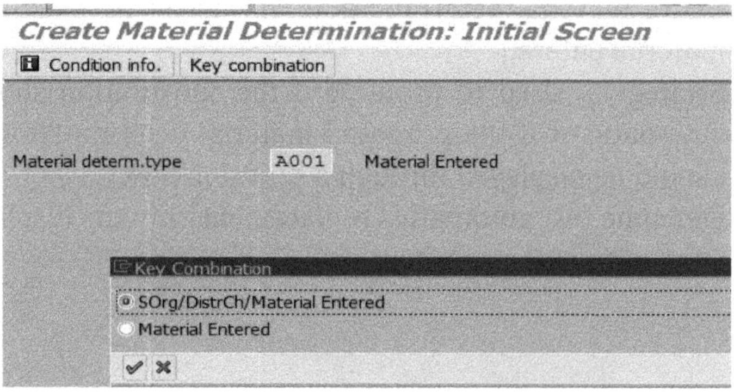

Create Material Determination: Initial Screen

Fig 13

Let us say we have replaced material 1000654 with 1000656 as occasion requires, for the sales org SFE1 and DC 01 only, while for SO SFE1 and DC 16 it is still available. So, we set up the condition record as with strategy 0005 for SFE1-01 so that 1000654 can be replaced with 1000656 should an order come:

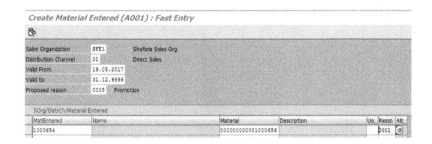

Fig 14

Now when we try to create the order for 1000654 in VA01 let us see what happens:

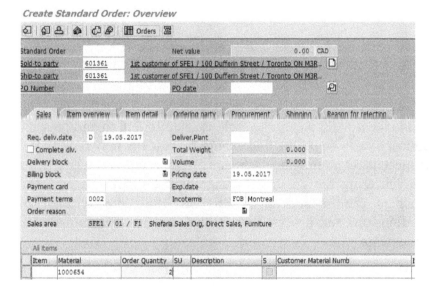

Fig 15

On Hitting Enter, the material 1000654 gets replaced with 1000656:

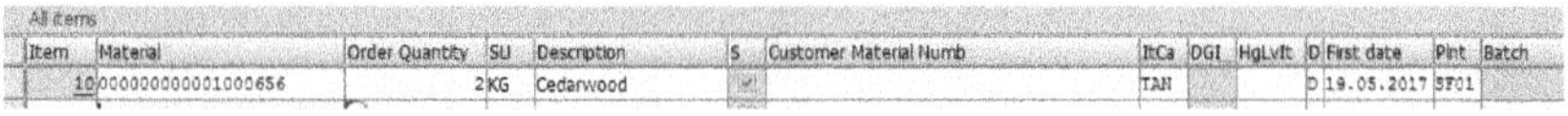

All items												
Item	Material	Order Quantity	SU	Description	S	Customer Material Numb	ItCa	DGI	HgLvIt	D	First date	Plnt	Batch
10	00000000001000656	2	KG	Cedarwood	✓		TAN			D	19.05.2017	SF01	

Fig 16

This is the effect of Material determination.

PARTNER DETERMINATION (C/U)

While the 4 main partners – sold to, ship to, bill to and payer will almost always be on the documents, a company may require more to meet its requirements – partners like sales representative, vendor for delivering the goods, clearing agent for customs etc. These partners can be set up in this SAP functionality and their relationships and process of how they will get determined in the documents.

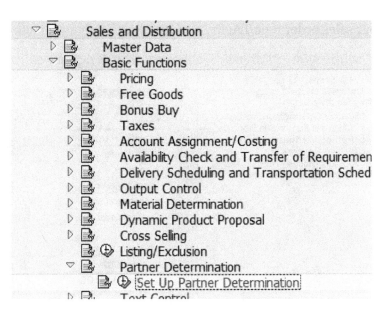

Fig 1

Let us see the setup of the partner determination for a sales document header. Double click on the 2nd option below:

Perfo	Name of Activity
	Set Up Partner Determination for Customer Master
	Set Up Partner Determination for Sales Document Header
	Set Up Partner Determination for Sales Document Item
	Set Up Partner Determination for Delivery
	Set Up Partner Determination for Shipment
	Set Up Partner Determination for Billing Header
	Set Up Partner Determination for Billing Item
	Set Up Partner Determination for Sales Activities (CAS)

Fig 2

For our sales order type TA:

Change View "Partner Determination Procedures": O

New Entries

Dialog Structure
▽ Partner Determination Procedure
  Partner Functions in Procedur
  Partner Determination Procedure
  Partner Functions
  Account Groups - Function Assig
  Partner Function Conversion

Partner Determination Procedures

Part.D	Name
EDL	SchedAgr w.ExtAgent
KAB	Release order
SM	Assortment
TA	Standard Order
Y02	partner deter proce
YAPP	Standard Order-Apple
ZA01	
ZA02	Standard Order
ZA03	Standard Order
ZOC	Standard Order OC

Fig 3

Double click on the Partner Functions in Procedure:

Change View "Partner Determination Procedures": Overview

New Entries

Dialog Structure
▽ Partner Determination Procedures
  Partner Functions in Procedure
  Partner Determination Procedure Assignment
  Partner Functions
  Account Groups - Function Assignment
  Partner Function Conversion

Partner Determination Procedures

Part.D	Name
EDL	SchedAgr w.ExtAgent
KAB	Release order
SM	Assortment
TA	Standard Order
Y02	partner deter proce

Fig 4

Standard SAP has provided many partner functions to be possible in the partner determination procedure TA – SP, BP, PY and SH.

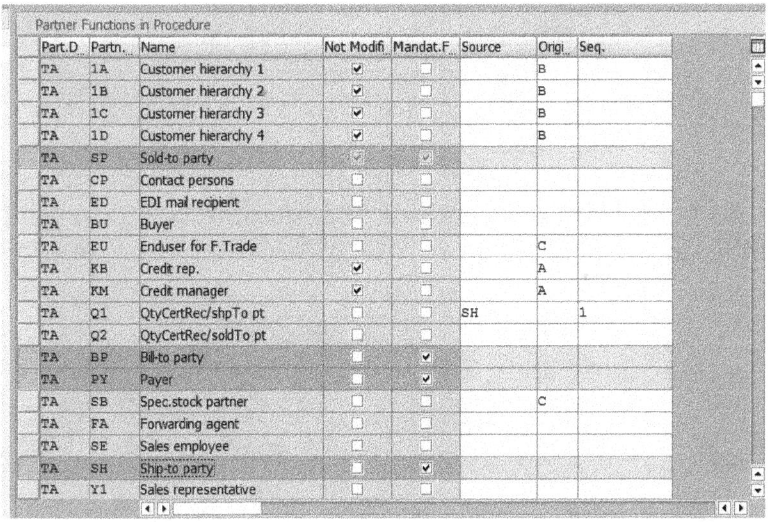

Partner Functions in Procedure

Part.D	Partn.	Name	Not Modifi	Mandat.F	Source	Origi	Seq.
TA	1A	Customer hierarchy 1	✓			B	
TA	1B	Customer hierarchy 2	✓			B	
TA	1C	Customer hierarchy 3	✓			B	
TA	1D	Customer hierarchy 4	✓			B	
TA	SP	Sold-to party	✓	✓			
TA	CP	Contact persons					
TA	ED	EDI mail recipient					
TA	BU	Buyer					
TA	EU	Enduser for F.Trade				C	
TA	KB	Credit rep.	✓			A	
TA	KM	Credit manager	✓			A	
TA	Q1	QtyCertRec/shpTo pt			SH		1
TA	Q2	QtyCertRec/soldTo pt					
TA	BP	Bill-to party		✓			
TA	PY	Payer		✓			
TA	SB	Spec.stock partner				C	
TA	FA	Forwarding agent					
TA	SE	Sales employee					
TA	SH	Ship-to party		✓			
TA	Y1	Sales representative					

Fig 5

Note that all 4 of them are mandatory partners i.e. if any of them is missing, the order can't be processed further. For example, remove the PY from the order and try saving it:

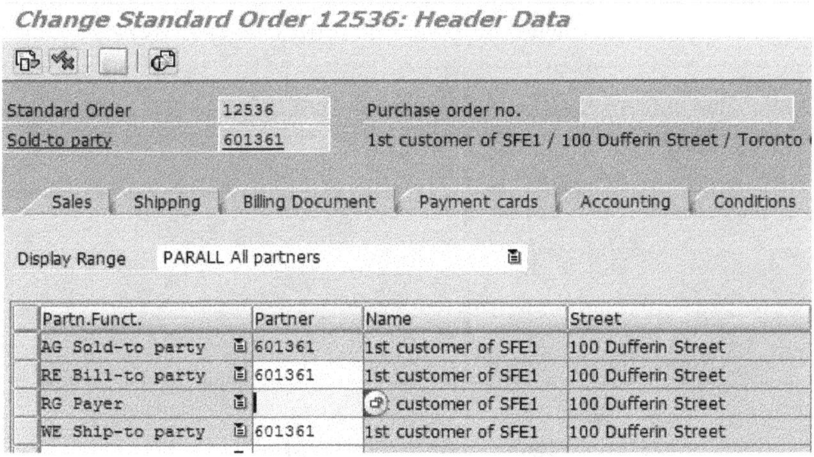

Fig 6

We get the error:

Payer must be filled in a Standard Order

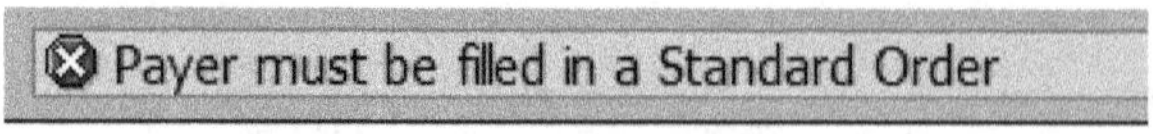

Fig 7

The sold to in this procedure, apart from being mandatory, is also non-modifiable, i.e. once entered and the order saved, it can't be modified at the partner tab.

Change Standard Order 12536: Header Data
Standard Order 12536
Purchase order no.
Sold-to party 601361
1st customer of SFE1 / 100 Dufferin Street / Toronto ON M...
Sales
Shipping
Billing Document
Payment cards
Accounting
Conditions
Account assignment
Display Range PARALL All partners
Partn.Funct. Partner Name Street Postal co... Cty
AG Sold-to party 601361 1st customer of SFE1 100 Dufferin Street M3R 4W2 Toronto
RE Bill-to party 601361 1st customer of SFE1 100 Dufferin Street M3R 4W2 Toronto
RG Payer 601361 customer of SFE1 100 Dufferin Street M3R 4W2 Toronto
WE Ship-to party 601361 1st customer of SFE1 100 Dufferin Street M3R 4W2 Toronto

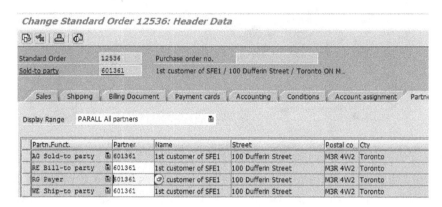

Fig 8

It can be changed on the main order entry screen though till the order gets processed further. The other use of this is that at line item levels, one can have different other partners, however, the sold to can't be changed:

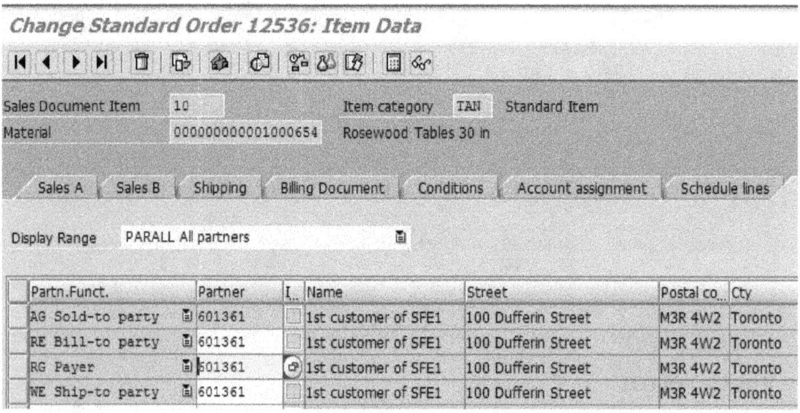

Change Standard Order 12536: Item Data
Sales Document Item 10
Item category TAN Standard Item
Material 000000000001000654
Rosewood Tables 30 in
Sales A
Sales B
Shipping
Billing Document
Conditions
Account assignment
Schedule lines
Display Range PARALL All partners
Partn.Funct. Partner I... Name Street Postal co... Cty
AG Sold-to party 601361 1st customer of SFE1 100 Dufferin Street M3R 4W2 Toronto
RE Bill-to party 601361 1st customer of SFE1 100 Dufferin Street M3R 4W2 Toronto
RG Payer 601361 1st customer of SFE1 100 Dufferin Street M3R 4W2 Toronto
WE Ship-to party 601361 1st customer of SFE1 100 Dufferin Street M3R 4W2 Toronto

Fig 9

Thus, one can create multiple line items for different ship to locations or bill to parties under the sale sold to party. These ship to's will because a delivery to get split and the bill to's and payers will cause invoice splits as we will see later in the course.

LOG OF INCOMPLETE ITEMS (U)

In this functionality, we define when a sales document is to be regarded as incomplete and how the system should respond when we create a document that has any missing data for example. Should it allow to be processed further, should it not even allow the user to save the document etc.

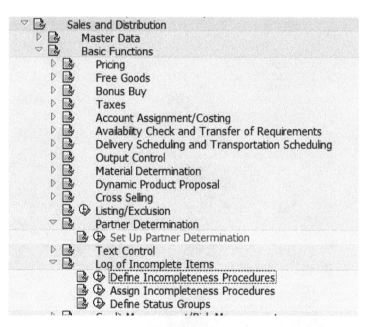

Fig 1

1. DEFINE INCOMPLETION PROCEDURE (C)

Let us define an incompletion procedure:

Fig 2

We notice there are various groupings of the incompletion procedures based on what purpose they will be used for:

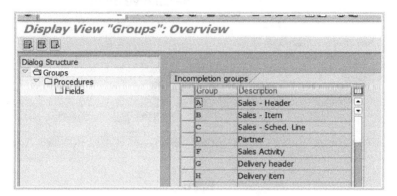

Fig 3

We will define a new one for the Sales- header. Select the Group A and double click on Procedures:

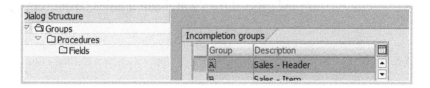

Fig 4

We see a procedure 11 exists already for a sales order:

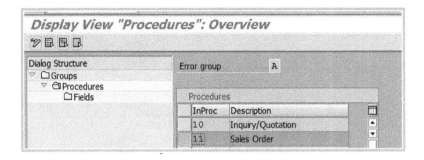

Fig 5

We can either create a new one or copy from 11 or append/delete a

field. Click on  to move into the Change mode:

Fig 6

Click on Copy -

We know we are limited to the name space beginning with a Y or a Z so we will name our new procedure Y2 and call it Sales Order (copy):

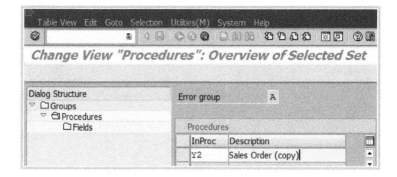

Fig 7

Hit Enter and Say Copy All:

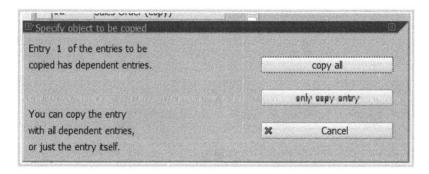

Fig 8

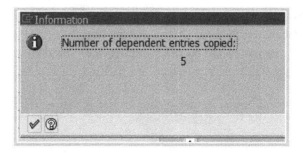

Fig 9

These 5 dependent entries are the underlying fields:

Change View "Procedures": Overview

New Entries

Dialog Structure	Error group	A
▽ ☐ Groups		
▽ ⊟ Procedures		
☐ Fields	Procedures	

InProc	Description	
Y2	Sales Order (copy)	

Fig 10

Double click on Fields:

Change View "Fields": Overview

New Entries

	Error proc.	Y2					
Dialog Structure	Incompletion fields						
▽ ☐ Groups							
▽ ☐ Procedures	Table	Fld name	Description	Scr.	Status	Warning	Seq.
⊟ Fields	VBAK	AUDAT	Document Date	KKAU	01	☐	
	VBAK	WAERK	Document Currency	KBUC	03	☐	
	VBKD	INCO1	Incoterms	KDE3	04	☐	
	VBKD	PRSDT	Pricing date	KKAU	04	☐	
	VBKD	ZTERM	Terms of Payment	KDE3	03	⊘ ☐	

Fig 11

Simply put these are the fields which if missing, will cause the document to be incomplete – those document types that will be attached to this incompletion procedure Y2. The field Status tells us the behavior of the system if that respective field is not populated. We can add our own field to it for example.to say the document will be incomplete if the order reason is not filled in. We would add that field and make the 6th entry using the [New Entries] button:

New Entries: Overview of Added Entries

	Error proc.	Y2					
Dialog Structure	Incompletion fields						
▽ ☐ Groups							
▽ ☐ Procedures	Table	Fld name	Description	Scr.	Status	Warning	Seq.
⊟ Fields	VBAK	AUGRU			02	⊘ ☐	

Fig 12

Hit Enter & Save the configuration.

Now, if we create a new order and do not populate the order reason, the order will remain incomplete assuming we are using the incompletion procedure Y2 for the document type being created and the incompletion log would show up like this:

When the order is being saved:

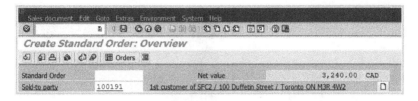

Fig 13

A window will pop up:

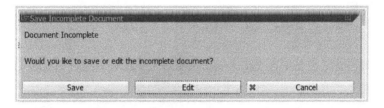

Fig 14

Click on [Edit] to see what is missing:

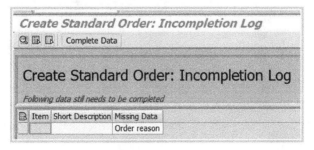

Fig 15

221

Alternatively, the incompletion log can also be seen on the main screen of the order:

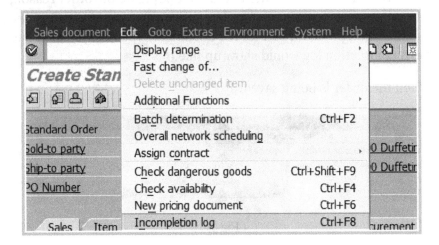

Fig 16

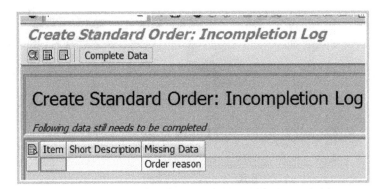

Fig 17

2. ASSIGNMENT OF INCOMPLETION PROCEDURES (C)

We will bypass the assignment of the incompletion procedure to the document type so as not to disturb the standard OR type order that we are using. The student is asked to create their own incompletion procedure and use it with the order type that was created to see the effects of these incompletion procedures.

3. DEFINE STATUS GROUPS

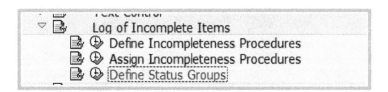

Fig 18

The status groups define the behavior of the system – we saw them being used earlier in the procedure itself:

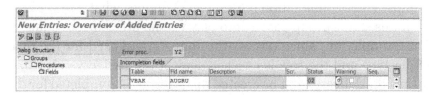

Fig 19

223

Here we see their usage:

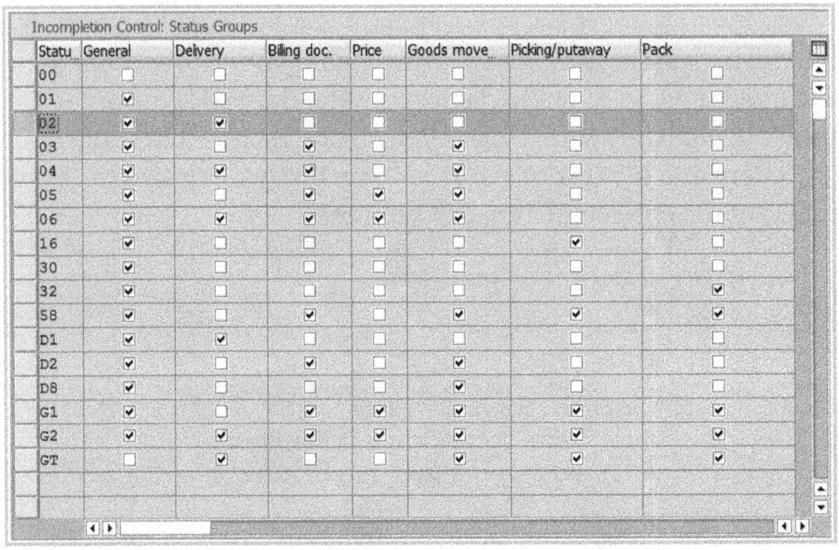

Incomplection Control: Status Groups

Statu	General	Delivery	Billing doc.	Price	Goods move	Picking/putaway	Pack
00							
01	✔						
02	✔	✔					
03	✔		✔		✔		
04	✔	✔	✔		✔		
05	✔		✔	✔	✔		
06	✔	✔	✔	✔	✔		
16	✔					✔	
30	✔						
32	✔						✔
58	✔		✔		✔	✔	✔
D1	✔	✔					
D2	✔		✔		✔		
D8	✔				✔		
G1	✔		✔	✔	✔	✔	✔
G2	✔	✔	✔	✔	✔	✔	✔
GT		✔			✔	✔	✔

Fig 20

The matrix may seem intimidating though it is really very simple. The columns define the activity in SAP and the rows define the status groups. Their combination (check mark) defines what will get held up if this status group comes into play via the preceding document. For example. in , since 02 was the status group used for the field Order type and the row is checked against the Delivery column, it means the delivery can't be created till the order is completed for the field order reason.

SALES DOCUMENT ITEM (C)

We saw the mechanics behind a sales order type earlier in the course. Now we will go one level lower and explore how items or lines are created. The sales document at the header level comprises of multiple lines, also called items. This item data from the sales order becomes the header data in a delivery or bill. The key driver behind how the item line in a sales order will behave in the order and in the subsequent documents is an item category. Item categories represent data at different planes. To understand this critical component of SD let us look at one such item category in more detail:

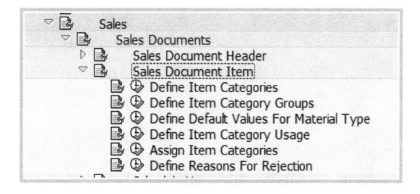

Fig 1

225

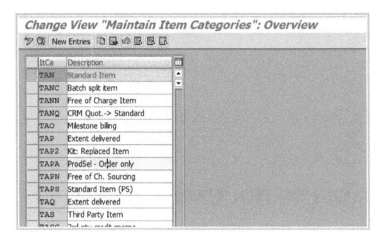

Fig 2

TAN is possibly the most widely used item category in product based industries. TAN represents a standard item.

Click on 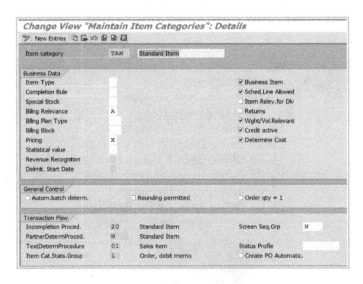 to see the details underlying TAN:

Fig 3

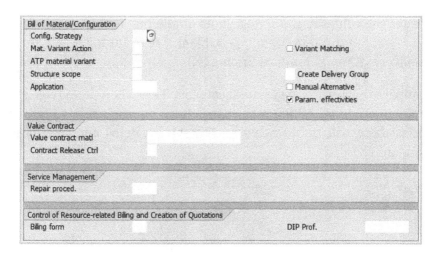

Fig 4

Some important fields to understand are:

- Item type – whether it is a standard product based item, a service or an item that has only a value etc.
- Billing relevance – if the item will require to be billed and if so, how? Since the data is carried from one document to the next in SAP, it is important to mark this field for this relevance for example. a product that is to be shipped out would need to be billed only once the delivery has taken place. Hence, for TAN, A is the suitable choice
- Pricing – Will the item be priced
- Schedule line allowed –a schedule line enables the order creator to determine delivery dates at time or order creation if the system is so set up. This helps in advising the customers of the delivery dates right when orders are placed without waiting to check with warehousing or production departments
- Determine Cost – if SAP should calculate the costs of this item based on the configurations. These costs will be needed at the time of profitability analysis

We see the values in the screen shots on the previous page for TAN – it is a standard item (item type = blank), relevant for billing from a delivery (A) and Standard Pricing (X).

Compare this with a service item category TAD where item type is A (Value item only), billing relevance is from an order related billing (B, as there will be no delivery of a service item) and pricing is standard (X)

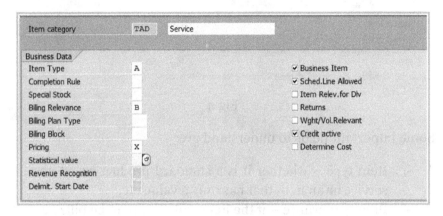

Fig 5

As we can imagine the entire behavior of how that line item on the sales order will depend on the item category that drives it.

As we have TAN and TAD, we have many more to represent the function they are supposed to achieve and based on that their setups will be different from each other.

1. ITEM CATEGORY GROUPS (C)

In an item category group, we group together different material types for item category determination from the SD point of view. The material types could be like finished goods, services, raw materials etc. if we were to sell them via the SD module, we would need to tell SAP how to treat them for pricing, shipping, billing etc. As we saw, this is done via item categories. We then, should be able to set up a process whereby SAP can automatically determine which item category to use in the sales order for the material in that line item. This is done by using item category groups, which, when used in conjunction with the sales order type, automatically proposes the item category. The item category groups are a part of the material master sales view and based on that this determination takes place.

Again, SAP has provided many such item category groups, the main ones being DIEN for service items and NORM for standard items:

ItCGr	Description
NLAG	Non-stock material
NORM	Standard item
SAMM	Generic material
SRVM	Service material CRM
SRVO	Service item CRM
SRVP	Service product CRM
TRMP	Packaging
VCIT	Value contract item
VERP	Packaging

Fig 6

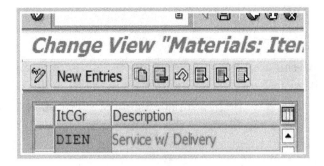

Fig 7

On their own they do not mean anything except acting as place holders in the material master.

2. ASSIGN ITEM CATEGORIES (C)

The next step is to make SAP recognize how to use the item categories which we do via the assignment node:

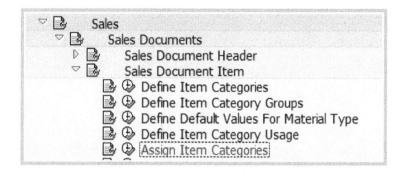

Fig 8

Fig 9

The above table states that when the order type is an OR, the item category group (from the material master) is NORM then the 'default' item category that SAP will propose in the order line item will be TAN. It can be manually over written with a TAP, TAQ or TANN. Obviously, if TAN is replaced with TAP or TAQ or TANN it will take on the behavior expected from one of these instead of from TAN.

As usual we can use SAP standard or create our own item categories beginning with a Y or Z. Changing any SAP standard item category is strongly advised against as it will get over written when an upgrade takes place.

SCHEDULE LINES

Schedule lines are created when an item is relevant for delivery i.e. it is a physical good rather than a service. In terms if hierarchy it is one level lower than the item category. A schedule line comprises of 2 things:

- Quantity
- Delivery date

A schedule line is a unique combination of the quantity and delivery date. For example. if a customer orders 100 units and we have available, 50 today, 30 tomorrow and 20, 5 days later, then, provided SAP is set up for schedule line determination, SAP will propose 3 different schedule lines for that line item in the order. Each schedule lines leads to a delivery on its own.

1. DEFINE SCHEDULE LINE CATEGORIES (C)

A schedule line category functions much like an item category except that its data relevance is limited to delivery only. Follow the path to create a new one or view an existing one:

Fig 1

Change View "Maintain Schedule

New Entries

SLCa	Description
AE	MRP
AN	ALE Standard
AQ	MRP
AT	Inquiry sched.line
BN	No MRP
BP	Deterministic MRP
BT	No inventory mgmt
BV	Consumption MRP

Fig 2

The standard schedule line category for standard delivery products is CP – Deterministic MRP. Its calculations follow the MRP process defined in the material master.

Sched.line cat.	CP	Deterministic MRP	
Business data			
Delivery block			
Movement Type	601	GD goods issue:delvy	☑ Item rel.f.dlv.
Movement Type 1-Step			
Order Type			☐ P.req.del.sched
Item Category			
Acct Assgt Cat.			
Transaction flow			
Incompl.proced.	30	Deliv-Rel.Sched.Line	
☑ Req./Assembly			
☑ Availablity			
☑ Prod.allocation			

Fig 3

A schedule line category can be used for an outbound delivery or for an inbound delivery (used to receive materials against Purchase orders or even otherwise).

In the above screen, the one important field is the movement type. Movement types are set up in MM and control how the updates will get done to the quantities and values of the material when movement thereof takes place with any movement type. The above, 601 is a standard movement type when an outbound delivery will be goods issued i.e. when the stocks will be depleted from the system.

For the most part, we should use the standard schedule line categories as they are simple objects and should be able to satisfy the requirements of any company. If necessary though, new ones can be created like all other configurations, using the name space beginning with Y or Z.

2. ASSIGNING SCHEDULE LINE CATEGORIES (C)

As always, we need to assign the schedule line categories to be able to use them.

Fig 4

In the same way as we determine the item categories from a sales order type, here we determine the schedule line categories from the item category being used in conjunction with the MRP type. The MRP type field can be found in the MRP1 view of the material master:

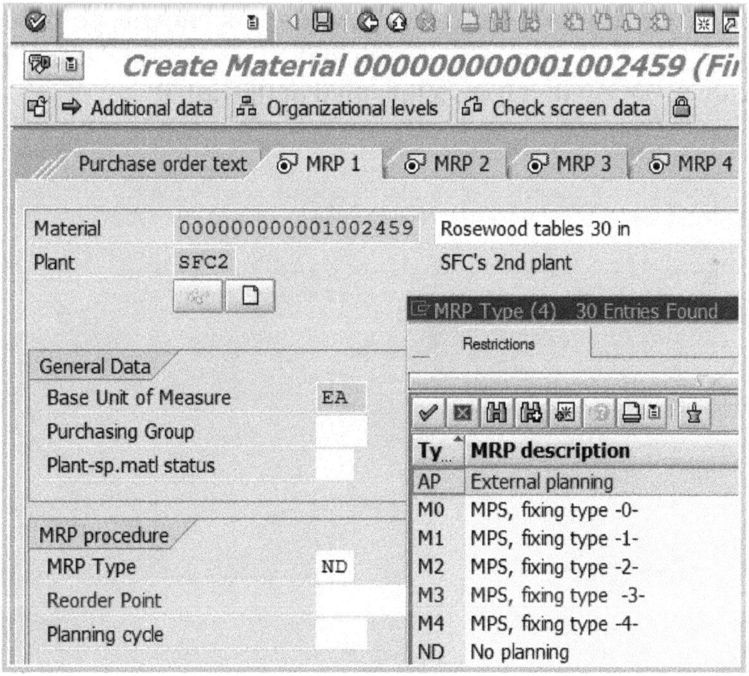

Fig 5

Since it is not necessary SAP has to be set up for MRP (Materials resource planning), we can leave the field blank in the configuration and in that case, SAP will determine the schedule line category without it, with only the item category:

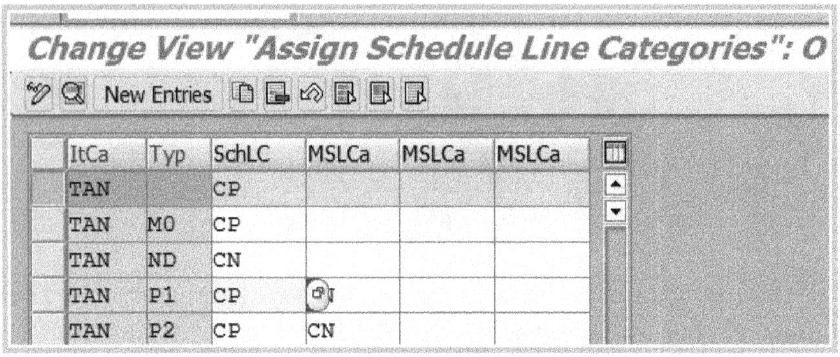

Change View "Assign Schedule Line Categories": O

New Entries

	ItCa	Typ	SchLC	MSLCa	MSLCa	MSLCa	
	TAN		CP				
	TAN	MO	CP				
	TAN	ND	CN				
	TAN	P1	CP				
	TAN	P2	CP	CN			

Fig 6

In the above example, with the MRO type blank, when the line item in the order has item category TAN, the system will propose the schedule line category CP. A schedule line is mandatory for a delivery to get created from a line item of the order.

CONSIGNMENT PROCESS IN SAP (C/U)

Many companies keep stock at their customers' premises for better service, flexibility and saving costs especially on transportation by shipping in bulk. This stock remains at the customer premises and is consumed by the customer as needed and replenished when it reaches re-order levels. Billing for these takes place based on consumption rather than on shipment. SAP has provided 4 standard order types that can be used for this process:

- Consignment fill up: CF
- Consignment Issue: CI
- Consignment Pick-up: CP
- Consignment returns: CONR

To use them for our sales area we need to assign them to it in configuration as we did for order types OR, RO, DR etc.

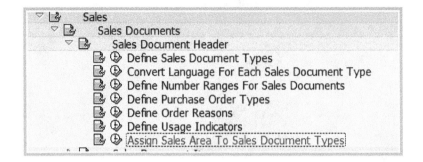

Fig 1

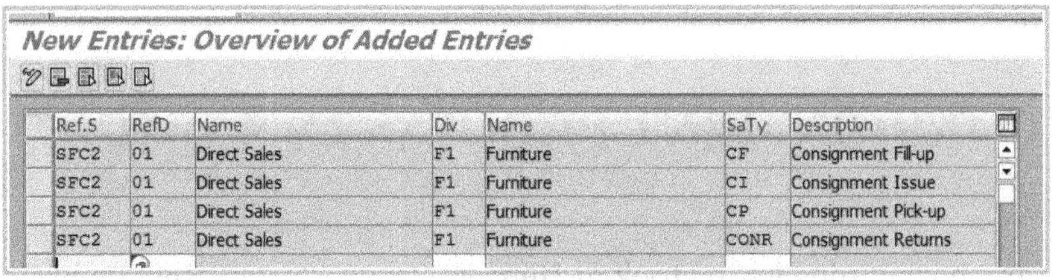

New Entries: Overview of Added Entries

Ref.S	RefD	Name	Div	Name	SaTy	Description
SFC2	01	Direct Sales	F1	Furniture	CF	Consignment Fill-up
SFC2	01	Direct Sales	F1	Furniture	CI	Consignment Issue
SFC2	01	Direct Sales	F1	Furniture	CP	Consignment Pick-up
SFC2	01	Direct Sales	F1	Furniture	CONR	Consignment Returns

Fig 2

Save the configuration in the transport.

To understand the complete Consignment cycle, we will create the 4 types of orders step wise and see the effect.

1. CONSIGNMENT FILL-UP (U)

Create an order type CF:

Create Sales Order: Initial Screen

🖸 Create with Reference	🐣 Sales	🐣 Item overview	🐣 Ordering party

Order Type	CF	Consignment Fill-up

Organizational Data

Sales Organization	SFE1	Shefaria Sales Org
Distribution Channel	01	Direct Sales
Division	F1	Furniture
Sales Office		
Sales Group		

Fig 3

Create Consignment Fill-up: Overview

🔙 | 🔲🔺 🔷 🗂️🖉 | ⊞ Orders | 🔀

Consignment Fill-up		Net value	0.00 CAD
Sold-to party	601361	1st customer of SFE1 / 100 Dufferin Street / Toronto ON M3R...	
Ship-to party	601361	1st customer of SFE1 / 100 Dufferin Street / Toronto ON M3R...	
PO Number		PO date	

Sales	Item overview	Item detail	Ordering party	Procurement	Shipping	Reason for rejection

Req. deliv.date	D 19.05.2017	Deliver.Plant		
☐ Complete dlv.		Total Weight	0 KG	
Delivery block		Volume	0.000	
Billing block		Pricing date	19.05.2017	
Payment terms	0002	Incoterms	FOB Montreal	
Order reason				
Sales area	SFE1 / 01 / F1	Shefaria Sales Org, Direct Sales, Furniture		

All items

Item	Material	Order Quantity	SU	Description	S	Customer Material Numb	ItCa
10	000000000001000...	100	CAR	Rosewood Tables 30 in			KBN

Fig 4

The main thing to note is that based on the order type CF, SAP auto determined a different item category KBN (instead of the usual TAN) as seen above. Also noteworthy is that the order is of 0 value, again auto determined as a consignment fill up order. Save the order:

Consignment Fill-up 12537 has been saved

Fig 5

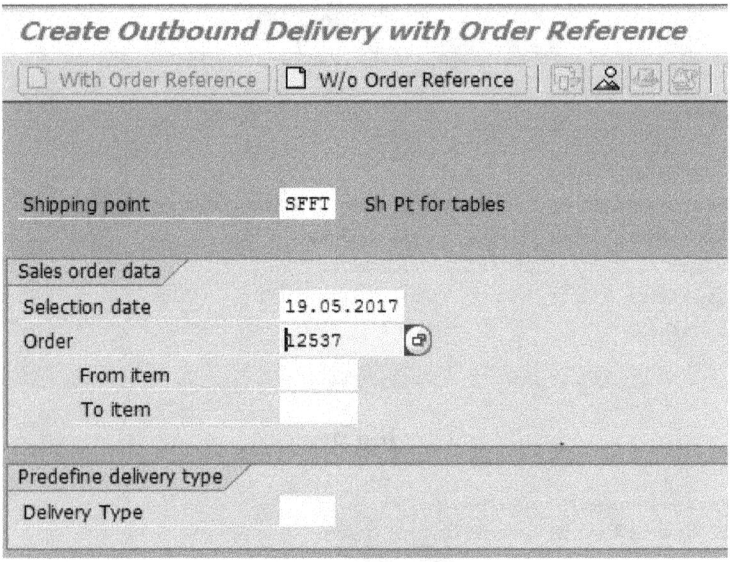

Create Outbound Delivery with Order Reference

| With Order Reference | W/o Order Reference | |

Shipping point   SFFT   Sh Pt for tables

Sales order data

Selection date   19.05.2017

Order   12537

   From item

   To item

Predefine delivery type

Delivery Type

Fig 6

Let us see the current stock of this material 1000654 in MMBE:

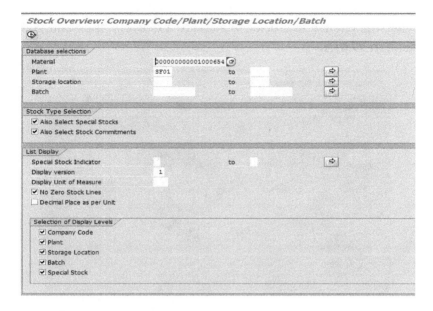

Fig 7

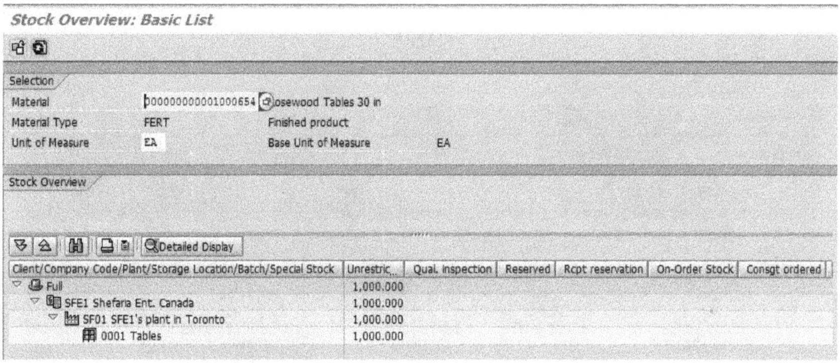

Fig 8

While the delivery process will be explained in greater detail in Logistics Execution, for the moment, we need to get this fill up order to view the change in stocks. We create a delivery, pick and goods issue it in VL01N:

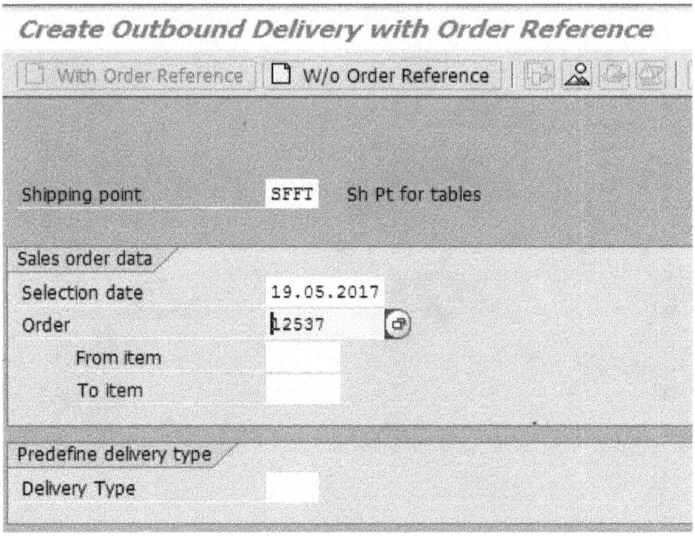

Create Outbound Delivery with Order Reference

| With Order Reference | W/o Order Reference | | | |

Shipping point   SFFT   Sh Pt for tables

Sales order data

Selection date   19.05.2017
Order   12537
     From item
     To item

Predefine delivery type

Delivery Type

Fig 9

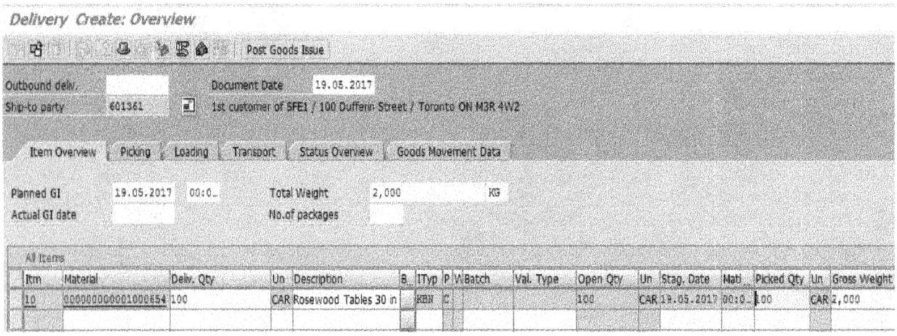

Delivery Create: Overview

| Post Goods Issue

Outbound deliv.   Document Date   19.05.2017
Ship-to party   601361   1st customer of SFE1 / 100 Dufferin Street / Toronto ON M3R 4W2

Item Overview | Picking | Loading | Transport | Status Overview | Goods Movement Data

Planned GI   19.05.2017   00:0..   Total Weight   2,000   KG
Actual GI date   No.of packages

All Items

Itm	Material	Deliv. Qty	Un	Description	B.	ITyp	P	W Batch	Val. Type	Open Qty	Un	Stag. Date	Matl	Picked Qty	Un	Gross Weight
10	600000000001000654	100	CAR	Rosewood Tables 30 in		KBN	C			100	CAR	19.05.2017	00:0..	100	CAR	2,000

Fig 10

Goods issue the delivery using the   button:

    Delivery 80015457 has been saved

Fig 11

Refreshing the MMBE screen for the new stock we see:

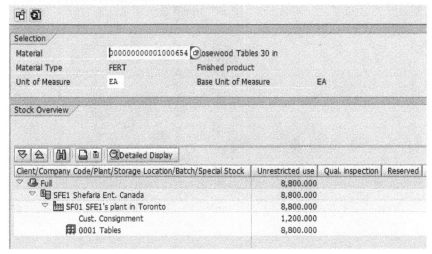

Fig 12

Thus, 1200 EA of this material 1000654 now resides as consignment stock with the customer leaving behind 8800 for other use in our own plant.

To see more details, highlight this 1200 line:

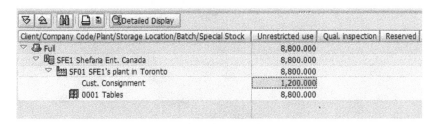

Fig 13

And click on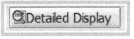

A new window opens telling us more details about the stock and the customer it is residing with:

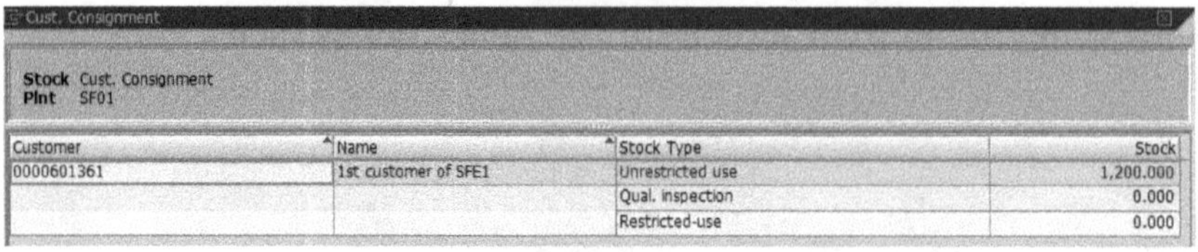
Cust. Consignment

Stock Cust. Consignment
Plnt SF01

Customer	Name	Stock Type	Stock
0000601361	1st customer of SFE1	Unrestricted use	1,200.000
		Qual. inspection	0.000
		Restricted-use	0.000

Fig 14

2. CONSIGNMENT ISSUE (U)

The customer may call up the next day advising is they will be consuming 30 CAR of this product. We now need to 'issue' this quantity to the customer. Note that the plant is still regarded as being in our own plant and company code, as seen in the screen shot in MMBE; only the physical location is the customer.

To create the consignment issue for quantity = 30 CAR, create the order type CI in VA01 for the same customer/material:

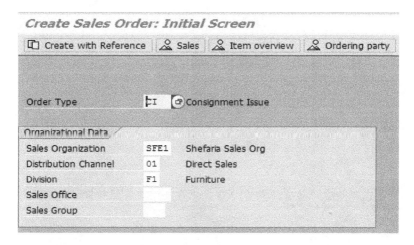

Fig 15

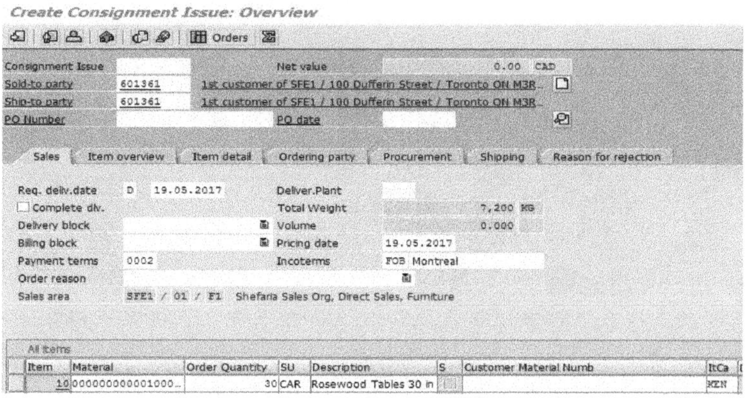

Fig 16

Note how the order now gets an item category as KEN and also has a value for the 30 CARs (not for 100 CAR which was sent to the customer).

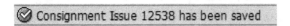

Fig 17

Using the same process as earlier, we create a delivery for this quantity in VL01N and goods issue it:

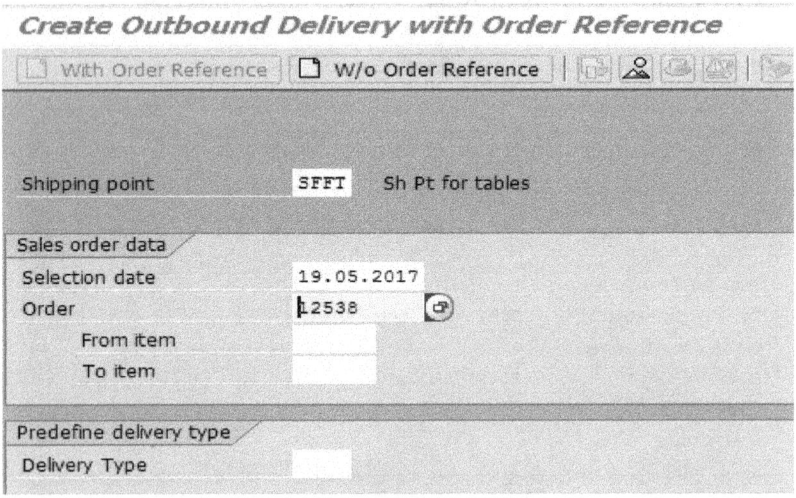

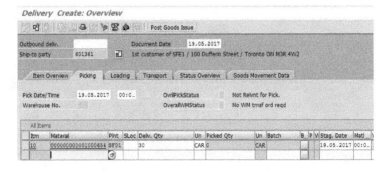

Fig 18

Fig 19

Note that the system is no longer asking us to pick this quantity. This is because the objective of this delivery is to move the stocks to the appropriate place and to invoice the customer for this usage of 30 CAR. The delivery was already picked when the consignment fill up occurred for 100 CAR.

Post the goods:

Fig 20

Let us now look at the stock situation again in MMBE:

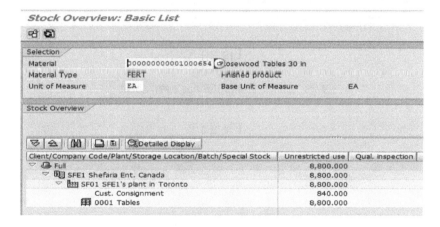

Fig 21

We notice the stock has reduced from 1,200 to 840, the different of 360 = 30 CAR * 12 EA = 360 EA

This delivery will get invoiced to the customer for payment. We will do billing in detail later, for the moment, we can just do one quick invoice in transaction VF01 using this delivery:

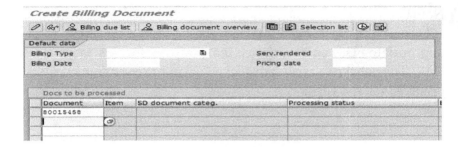

Fig 22

Hit Enter & Save.

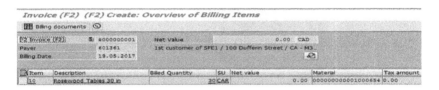

Fig 23

Fig 24

3. CONSIGNMENT PICKUP (U)

A consignment pick up is used when there is left over material and needs to be brought back as the customer will not be using it. This may be due to over stock or pre-agreed terms or due to possibility of expiration of the product etc.

In the same way, in VA01, create the order type CP for 45 CAR of this product as that is what will be brought back:

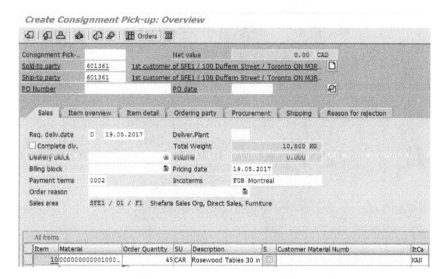

Fig 25

Once again SAP has determined a new item category KAN and not assigned any value to this order because it was never invoiced. This is a part of the quantity still lying unused with the customer.

Save the order.

Fig 26

Note that the numbering sequence has changed. Though it is possible to assign the same numbering sequence, a different one is a better choice as the consignment pick up is in reality a return order.

As before, we will create a new delivery for this consignment pick up in t code VL01N:

Create Outbound Delivery with Order Reference

| With Order Reference | W/o Order Reference | | | | |

Shipping point	SFFT	Sh Pt for tables

Sales order data

Selection date	19.05.2017
Order	60000128
From item	
To item	

Predefine delivery type

Delivery Type	

Fig 27

Returns delivery Create: Overview

| | | | Post Goods Receipt |

Outbound deliv.		Document Date	19.05.2017	
Ship-to party	601361	1st customer of SFE1 / 100 Dufferin Street / Toronto ON M3R 4W2		

| Item Overview | Picking | Loading | Transport | Status Overview | Goods Movement Data |

Pick Date/Time	19.05.2017	00:0...	OvrllPickStatus	Not Relvnt for Pick.
Warehouse No.			OverallWMStatus	No WM trnsf ord reqd

All Items

Itm	Material	Plnt	SLoc	Deliv. Qty	Un	Picked Qty	Un	Batch
10	000000000001000654	SF01		45	CAR	0	CAR	

Fig 28

SAP automatically creates a returns delivery as above and this time, after defining the storage location where we want to receive these

250

goods, instead of a goods issue, we do a good receipt by clicking on

Post Goods Receipt

⊘ Returns delivery 84000041 has been saved

Fig 29

Note the delivery # also follows a different series as it is a returns delivery, not an outbound delivery.

Let us look at the stocks again in MMBE:

BEFORE:

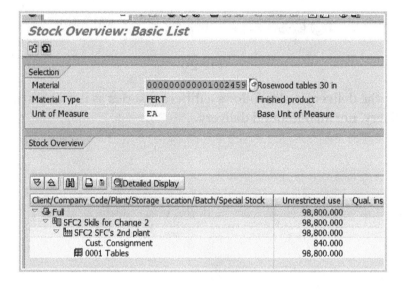

Fig 30

AFTER:

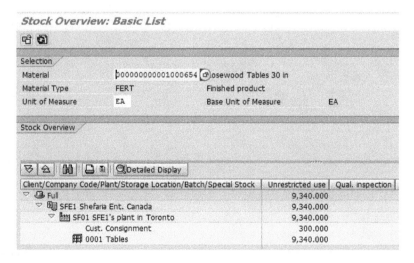

Fig 31

We see that because of this return of 45 CAR (= 45*12 = 540 EA) the consignment stock at the customer has depleted to 300 and the stock in the storage location has increased by the same amount to 9,340 EA.

4. CONSIGNMENT RETURN (U)

This is the last type of the consignment order in the consignment landscape. A consignment return occurs when a customer returns goods already bought (for which he was invoiced already) back to us. In out example, we had invoiced the customer 30 CAR earlier. If the customer were to return 10 CAR of these back to us, a consignment return would be created in VA01 using the order type CONR:

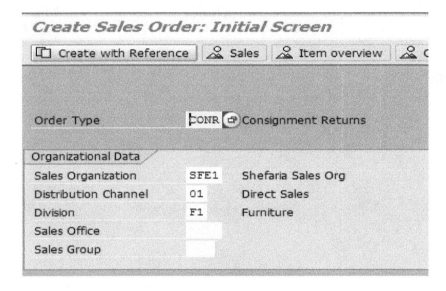

Fig 32

As a standard SAP process, all credits are given a billing block automatically and all returns require a return reason:

☐ Complete dlv.		Total Weight		0.000
Delivery block		Volume		0.000
Billing block	08 Check credit memo	Pricing date	19.05.2017	
Payment terms	0002	Incoterms	FOB Montreal	
Order reason				
Sales area	SFE1 / 01 / F1	Shefaria Sales Org, Direct Sales, Furniture		

Fig 33

These can be de-activated but for prudence's sake, all companies prefer to let them remain for reasons of accountability. Give an appropriate reason and give the material and quantity details:

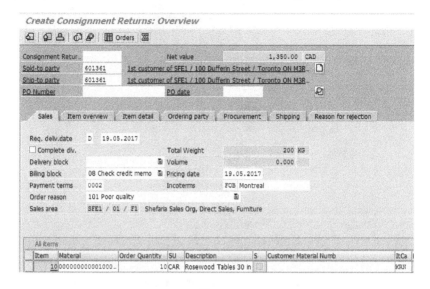

Fig 34

Yet again, as we notice, based on order type CONR, SAP applied the item category KRN to this line. Save the order and gave it a value as we will need to credit the customer with this amount.

Fig 35

Since this too is a physical return of goods, we need to create another delivery and receive the stock into 0001 storage location. We do it in VL01N again using this consignment return order:

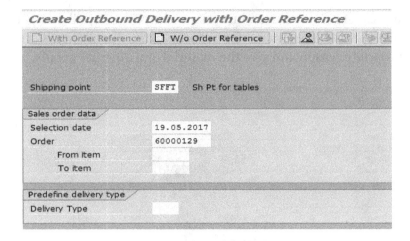

Fig 36

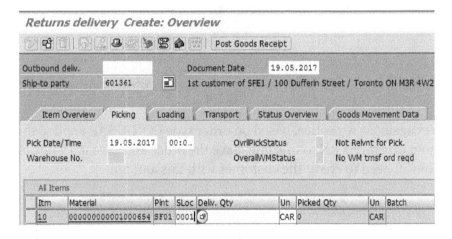

Fig 37

Post goods receipt.

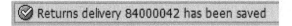

Fig 38

View the stock again:

BEFORE:

Client/Company Code/Plant/Storage Location/Batch/Special Stock	Unrestricted use
▽ 📖 Full	9,340.000
▽ 📑 SFE1 Shefaria Ent. Canada	9,340.000
▽ 📊 SF01 SFE1's plant in Toronto	9,340.000
Cust. Consignment	300.000
📇 0001 Tables	9,340.000

Fig 39

AFTER:

Client/Company Code/Plant/Storage Location/Batch/Special Stock	Unrestricted use	Qual.
▽ 📖 Full	9,340.000	
▽ 📑 SFE1 Shefaria Ent. Canada	9,340.000	
▽ 📊 SF01 SFE1's plant in Toronto	9,340.000	
Cust. Consignment	420.000	
📇 0001 Tables	9,340.000	

Fig 40

We notice that due to the return the customer consignment stock quantity has increased by 10 CAR (120 EA) while the storage location stock remains unaffected. Once the QC department has passed its judgement on this stock, it will get moved out of the customer consignment.

The customer is now to be credited for this quantity of 10 CAR. This is done in billing again in t code VF01 using this consignment returns order 60000129 after removing the billing block from it:

Create Billing Document

🖉 🔍 👤 Billing due list   👤 Billing document overview   📖 📑 Selection list   ⊕ 📥

Default data				
Billing Type		📄	Serv.rendered	
Billing Date			Pricing date	

Docs to be processed			
Document	Item	SD document categ.	Processing status
60000129			
	📝		

Fig 41

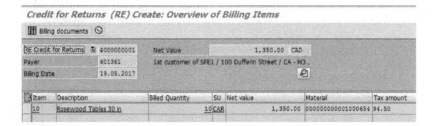

Fig 42

Save.

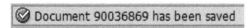

Fig 43

BILLS OF MATERIALS (U)

Often materials comprise of components, all of which need to be shipped though the order may be created only for the main item. The main item automatically pulls in the sub-items when entered in the sales order. The relationship between the main item and its sub-items is set up in a bill of material. Again, the primary driver of this relationship is an item category. In standard SAP, an item category group ERLA has been provided to represent the main item if the main item is an assembly. In this case, the pricing is maintained for the assembled product and it is also the one delivered. The sub-items do not get delivered and are not relieved from inventory.

If the material is to be non-assembly type and we need to ship, price and maintain inventory of the individual components and not the main item, then we use the item cat group LUMF instead of ERLA.

It is best understood with an example. A typical BOM could be created for any product that has sub-components for example. a computer that would have a hard drive, a keyboard and a monitor. The computer then would have ERLA:

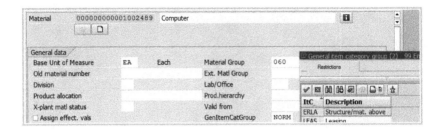

Fig 1

Its components are:

1002490 - Hard Drive
1002491 – Keyboard and
1002492 – Monitor

We need to establish a relationship between them so that SAP can understand that 1002489 comprises of 3 components – 1002490 to 1002492. We do this via a BOM – use transaction code CS01 or follow the path:

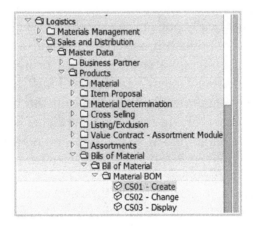

Fig 2

Create a BOM with usage 5 for the computer – Sales & Distribution:

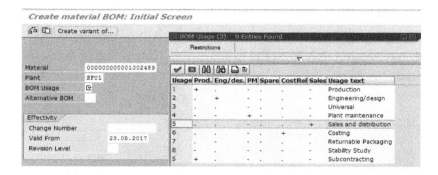

Fig 3

Enter how much of each component is needed per one computer:

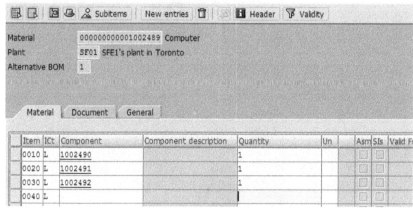

Fig 4

Save the BOM.

Fig 5

Similarly, another BOM was created for the non-assembled material 1002498 that has item category group LUMF.

When we create the sales order, and enter the material # 1002489, the system automatically pulls in the rest. In the order below, we have 2 materials – 1002489 which is an assembled computer and 1002498 which is a non-assembled one (sub-components being shipped separately). Note the difference in the pricing of the 2 groups based on different item categories of the sub-items that are determined because of ERLA and LUMF:

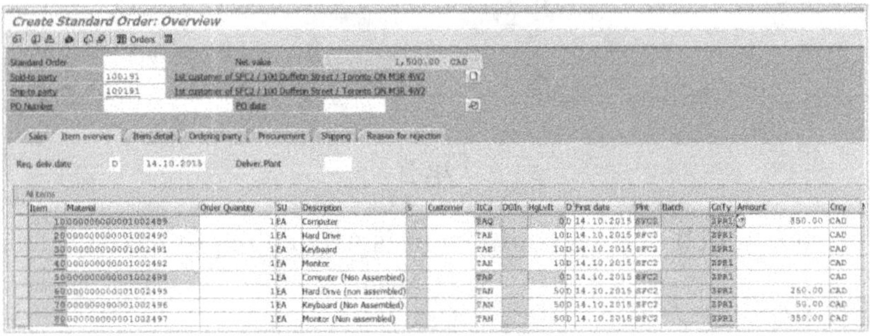

Fig 6

Based on the item category determination table:

SaTy	ItCGr	Usg.	ItmCatHItm	DfItC	MItCa	MItCa
OR	ERLA			TAQ		
OR	ERLA		TAP	TAE		
OR	ERLA		TAQ	TAE		
OR	LUMF			TAP		
OR	LUMF		TAP	TAN		

Fig 7

262

BILLING (C/U)

Billing in SAP is a function performed in Sales and Distribution. However, in many companies, billing is in reality, done by the Finance or Accounting department. Thus, we will cover billing to some extent in this course.

In SAP, Billing is a very large sub-module and the term is used as a very generic term to encompass all invoicing, credit/debit memos, pro-forma invoices, inter-company invoicing etc. There are many kinds of billing documents that are set up in SAP to represent different requirements. Further, depending on the process, billing may be done with reference to a delivery where actual physical goods are invoiced or directly from a sales order in cases of services or debit/credit memos.

We will go through in some detail with 2 kinds of billing:

16. Invoicing wrf deliveries i.e. when tangible, physical goods are sold
17. Invoicing wrf services when services are provided

We will also see how pro-forma invoices are created and debit or credit memos processed in SAP. As also how data is passed from the SD module to the FI module once billing has taken place.

There are many transactions to do billing. Billing for a single or a few transactions can be done by VF01. Large scale billing i.e. for many customer and/or documents is done in VF04. VF06 is utilized for creating background jobs for high volume billing. Depending on need, invoicing jobs are set up to run in the background or invoicing is done by the users themselves.

In the transaction cycle in the Sales & Distribution module, a transaction typically begins with a sales order or a credit/debit memo request. This sales order may get converted directly into an invoice if it is a services business of via a delivery into invoice if it is shipment of tangible products.

Here, we will understand the order and the customer master's invoicing tab under sales area data in more detail.

A customer master has the following fields under the Sales Area data which are significant in accounting:

Customer	601361	1st customer of SFE1	Toronto
Sales Org.	SFE1	Shefaria Sales Org	
Distr. Channel	01	Direct Sales	
Division	F1	Furniture	

Sales | Shipping | Billing Documents | Partner Functions

Billing document
☐ Subs. invoice processing   ☑ Rebate   ☐ Price determin.
Invoicing dates | ☞
InvoicingListDates

Delivery and payment terms
Incoterms   FOB   Montreal
Terms of payment   0002   Paym.guar.proc.
Credit ctrl area   SFE1

Accounting
Acct assgmt group   01   Domestic revenues

Fig 1

Invoicing dates – sometimes customers may insist on getting one invoice for the entire period if there are lots of transactions. This field can be populated with a calendar that will define the billing date of the invoices. This date will then default into every sales order and invoicing will take place with that same billing date for all the sales orders. The billing date is a precursor to the Baseline date from where the credit terms of the customer begin. Normally it is kept the same as the billing date though it can be altered. Every invoice in standard SAP leads to an accounting document which is what is reflected in a customer's AR. Usually companies prefer to keep it the same as the invoice number though it can be kept different as per need.

InvoiceListDates – invoices, when in a high number can be combined into an invoice list. An invoice list is merely a 'list' of the invoices. It is not an accounting document. While pricing can be done in an invoice list and it becomes useful in cases of rebate processing, most organizations will prefer not to do it as it is double maintenance. A calendar similar to the one described earlier is maintained in this field to combine the invoices on that date.

Incoterms - Incoterms are internationally agreed shipping terms and have a strong bearing on the freight of the product. Depending on the Inco terms, the freight costs may be a part of the invoice or may not be. Thus, these terms get to play a role in the invoking module.

Terms of Payment – When defined, these are the credit terms of the customer. The invoice will get due based on these terms which will get applied to the baseline date.

Credit control area – when set, this CCA is the umbrella under which the customer's credit limits are set up. The exposure of open AR, orders not yet executed or in the pipe line, all may together be a part of these credit limits which will get depleted as more and more invoicing takes place. Credits will, in the opposite way, release more credit limits of the customers.

Account Assignment group – is often used to define the G/L accounts to which the revenue relating to product sales, freight, surcharges/discounts etc. will be directed to.

Taxes					
Country	Name	Tax category	Name	Tax ...	Description
CA	Canada	CTX1	GST (Canada)	1	GST Only
CA	Canada	CTX2	PST (Canada)	0	Tax exempt
CA	Canada	CTX3	PST-Que & Mar(Base+)	0	Tax exempt

Fig 2

The implication of the tax setup was already discussed in the section of Taxes.

Among the check buttons, one is very important:

Fig 3

If this is not checked the customer will not be entitled to rebates.

2 DIFFERENT TYPES OF BILLINGS AND BILLING TYPES (U)

The Billing type defines the purpose and behavior of how the transaction will get billed. Standard SAP has many billing types and they can be made to follow different numbering sequences. Many companies may also prefer this numbering sequence set up by company codes only for the purpose of identification and separation. The more common billing types in SAP are:

F2   Invoice (F2)
F5   Pro Forma for Order
F8   Pro Forma wrf Dlv
G2   Credit Memo
IG   Internal Credit Memo
IV   Intercompany billing
L2   Debit Memo
LG   Credit memo list
LR   Invoice list
LRS   Cancel invoice list
S1   Invoice Cancellation

We will look at F2, G2 and F5, the 3 satisfying different purposes.

F2 invoice can be created from a goods issued delivery only or from a sales order only. In the former case, the Actual goods issue date in the delivery serves to become the billing date in the invoice. In the latter case, the billing date flows from the sales order itself.

i.   Invoicing from a delivery (U)

We have a delivery 80015042 that has been goods issued.

The billing that that the invoice of this delivery will assume is under the Goods movement tab in the delivery in transaction VL03N:

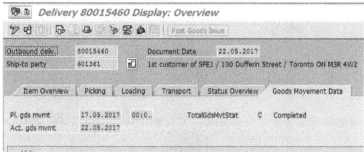

Fig 4

Using the transaction F2 we will create the invoice from this delivery. In the VF01 screen, enter this delivery number:

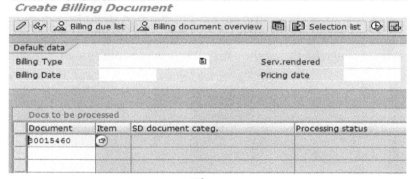

Fig 5

There is normally no need to enter the Billing type unless a billing type different from the system proposed one is required and in that case, certain configurations must be set up already for the billing to happen.

The open fields are the default criteria that can be changed and/or applied to all the deliveries being invoiced in this transaction.
A drop down of the Billing type will give the choices available:

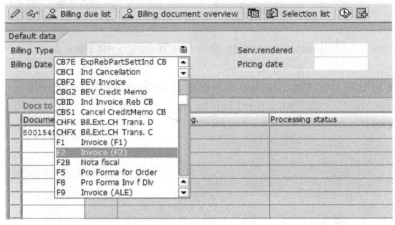

Fig 6

We can enter any dates in the other 3 fields though the billing data must be in the open period for the document to post to accounting. There is no need to define any of this data as it comes from the sales order and/or from the delivery into this invoice.

Multiple deliveries can be entered in the screen at the same time and depending on the configuration set up, some of them may combine to create one invoice for example. if the customers, billing dates, pricing etc. are the same, they may be a case to combine on the same invoice:

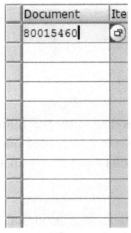

Fig 7

If there are multiple lines on the delivery and we need to create separate invoices for each line or a combination of lines, or we simply want to invoice only a limited number now and the rest later, the button ▣ Selection list can be used to 'select' the line items we want to invoice now.

In our example, we will invoice the entire delivery of 1 line. With the delivery # entered in the screen, Hit Enter:

At the bottom of the screen a message comes up briefly:

Processing of Document 0080015460

Fig 8

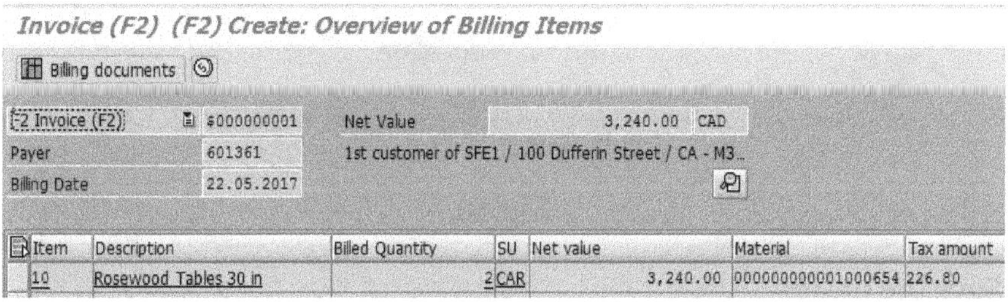

Invoice (F2) (F2) Create: Overview of Billing Items

⊞ Billing documents ⊙

F2 Invoice (F2)	▣ &000000001	Net Value	3,240.00 CAD	
Payer	601361	1st customer of SFE1 / 100 Dufferin Street / CA - M3...		
Billing Date	22.05.2017		▣	

Item	Description	Billed Quantity	SU	Net value	Material	Tax amount
10	Rosewood Tables 30 in	2	CAR	3,240.00	00000000001000654	226.80

Fig 9

The invoice will get most of the data from the delivery and/or order and may re-determine some depending on how configurations are set up.

ii. Invoicing from an Order (U)

In businesses which do not sell any tangible goods but provide services, orders are created and invoiced directly when the services are completed or based on any other billing plan/schedule. The order is created in the transaction VA01. We create a sales order for 50 hours of service:

Fig 10

Save the order:

Fig 11

Now this order 12540 can be invoiced in VF01 as we did the delivery earlier:

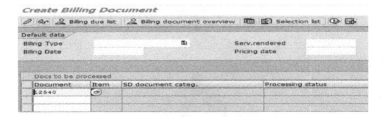

Fig 12

Save:

Fig 13

iii.   Important fields on a Billing Document (U)

Most of the header data in the billing document defaults from the customer master and most of the line item data, from the material master. In the above example, save the billing document first:

Fig 14

VF02 is the transaction to make any changes in the existing billing document. VF03 is the transaction to display the billing document.

Payer:

Fig 15

As far as Accounting is concerned, the Payer is the only significant customer. As we saw earlier, a customer master has 4 primary partner functions:

- Sold to party; the party that usually is the main customer that drives the purchases
- Ship to party; the location of the customer where goods are shipped to or services performed at
- Bill to; where the invoice is sent
- Payer; the one who pays and in whose name the AR is created

Billing Date:

Billing Date   22.05.2017

Fig 16

This is the date when the baseline date usually begins i.e. when the credit terms of the customer begin.

Under the section, Header>Header:

274

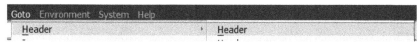

Fig 17

Company code:

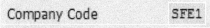

Fig 18

This is the company code responsible for the sales organization that did the transaction. This company code holds the AR and the receivables will form a part of its current assets.

On the Conditions tab, once can see the value of the document along with the taxes:

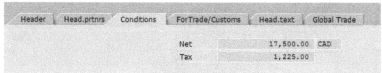

Fig 19

The accounting document of this invoice can be reached via the accounting tab:

Fig 20

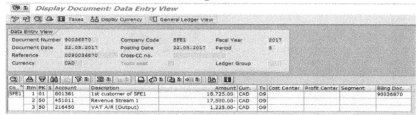

Fig 21

At the line item level, the important fields are:

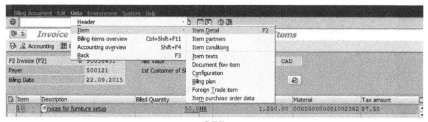

Fig 22

Service Rendered Date:

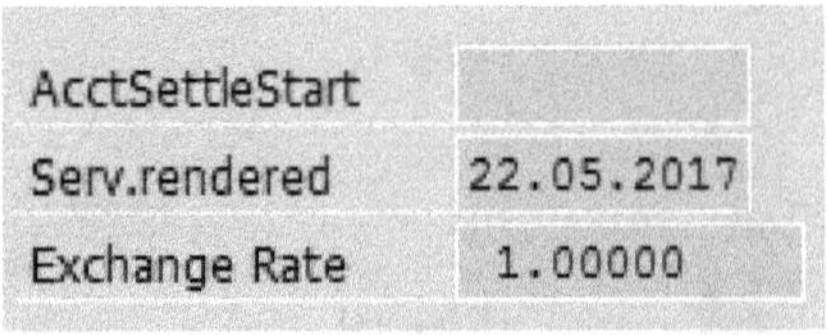

AcctSettleStart	
Serv.rendered	22.05.2017
Exchange Rate	1.00000

Fig 23

This is the date on which taxes are calculated i.e. the taxes existing on that date in SAP (or external systems) are the valid taxes for this transaction. It is independent of the billing date or date when the order created.

iv.   Pro-forma invoices (U)

Occasionally the customer may require a pro-forma invoice for purpose of getting prior approvals for imports, or for customs or bank funding in cases of capital goods etc. 2 standard pro-forma invoices exist in SAP – the F5 created from a sales order and F8 with reference to a delivery. The delivery does not have to be goods issued for this purpose. Pro-forma invoices do not create accounting entries i.e. they never hit AR.

From order, type F2:

Create the sales order in VA01, all that is needed to enter are the customer #, material and quantity:

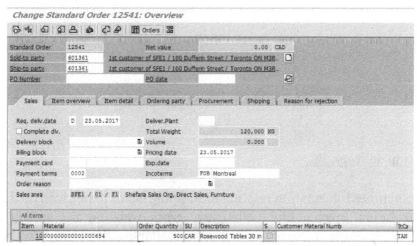

Fig 24

Save -

In VF01, enter the order # in the Document field and choose F5:

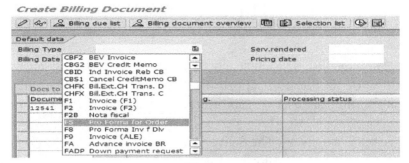
Fig 25

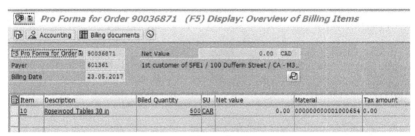
Fig 26

Save

Fig 27

From delivery, F8:

Sometimes information relating to shipping needs to be given on the pro-forma invoice like palletizing, gross weights, net weights, transporter etc. and some of it may be available only in the delivery. In those cases, a delivery is created from the sales order and the pro-forma created wrt to that delivery instead of from the order. Unlike the real invoice, for a pro-forma invoice the delivery need not be goods issued for the pro-forma to create.

Create the order in VA01 and then the delivery in VL01N using that sales order.

Delivery Create: Overview

Fig 28

Save

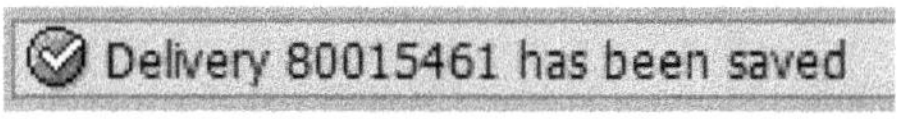

Delivery 80015461 has been saved

Fig 29

Use this delivery # in VF01, choosing F8 as the Billing type:

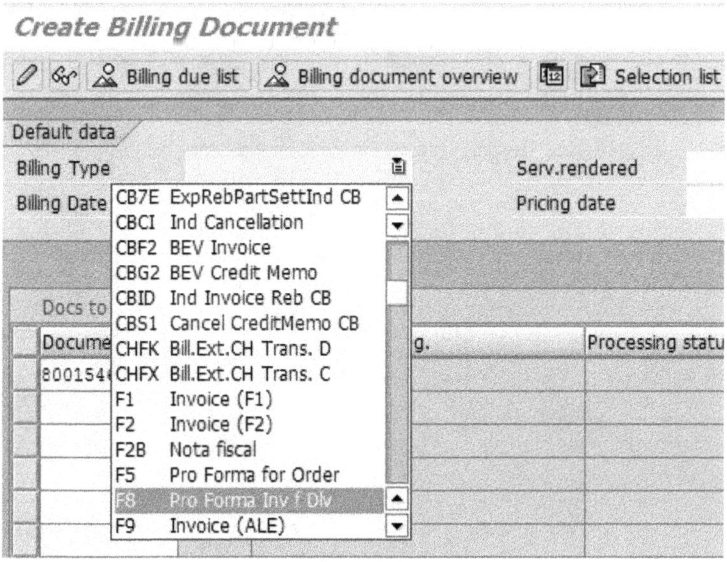

Create Billing Document

| | | Billing due list | | Billing document overview | | Selection list |

| Default data | | | | | |

Billing Type				Serv.rendered	
Billing Date	CB7E ExpRebPartSettInd CB			Pricing date	
	CBCI Ind Cancellation				
	CBF2 BEV Invoice				
	CBG2 BEV Credit Memo				
	CBID Ind Invoice Reb CB				
Docs to	CBS1 Cancel CreditMemo CB				
Docume	CHFK Bill.Ext.CH Trans. D		g.	Processing statu
800154	CHFX Bill.Ext.CH Trans. C				
	F1 Invoice (F1)				
	F2 Invoice (F2)				
	F2B Nota fiscal				
	F5 Pro Forma for Order				
	F8 Pro Forma Inv f Dlv				
	F9 Invoice (ALE)				

Fig 30

Press Enter – the following message will appear:

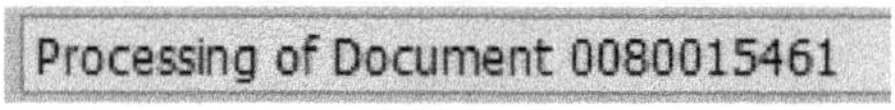

Processing of Document 0080015461

Fig 31

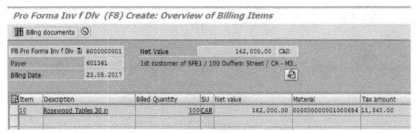

Fig 32

Save

Fig 33

3. VIEWING AN INVOICE (U)

Although the content of the actual invoice will vary depending on the company's requirements, the process to view them is the same. SAP offers the ability to 'preview' the invoices before the user can decide whether to print or not. Printing can be done in mass scale or individually depending on the volumes.

To look up an individual invoice on the screen go to VF03 (display):

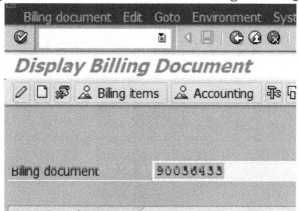

Fig 34

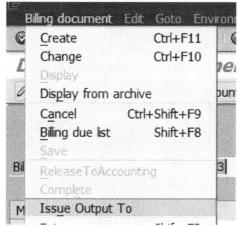

Fig 35

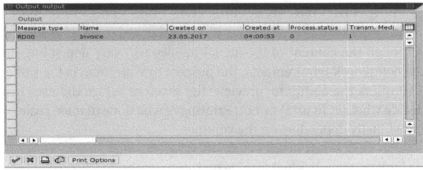

Fig 36

Every company will have its own Message type (also called Outputs) and often there will be multiple (usually different formats and reasons thereof). With the appropriate Output highlighted, click on the button

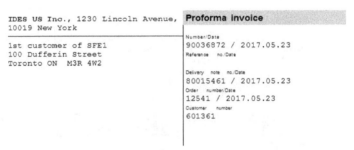

Fig 37

Use scrolling keys to see all the pages if there are multiple.

Cancelling a Billing Document is done in transaction VF11 which looks like VF01 except for a different header and that here you have to enter the billing document that needs to be cancelled instead of the order # or delivery #:

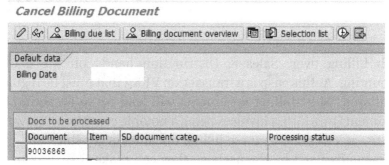

Fig 38

Hit Enter and Save.

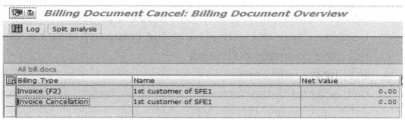

Fig 39

Document 90036873 saved

Fig 40

Once an existing billing document is cancelled, it releases the order or the delivery to get billed again. For the most part, in SAP, it is not possible to cancel a preceding document without first cancelling the subsequent document. Thus, it is very important that the data is good from the origin itself, as SAP can be very unforgiving if the data is wrong.

4 RELEASING BILLING DOCUMENTS TO ACCOUNTING (U)

With Billing over, Sales & Distribution hands off the data to accounting. At this cusp is a transaction VFX3 that must be regularly monitored. Most billing documents will lead up to an accounting document (pro-forma invoices being a notable exception). However, due to various reasons these billing documents get stuck and must be manually fixed by the users so they can make their way to AR. Some reasons for this are:

1. Old document, billing date is in a closed period.
2. Customer was not extended in the company code i.e. does not have company code data
3. Pricing was not correct
4. G/L account determination for revenue/freight etc. does not exist or is incorrect
5. For exports, certain mandatory foreign trade related data is missing
6. Tax calculations are not correct

And some more that may occur due to company specific custom transactions and data. This data will need to be fixed before these documents can be posted and in some cases, documents will need to be cancelled to re-create them with the right data.

LOGISTICS EXECUTION (C/U)

Logistics Execution module comprises of 2 primary sub-modules:

A) Delivery

B) Shipment

After an order is created, the first step in executing it is to create a delivery from it if it happens to be a physical product that needs to be shipped. Different order types lead to different kinds of deliveries. Deliveries are also created from Stock transport orders and Purchase orders that originate out of MM hence LE has been made a separate module on its own rather than keeping it confined to SD.

SAP has provided some standard delivery types that can be used for different transactions. The determination of a delivery type for an order or purchase order type is set up in the configuration of the order and Purchase order for example. in the order type OR that we have been using, SAP has provided delivery type LF to use with it:

Shipping			
Delivery type	LF	Delivery	Immediate delivery
Delivery block			
Shipping conditions			
ShipCostInfoProfile	STANDARD	Standard freight information	

Fig 1

However new delivery types can be and are often defined for business purposes.

For a delivery, the highest org unit is a shipping point. A shipping point can be used by multiple plants and it must be assigned to at least one plant. A shipment has a physical address, one of its elements being a transportation zone which will be used to determine the route the delivery will take. One delivery can have only one shipping point from where it will originate.

A delivery document has a structure very similar to the sales documents type- the delivery document contains header and item data. A delivery document is usually created with reference to the sales document type but it is not always the case. The list of standard delivery document types are as follows:

Delivery wrf to order - LF
Delivery without reference - LO
Returns delivery - LR
Returns delivery from a purchase order - RL
Replenishment delivery – NL

DELIVERY DOCUMENTS (C/U)

1. DEFINING DELIVERY TYPES (C)

The delivery document type can be created or accessed through IMG screen (Logistics execution- Shipping- Deliveries- Define Delivery Types) or the transaction code oVLK.

Define Delivery Types

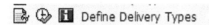

Fig 1

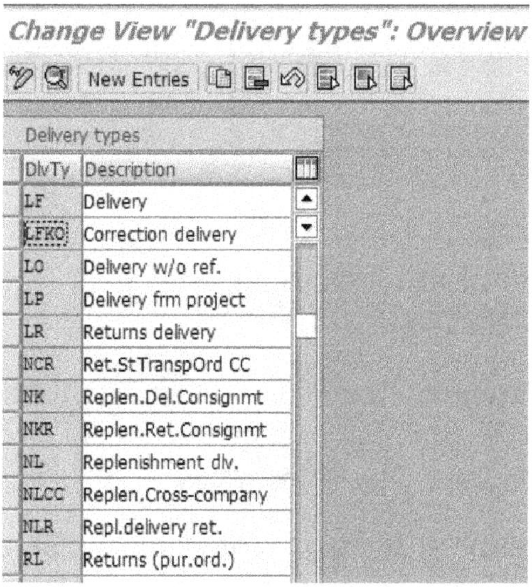
Change View "Delivery types": Overview
New Entries
Delivery types
DlvTy
Description
LF
Delivery
LFKO
Correction delivery
LO
Delivery w/o ref.
LP
Delivery frm project
LR
Returns delivery
NCR
Ret.StTranspOrd CC
NK
Replen.Del.Consignmt
NKR
Replen.Ret.Consignmt
NL
Replenishment dlv.
NLCC
Replen.Cross-company
NLR
Repl.delivery ret.
RL
Returns (pur.ord.)

Fig 2

A new delivery document can be created by copying the standard delivery document types and modifying them as per the requirements.

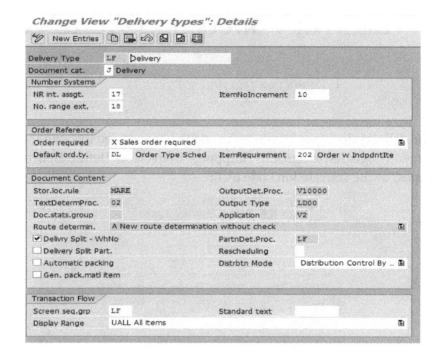

Fig 3

A few important fields in the configuration of delivery document types are as follows:

Document Category- It is an important field that identifies what document type is used. For example, A stands for Inquiry, B for quotation, C for order, J for delivery etc.

Number systems - It gives the user the option to use number range according to his/her preference. Also, the item no. increment for delivery document can be defined here. To define the number range, follow the IMG path or use t-code VN01. Logistics Execution -> Shipping -> Deliveries -> Define Number Ranges for Deliveries

Order reference - This setting enables the user to create delivery document type without reference to a sales document type. For this a pseudo sales document type must be specified in the default order type.

Document content -The settings in the document content screen are not configurable from this view. They are determined by the individual settings which assign them to delivery document type. Some of the functions include storage location determination, output determination, split delivery etc.

Transaction Flow – In this section the sequence of the screens in which they are displayed and display of delivery items can be configured i.e. you can limit the display to main items in the delivery.

2. DELIVERY ITEM CATEGORIES (C)

A delivery item category determines how an item is to behave in the delivery document type. A delivery item category is very similar to sales item category except that it has its own control features.

i.   Delivery Item Category determination (C)

 A delivery item category can be defined through the transaction code oVLP and using the following menu path: Logistics Execution -> Shipping -> Deliveries -> Define Item Categories for Deliveries

Fig 4

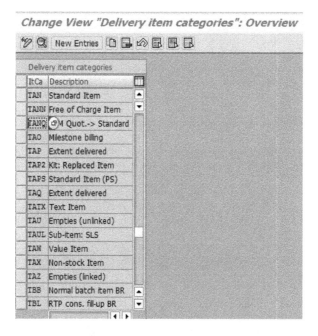

Fig 5

The SAP-defined item category can be used by assigning them to the delivery document types. Alternatively, new delivery document types can be created by copying the existing entries and modifying them as per the requirements. The new item category must begin with the prefix Y or Z.

Change View "Delivery item categories": Details

New Entries

| Item Category | TAN | Standard Item |
| Document cat. | J | Delivery |

Material/Statistics
☑ Mat.no.'0' allowed
ItemCat.stat.group   Stk determ.rule

Quantity
Check quantity 0   A   Note about the situation   AvailCkOff
Check minimum qty   A   Note about the situation   Roundng
Check overdelivery

Warehouse Control and Packing
☑ Relevant for picking   Packing control
☑ StLocation required   ☐ Pack acc. batch itms
☑ Determine SLoc
☐ Don't chk st. loc.
☐ No batch check   ☑ AutoBatchDeterm

Transaction Flow
TextDetermProcedure   02   Standard text

Fig 6

Material/Statistics -The material number 0 allowed is used for creating item without item reference, mainly used for text items. The stock determination group is used with stock determination group to decide stock determination strategy.

Quantity - The check quantity 0 field determines if the system reacts with warning or error message for the item that has zero quantity. The check minimum quantity field checks the minimum delivery quantity specified in material master or customer material info records and reacts accordingly. The check over delivery issues a warning or error message if the delivery quantity exceeds one maintained in customer material info record or material master.

291

Warehouse control and packaging - The picking indicator is used to mark the item relevant for picking except for non-stock, value, and service items. The StLocation required necessitates entering storage location for the processing of delivery and Determine StLocation is used for automatic determination of the storage location. The Auto Batch Determ indicator is used for carrying automatic batch determination for the line item in the delivery.

ii.   Delivery Item Category determination (C)

The item category in the delivery document is copied from the item category used in the sales order. Alternatively, the item category of items that have no reference to a sales document (packaging items) is determined by the delivery item category determination table.
The item category is determined by the delivery type, the item category group of the material, usage of the item and the item category of the higher level item.

Change View "Delivery item category determination": Overview

New Entries

Delivery item category determination

DlvT	ItCG	Usg.	ItmC	ItmC	MItC	MItC	MItC	MItC	MItC	MItC	MItC	MItC	MItC	MItC	I
LF		TEXT		TATX											
LF	LEIH			TAL											
LF	LEIH	PACK		TAL											
LF	LUMF		TAP												
LF	NORM			DLN											
LF	NORM	C		TAN											
LF	NORM	CHSP		TAN											
LF	NORM	CHSP	KLN	KLN											
LF	NORM	CHSP	TANN	TANN											
LF	NORM	PACK		DLN	DLX	DLP	KEN								
LF	NORM	PSEL	TAX	TAPS											
LF	VERP			ZDLP											
LF	VERP	PACK		ZDLP	DLN	DLP	KEN								
LO		TEXT		DLTX											
LO	DIEN			DLX	DLX										
LO	LEER			DLN											
LO	LEER		DLNG	DLNZ											

Fig 7

3. SHIPPING POINT DETERMINATION (C)

Shipping point represent the highest organizational unit for logistics execution and point of departure or receipt of materials. No delivery can be made without the shipping point. The shipping point is determined based on the entries maintained in the shipping point determination table. The shipping point is determined based on the combination of plant, shipping conditions and material loading group.

i)   Shipping conditions (C)

The shipping conditions are maintained in the customer master or can be manually entered in the sales order. The shipping conditions can also be defaulted for a sales document type. The shipping conditions can be defined using following menu path:

Logistics Execution -> Shipping -> Basic Shipping Functions -> Shipping Point and Goods Receiving Point Determination -> Define Shipping Conditions by Sales Document Type

Define Shipping Conditions

Fig 8

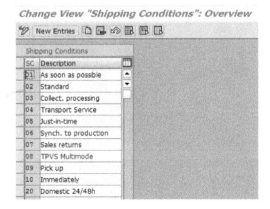

Fig 9

293

ii) Material Loading Group (C)

The loading group used for shipping point determination is maintained in the material master. The material loading group can be defined using the following menu path:

Logistics Execution -> Shipping -> Basic Shipping Functions -> Shipping Point and Goods Receiving Point Determination -> Define Loading Groups

Define Loading Groups

Fig 10

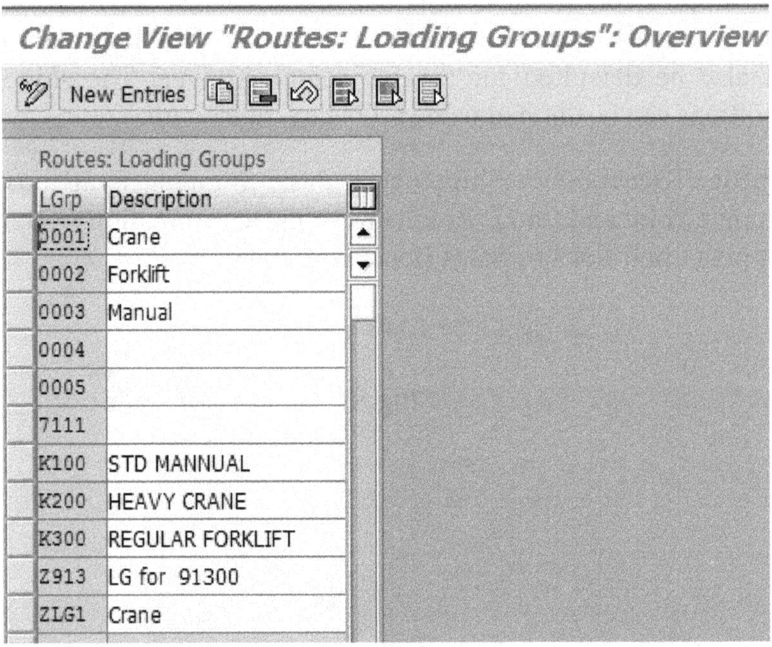

Change View "Routes: Loading Groups": Overview

🖉 New Entries 🗋 🖫 🖎 🖫 🖫 🖫

Routes: Loading Groups

	LGrp	Description	
	0001	Crane	▲
	0002	Forklift	▼
	0003	Manual	
	0004		
	0005		
	7111		
	K100	STD MANNUAL	
	K200	HEAVY CRANE	
	K300	REGULAR FORKLIFT	
	Z913	LG for 91300	
	ZLG1	Crane	

Fig 11

iii) Assign Shipping point (C)

The shipping point and manual shipping point is assigned to the combination of shipping condition, loading group and plant in the shipping point determination table.

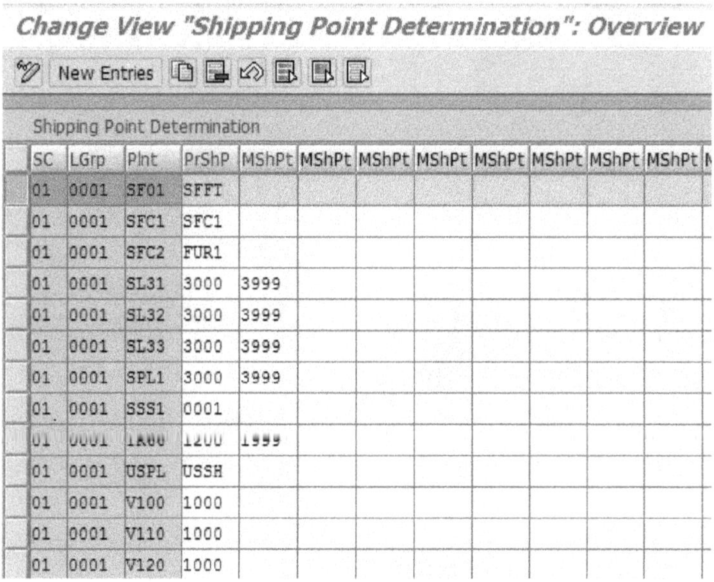

SC	LGrp	Plnt	PrShP	MShPt	MShPt	MShPt	MShPt	MShPt	MShPt	MShPt	MShPt	N
01	0001	SF01	SFFI									
01	0001	SFC1	SFC1									
01	0001	SFC2	FUR1									
01	0001	SL31	3000	3999								
01	0001	SL32	3000	3999								
01	0001	SL33	3000	3999								
01	0001	SPL1	3000	3999								
01	0001	SSS1	0001									
01	0001	1R00	1200	1999								
01	0001	USPL	USSH									
01	0001	V100	1000									
01	0001	V110	1000									
01	0001	V120	1000									

Fig 12

iv Goods receiving point for inbound deliveries (C)

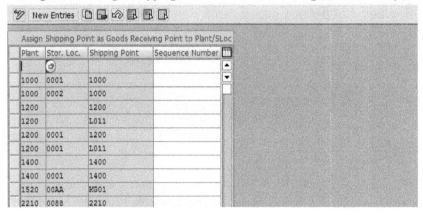

Fig 13

4. DELIVERY BLOCKS (C)

Delivery blocks are used for blocking the delivery from being created and also prevents assignment of stocks to the sales documents that are blocked.

i) Blocking reasons (C)

The blocking reason help to block the deliver based on different parameters. The blocking can be configured using t-code OVLS or the following menu path:

Logistics Execution -> Shipping Deliveries -> Define Reasons for Blocking in Shipping ->Deliveries: Blocking Reasons/Criteria

Change View "Deliveries: Blocking Reasons/Criteria": Overview

New Entries

Deliveries: Blocking Reasons/Criteria

DB	Delivery block descr	Order	Conf.	Print	DDueList	Pick	Good
01	Credit limits		✓			✓	✓
02	Political reasons						
03	Bottleneck material						
04	Export papers missng						
05	Check free of ch.dlv						
06	No printing			✓			
07	Change in quantity						
08	Kanban Delivery	✓			✓		
41	QM Block					✓	✓
42	Delta Usage Date				✓	✓	✓
43	Select Goods First				✓	✓	✓
44	'Pre-production'				✓	✓	✓
90	Internet				✓	✓	✓
91	Customer Request				✓	✓	✓
97	DEA: Check Form 222					✓	✓
98	DEA: Qty Tolerance					✓	✓

Fig 14

Order: This block will block a sales order from delivery processing. It can be maintained in the customer master or can be manually entered in the sales order.

Confirmation: This option will block the confirmation of stock after an availability check. Although the requirement is transferred to the MRP list, consumption of stock does not occur.

Print: This reason will block the output of the document.

Delivery Due List: This setting blocks the sales document from being automatically processed by delivery due list.

Picking: This setting blocks the goods from being picked.

Goods issue: This option blocks the goods issue of the delivery document.

These delivery blocks must be assigned to the delivery types as shown below:

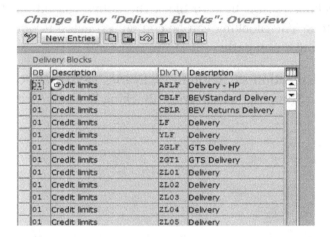

Fig 15

ii Delivery Block at header level (C)

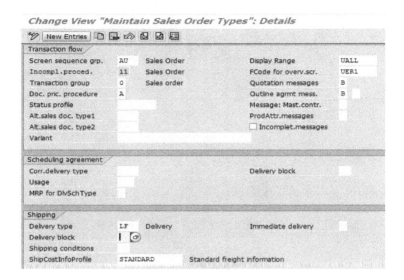

Fig 16

The block at header level can set through the shipping section of the sales document type. This blocks a specific order type as per the assigned block reason.

iii Delivery Block at Schedule Line Level (C)

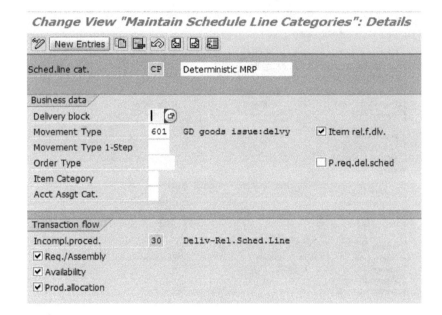

Fig 17

This function is used to block a certain portion of schedule lines in a sales document. This can be configured from the business data section of sales schedule line categories.

iv) Delivery block at Customer/Header level (C)

This option helps to block a customer from delivery processing for a particular sales area or all sales area. This can be done through t-code VD05.

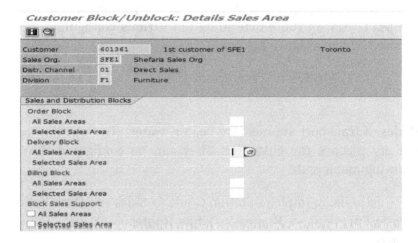

Fig 18

5. ROUTE DETERMINATION (C)

Route determination is the logistics process whereby one can assign a specific route using different shipment types and carriers. It is automatically proposed in the sales order for each sales item. The route may also be determined in the delivery based on the weight groups. To set up route determination various configurations are required which is shown below:

i) Modes of Transport (C)

Modes of transport are medium i.e. air, water, road etc. through a delivery reaches the customer. They can be configured through following menu path:

SAP Customizing Implementation Guide -> Sales and Distribution -> Basic Functions -> Routes-> Define Routes -> Define Modes of Transport

Change View "Mode of Transport": Overview

New Entries

Mode of Transport

ShTy	Description	SType	Description
01	Road	1	Road
02	Rail	2	Rail
03	Sea	4	Sea
04	Inland Waterway	3	Inland waterway
05	Air	5	Air cargo
06	Postal Service	1	Road

Fig 19

The mode of transport (column ShTy) must be transportation category (SType) assigned to it.

ii) Shipping Types (C)

Shipping types are the actual vehicles used for transportation such as train, truck etc. It can be defined using the following menu path:

SAP Customizing Implementation Guide -> Sales and Distribution -> Basic Functions -> Routes -> Define Routes -> Define Shipping Types

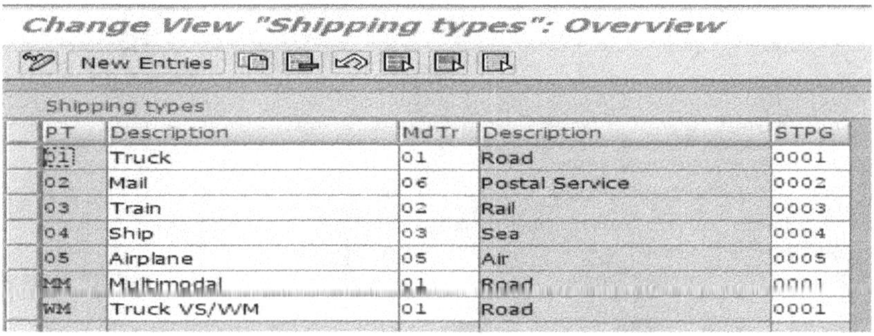

PT	Description	MdTr	Description	STPG
01	Truck	01	Road	0001
02	Mail	06	Postal Service	0002
03	Train	02	Rail	0003
04	Ship	03	Sea	0004
05	Airplane	05	Air	0005
MM	Multimodal	01	Road	0001
WM	Truck VS/WM	01	Road	0001

Fig 20

In the above figure, column PT represents the shipping types, Md Tr represents mode of transport and STPG is shipping type procedure group used to calculate costs relating to transportation.

303

iii) Transportation connection points (C)

Transport connection points such as railway stations, airports, harbours etc. are the places where various transportation types connect. They can be defined using the following menu path:

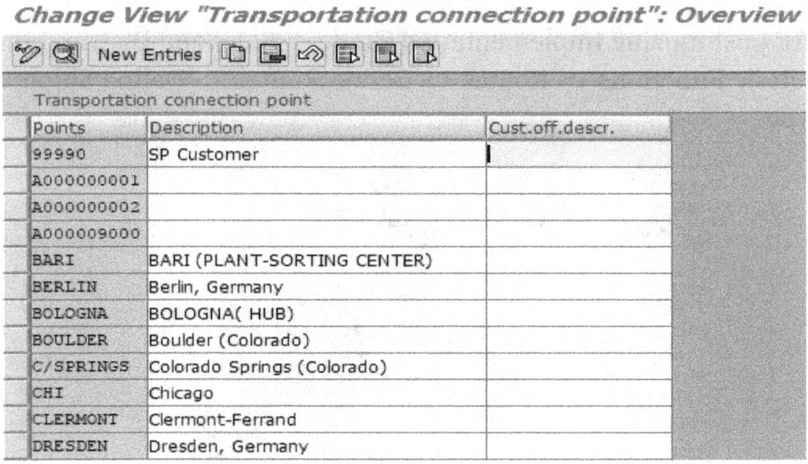

Change View "Transportation connection point": Overview

New Entries

Transportation connection point

Points	Description	Cust..off.descr.
99990	SP Customer	
A000000001		
A000000002		
A000009000		
BARI	BARI (PLANT-SORTING CENTER)	
BERLIN	Berlin, Germany	
BOLOGNA	BOLOGNA(HUB)	
BOULDER	Boulder (Colorado)	
C/SPRINGS	Colorado Springs (Colorado)	
CHI	Chicago	
CLERMONT	Clermont-Ferrand	
DRESDEN	Dresden, Germany	

Fig 21

iv) Routes and Stages (C)

In this step, we can define routes with stages and connection points. This can be done through the following menu path:

SAP Customizing Implementation Guide -> Sales and Distribution -> Basic Functions -> Routes -> Define Routes -> Define Routes and Stages

Change View "Routes": Overview

Route	Description	ST	PL	Un	ServcAgent	TransitDur	Trav.dur	Transit.Tm	Tr.lead tim	Cal	Distance		Unit	MoT	D	TR
000001	Northern Route															
000002	Southern Route															
000003	Eastern Route	03	01	01												
000004	Western Route															
000012	North-south Route															
000015	SP - Milano-Bologna(Hub)-Bari	01	01	01		1.00	:01	1.00	:01	IT	210		KM	3		
000021	South-north Route															
000034	East-west Route															

Fig 22

We will define a new route using existing route 000003(Eastern Route). The new route created is ZSFFT (New route for Shefaria Enterprises). Once the route is defined, we need to process of route determination.

Change View "Routes": Details of Selected Set

Route	ZSFFT	
Identification		
Description	New route for Shefaria Enterprises	
Route ID		
Processing		
Service agent		
ModeOfTr-Border		
Shipping type	03 🚃 Train	Distance
ShTypePreLeg	01 🚚 Truck	
ShTypeSubLeg	01 🚚 Truck	☑ Rel.transport
Scheduling		
TransitTime	1	Factory cal.

Fig 23

305

6. ROUTE DETERMINATION (C/U)

SAP determines the route based on the following parameters:

• The country and departure zone (taken from the shipping point)
• The country and receiving zone of the Ship-to Party
• The shipping conditions as in the sales order
• The transportation group of the material master record
• The weight group (optional and only relevant in the delivery)

So, let us set up each of the parameter for route determination.

i) Transportation zones

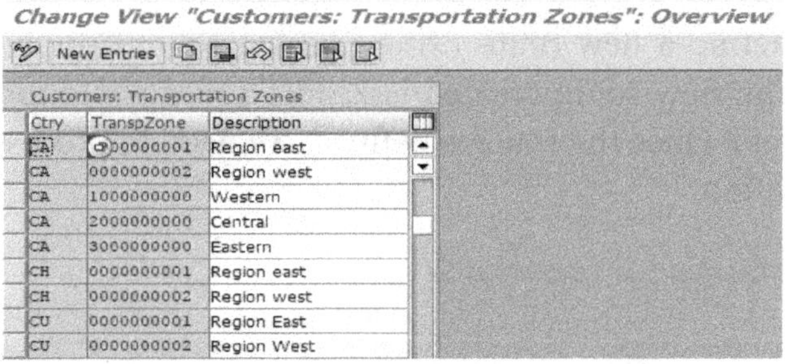

Fig 24

Now, we will define a new transportation zone(ZSFFT1) using the existing one.

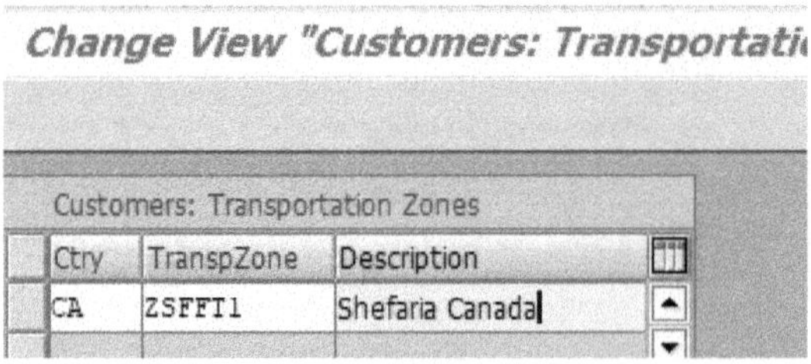

Fig 25

ii) Assignment: Departure Country/Zone to Shipping Point (C)

Next, the defined transportation zone is assigned to our shipping point SFFT.

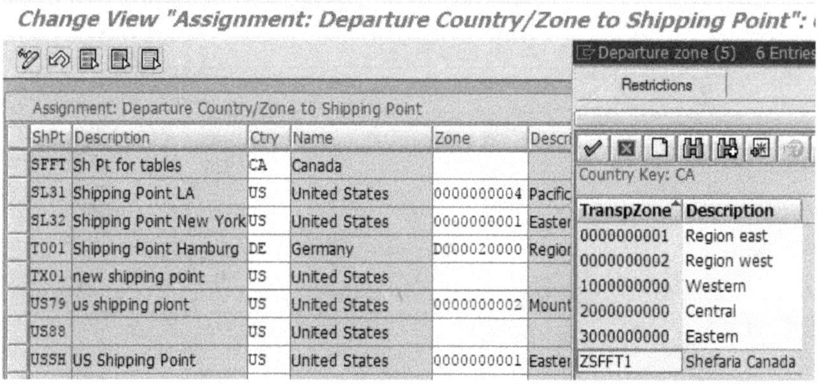

Fig 26

iii) Transport Groups (C)

The next parameter to be defined is the transport group. In our case we will be using standard transport groups.

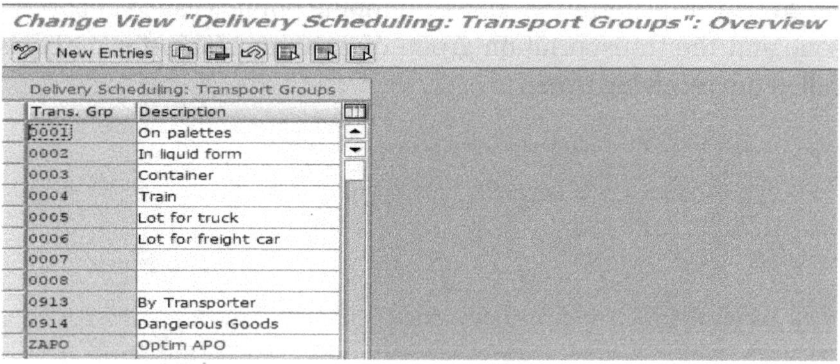

Fig 27

iv) **Weight Groups (C)**

Weight groups is considered for route determination in case of deliveries. New weight groups can be defined as per the requirements.

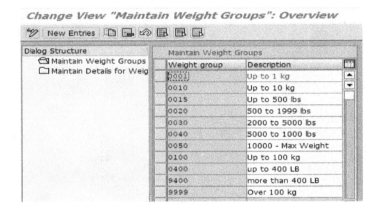

Fig 28

v) **Maintain route determination (C)**

Since, we have defined all the parameters for route determination, we can proceed to maintain route determination table. It is to be noted that transportation zone of shipping point is called departure zone and the transportation group of customer (ship-to- party) is called the receiving zone.

Change View "Ctry of dep./dep. zone and ctry of dest./recv.zone": Over

New Entries

CDep	Name	DepZ	Description	DstC	Name	RecZ	Description
				CA	Canada	1000000000	Western
				CA	Canada	2000000000	Central
				CA	Canada	3000000000	Eastern
				US	United States	0000000003	Central
AT	Austria	0000000001	Region east	AT	Austria	0000000001	Region east
AT	Austria	0000000001	Region east	AT	Austria	0000000002	Region west
AT	Austria	0000000002	Region west	AT	Austria	0000000001	Region east
AT	Austria	0000000002	Region west	AT	Austria	0000000002	Region west

Fig 29

We will be using ZSFFT1 (Shefaria Canada) as the departure zone and 0000000001(Region east) as the receiving zone.

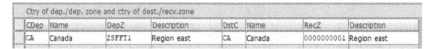

Ctry of dep./dep. zone and ctry of dest./recv.zone							
CDep	Name	DepZ	Description	DstC	Name	RecZ	Description
CA	Canada	ZSFFT1	Region east	CA	Canada	0000000001	Region east

Fig 30

Dep.country/Zone	CA	/	ZSFFT1		Canada / Shefaria Canada
Dest.country/Zone	CA	/	0000000001		Canada / Region east

Route Determination Without Weight Group (Order)					
SC	Description	TGroup	Description	Proposed ro...	Description
01	As soon as possible	0001	On palettes	000001	Northern Route
		0002	In liquid form	000002	Southern Route
02	Standard	0001	On palettes	000001	Northern Route
		0002	In liquid form	000003	Southern Route

Fig 31

Dep.country/Zone	CA	/	ZSFFT1	Canada / Shefaria Canada
Dest.country/Zone	CA	/	0000000001	Canada / Region east

Route Determination with Weight Group (Delivery)							
SC	Description	TGroup	Description	WgtGr	Description	Actual route	Description
01	As soon as possible	0001	On palettes	0010	Up to 10 kg	000001	Northern Route
				0100	Up to 100 kg	000002	Southern Route
				9999	Over 100 kg	000003	Eastern Route

Fig 32

Now that we have finished the configuration of route determination, we would run a scenario to better understand the process. We will use the table below to visualize different scenarios:

Customer: 601361
Material: 1000654

Scenario	Customer-Rcv. zone	Shp. point Depart. zone	Material Trnspt. Grp	Sales order	Route	Delivery	Weight Group	Route
1	0000000001	ZSFFT1	0001		000001	8001 5464	0010	000001
2	0000000001	ZSFFT1	0001	1254 7	000001		0100	000002
3	0000000001	ZSFFT1	0001		000001		9999	000003

vi) Maintain transportation zone in customer master (U)

Transportation zone is maintained in General data – address tab of the customer master. It is to be noted that transportation zone is picked from ship-to-party, hence this data is to be maintained for ship-to-party if it differs from sold-to-party.

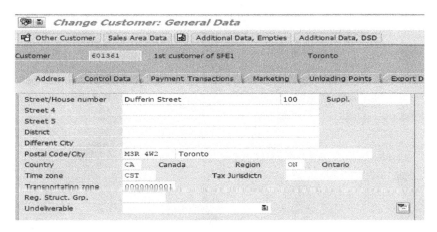

Fig 33

vii) Maintain transporting group in material master (U)

Transporting group of material master can be maintained through Sales: General/Plant view.

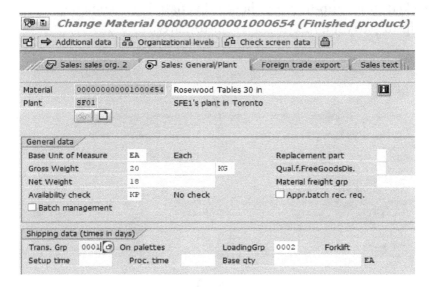

Fig 34

viii) Create sales order (U)

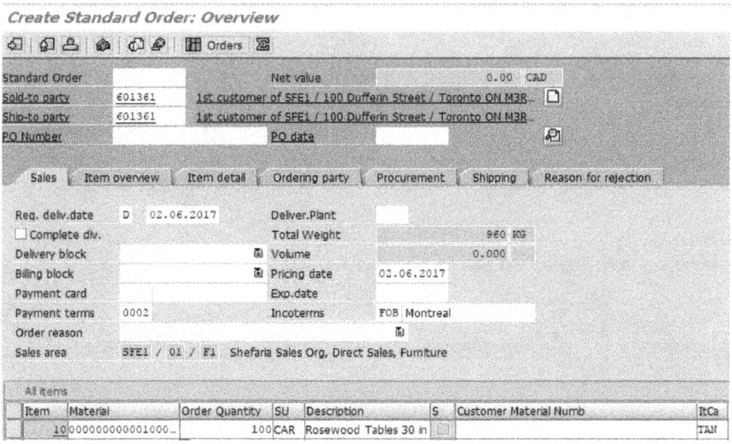

Fig 35

Check the shipping condition in Header- Sales data

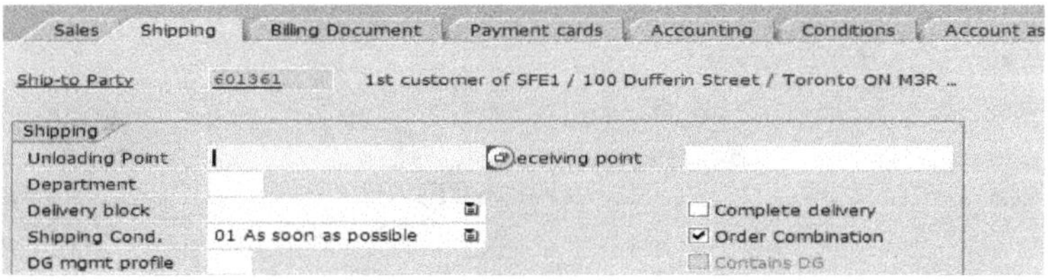

Fig 36

In the Item- Shipping tab, the route determined can be checked.

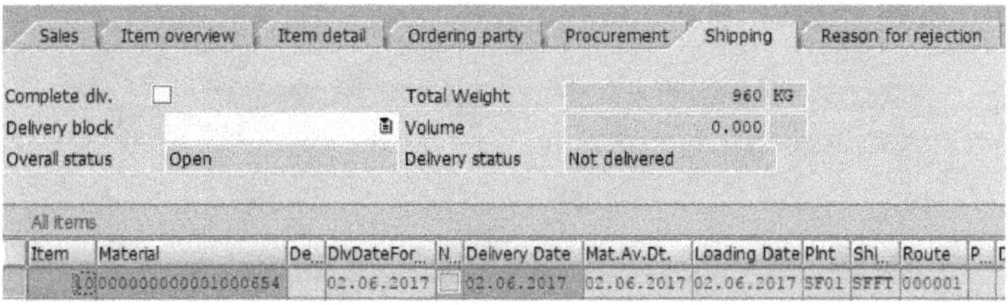

Fig 37

Save - sales order: 12547

ix) Create delivery (U)

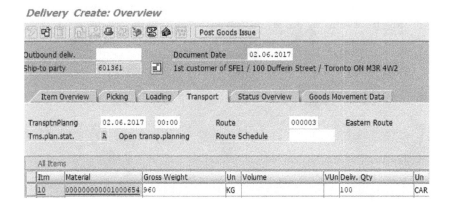

Fig 38

The route determined is **000003** since Gross weight is above 100kg (weight group:9999). Now let's change deliver quantity for verifying effect on route determination.

Delivery Create: Overview

			Post Goods Issue

Outbound deliv.
Document Date   02.06.2017
Ship-to party   601361   1st customer of SFE1 / 100 Dufferin Street / Toronto ON M3R 4W2

Item Overview | Picking | Loading | Transport | Status Overview | Goods Movement Data

TransptnPlanng   02.06.2017   00:00   Route   000003   Eastern Route
Trns.plan.stat.   A   Open transp.planning   Route Schedule

All Items

Itm	Material	Gross Weight	Un	Volume	VUn	Deliv. Qty
10	000000000001000654	9.600	KG			1

Information

ℹ Route 000001 was re-determined

✓ ⑫

Fig 39

Route 000001 is determined as weight less than 10 kg.

Further, changing the quantity of delivery items:

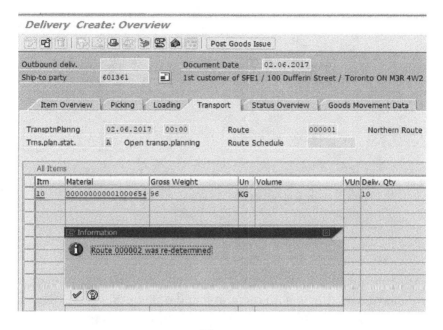

Fig 40

Delivery no.: 80015464

Delivery 80015464 has been saved

Fig 41

TRANSPORTATION

Transport is an essential function in logistics execution which ensures that the shipments are dispatched without delay and arrive on schedule. It affects both incoming and out coming goods. Hence, the shipment costs should be kept to a minimum so that price of a product is competitive.

In this section, we would be using outbound shipments based to transportation planning and process.

The basic elements of the shipment processing discussed henceforth include:

- Function of organisation unit Transportation planning point
- Function of shipment document
- Output determination
- Reports available in shipment processing

Transportation planning point is the point for carrying out the transportation planning and shipment execution. Each shipment must be assigned to a specific transportation planning point for transportation activities. It is independent of other organisational units except for company code. It is not necessary to assign trans. planning point to company code for transportation planning however it is required for shipment costing and settlement. It can be created though SAP IMG screen:

Fig 1

Change View "Transportation planning points": Overview

TPPt	Description	CoCd
0001	Transp. (common)	1000
0007	APO Europe	1000
1000	Trsp. Hamburg Truck	1000
1010	Trsp. Intern. Sea	1000
1011	Trsp. Hamburg Train	1000
1200	Trsp. Dresden Truck	1000
2200	Trsp. France Truck	2200
2700	Trsp. Hamburg Truck	2700
3000	Trsp. NY Truck	3000
3011	Trsp. NY Train	3000
3050	Trsp. NY Air	3000
3200	Trsp. Atlanta Truck	3000

Fig 2

We would copy the existing transportation planning point, change it according to our requirements and assign to our company code SFE1.

Fig 3

2. SHIPMENT TYPES (C)

The shipment type contains all the important control features for a shipment, such as the number range, whether the shipment is inbound or outbound, how leg determination is performed, and which leg indicator has been set for a shipment of this type.

The SAP system supports three types of shipments:

- Individual shipment
- Collective shipment
- Transportation chain

An individual shipment includes:
- One or more deliveries
- One point of departure
- One destination
- Ono modo of transport

A collective (or milk-run) shipment includes:
- One or more deliveries
- Several points of departure
- Several destinations
- One mode of transport

Transportation chain
- One or more deliveries
- Several points of departure
- Several destinations
- Multiple modes of transport

The shipment type can be defined via the menu path:
Logistics Execution-> Transportation-> Shipments-> Define Shipment Types

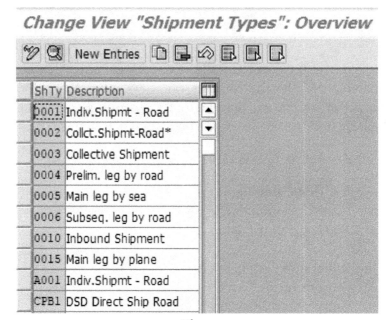

Change View "Shipment Types": Overview

New Entries

ShTy	Description
0001	Indiv.Shipmt - Road
0002	Collct.Shipmt-Road*
0003	Collective Shipment
0004	Prelim. leg by road
0005	Main leg by sea
0006	Subseq. leg by road
0010	Inbound Shipment
0015	Main leg by plane
A001	Indiv.Shipmt - Road
CPB1	DSD Direct Ship Road

Fig 4

Change View "Shipment Types": Details

New Entries

Shipment type	0001	Indiv.Shipmt - Road
Document cat.	8	Shipment

Number Systems

NR int. assgt.	01	No. range ext.
Scr.seq.group	T	

Document Content

ShpmtComplType	1 Loaded outbound ship...	Shipping type	01 Truck
Service Level	1 Load	ShTypePrelimLeg	
ProcessControl	1 Individual shipment usi...	SubseqLegShType	
Leg indicator	4 Direct leg		
Adopt route	Adopt all stages		
Determine legs	1 1: Legs determined according to departure point & itinerary		
GR-RelevanceInd	Normal		

Control

Application	V7	TextDetermProc.	03	PartnDet.Proc.	ZSFE
OutputDet.Proc.	V7STRA	Deadlines	MIG TRA		
Pick check	B No check regarding full picking				
SplProfBefPlng					
SplProfAfterPlg					
☐ HUs relevant for DI generation					

Fig 5

320

The shipping document is the central element of transportation planning and shipment completion. It contains all the information necessary for carrying out transportation. It can be created via the transaction code VT01n.

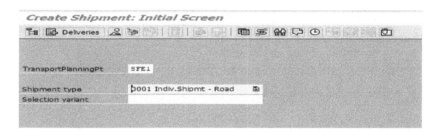

Fig 6

Fig 7

First, we would set up all the functions required for the shipment processing, before moving to create our first shipment document.

4. FREIGHT CODES AND FREIGHT CODE SETS; FREIGHT CLASSES (C)

Freight code is used by forwarding agents to classify the goods they transport. Freight codes are specified in the transportation papers, and some are specific to rail or road transportation.

Freight code sets are the set of freight codes used specifically when referring to rail and road transport.

Freight classes are made up of one or more freight codes and are one of the criteria for shipment costing.

Freight code is determined in two steps:

Step 1: Determination of Freight code set

Automatic freight code set determination is done based on the following factors:

- Country of origin
- Shipping type (truck, rail, etc.)
- Forwarding agent freight group in the vendor master

Step 2: Determination of Freight code

Automatic Freight code is determined based on the following factors:
- Freight code set determined in step 1
- Freight group in material master

The setup of freight code determination is configured via following menu path:

Logistics Execution-> Transportation -> Basic Transportation Functions -> Maintain Freight Code Sets and Freight Codes

i) Define material freight groups (C)

Material freight can be defined by copying and modifying the existing one.

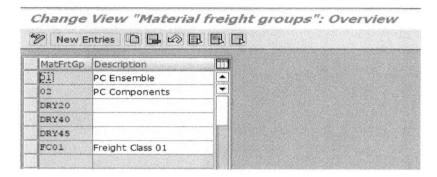

Fig 8

ii Define forward agent freight groups *(C)*

The standard forwarding agents shown below could be used or new ones can be defined using the existing ones.

Fig 9

iii Determine freight code set (C)

The criteria for freight code set determination is maintained in the following table:

Change View "Determine Freight Code Set": Overview

New Entries

CarFrgtG	Description	DCy	ST	FrCSet	Description
01	Carrier - Road	DE	01	01	Carrier association
01	Carrier - Road	US	01	01	Carrier association
01	Carrier - Road	US	04	01	Carrier association
02	Train	DE	03	02	Train
04	LTL Carriers	US	01	09	LTL Freight Class

Fig 20

We will maintain an entry for departure country as Canada.

Change View "Determine Freight Code Set": Overview of Selected Set

CarFrgtG	Description	DCy	ST	FrCSet	Description	
01	Carrier - Road	CA	01	01	Carrier association	

Fig 21

Next, the freight code determination is maintained using the freight code set 01(in the screenshot above) and the material freight group.

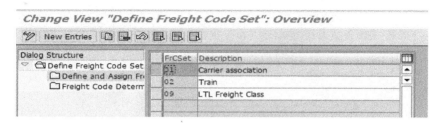

Fig 22

The freight code for freight code set 01 is shown below:

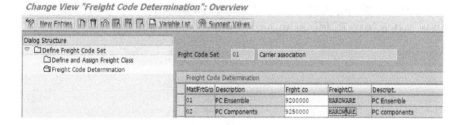

Fig 23

A freight class is a group of freight codes used to calculate shipment costs. It is assigned to the freight code.

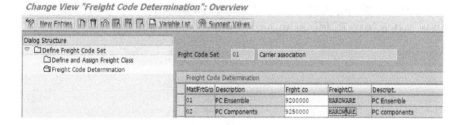

Fig 24

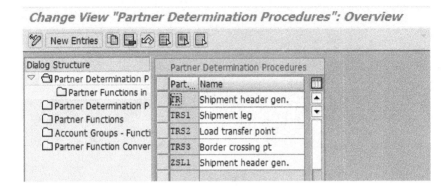

Fig 25

Copy the existing partner determination and modify to define a new procedure ZSFE as shown below:

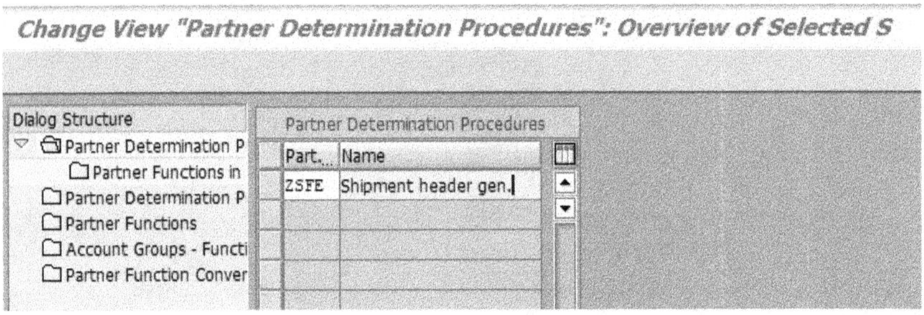

Fig 26

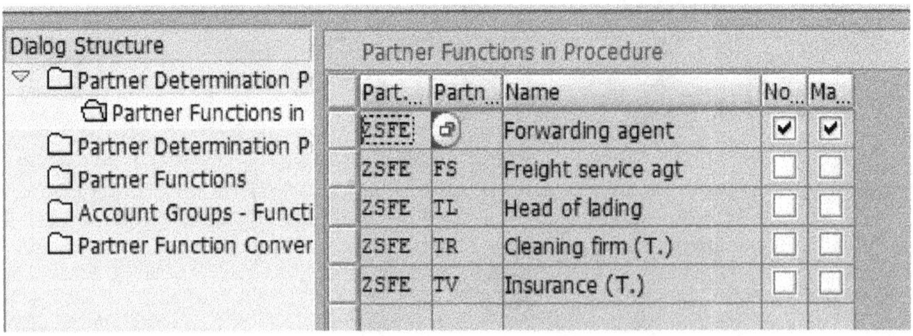

326

Fig 27

Assign the partner determination procedure to the shipment type as shown below:

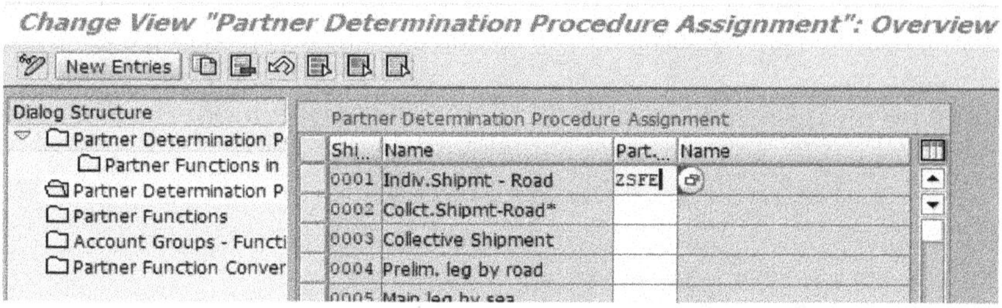

Change View "Partner Determination Procedure Assignment": Overview

Dialog Structure	Partner Determination Procedure Assignment				
▽ ☐ Partner Determination P	Shi..	Name	Part...	Name	
☐ Partner Functions in	0001	Indiv.Shipmt - Road	ZSFE		▲
☐ Partner Determination P	0002	Collct.Shipmt-Road*			▼
☐ Partner Functions	0003	Collective Shipment			
☐ Account Groups - Functi	0004	Prelim. leg by road			
☐ Partner Function Conver	0005	Main leg by sea			

Fig 28

The output determination procedure is used to relay messages in form of print/email/EDI/fax to various business partners involved in the shipment processing.

It can be maintained through SAP IMG screen as follows:

i) Define condition table (C)

Condition table contains the sap field which are searched for in shipment document to trigger the message. We will be using standard condition table 17 for our purpose.

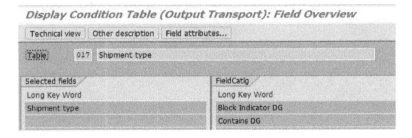

Fig 29

ii) Define Output types (C)

Output types are the message types which determine the message type, texts and the partners to which the message is to be delivered. We would be using predefined output types for our purpose.

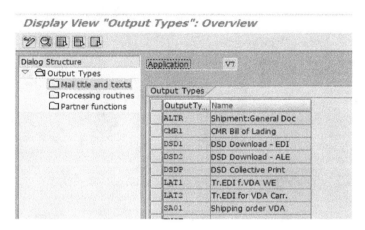

Fig 30

iii. Define Access sequence (C)

Access sequence defines the order/sequence in which the condition table are accessed until the search criteria is fulfilled. Here, we would be using the standard access sequence for our purpose. It is shown below in the picture:

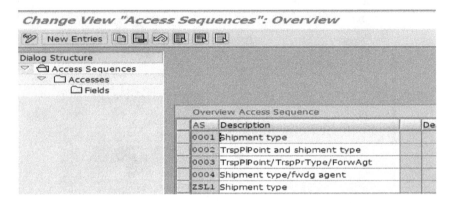

Fig 31

The accesses refer to the condition tables assigned to the given access sequence. In this case, the condition table being used is 17.

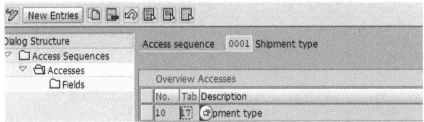

Fig 32

This section below shows the field label and SAP structure to which the field is referring to:

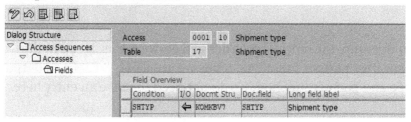

Fig 33

331

iv. Assign output types to partner function (C)

In this step, the output types defined above are assigned to the respective partner functions. Since we are using predefined output type and partner function, we do not need to make an entry here.

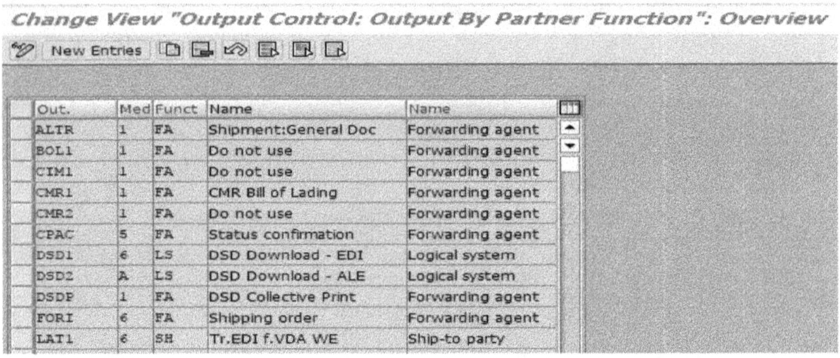

Change View "Output Control: Output By Partner Function": Overview

New Entries

Out.	Med	Funct	Name	Name	
ALTR	1	FA	Shipment:General Doc	Forwarding agent	▲
BOL1	1	FA	Do not use	Forwarding agent	▼
CIM1	1	FA	Do not use	Forwarding agent	
CMR1	1	FA	CMR Bill of Lading	Forwarding agent	
CMR2	1	FA	Do not use	Forwarding agent	
CPAC	5	FA	Status confirmation	Forwarding agent	
DSD1	6	LS	DSD Download - EDI	Logical system	
DSD2	A	LS	DSD Download - ALE	Logical system	
DSDP	1	FA	DSD Collective Print	Forwarding agent	
FORI	6	FA	Shipping order	Forwarding agent	
LAT1	6	SH	Tr.EDI f.VDA WE	Ship-to party	

Fig 34

v) Maintain output determination procedure (C)

We would be using output determination procedure V7STRA for our purpose.

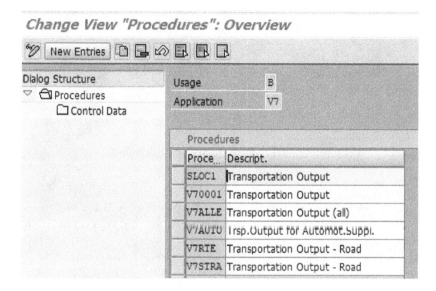

Fig 35

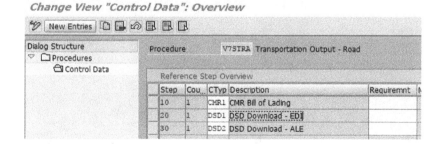

Fig 36

vi) Assign output determination procedure (C)

Here we assign the output determination procedure to the shipment type:

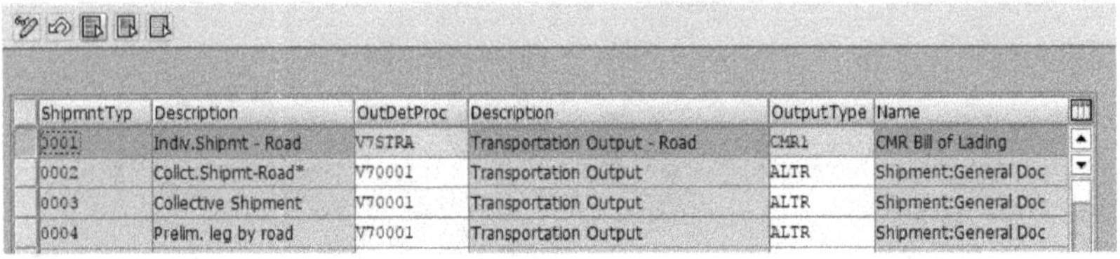

Change View "Transport: Types - Output Determination": Overview

ShipmntTyp	Description	OutDetProc	Description	OutputType	Name
0001	Indiv.Shipmt - Road	V7STRA	Transportation Output - Road	CMR1	CMR Bill of Lading
0002	Collct.Shipmt-Road"	V70001	Transportation Output	ALTR	Shipment:General Doc
0003	Collective Shipment	V70001	Transportation Output	ALTR	Shipment:General Doc
0004	Prelim. leg by road	V70001	Transportation Output	ALTR	Shipment:General Doc

Fig 37

vii) Maintain condition record (U)

Now, we need to maintain condition record via VV71 for output determination.

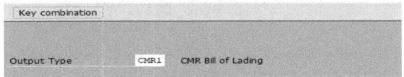

Fig 38

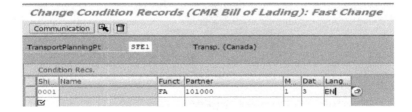

Fig 39

Fig 40

viii) Define Print Parameters (U)

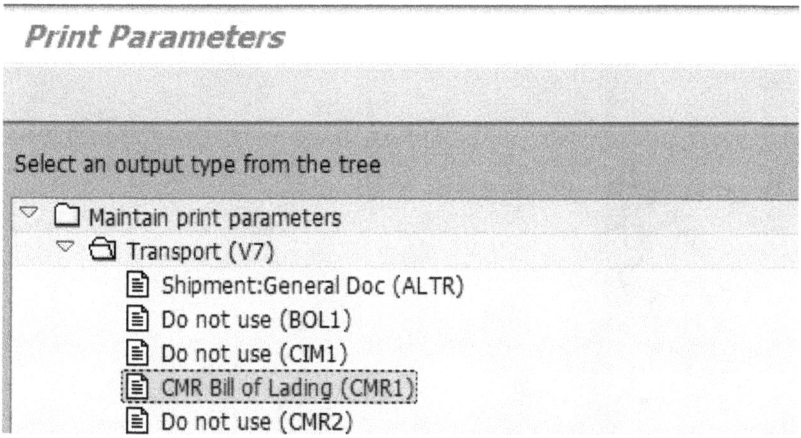

Print Parameters

Select an output type from the tree

▽ 🗀 Maintain print parameters
   ▽ 🗃 Transport (V7)
      📄 Shipment:General Doc (ALTR)
      📄 Do not use (BOL1)
      📄 Do not use (CIM1)
      📄 CMR Bill of Lading (CMR1)
      📄 Do not use (CMR2)

Fig 41

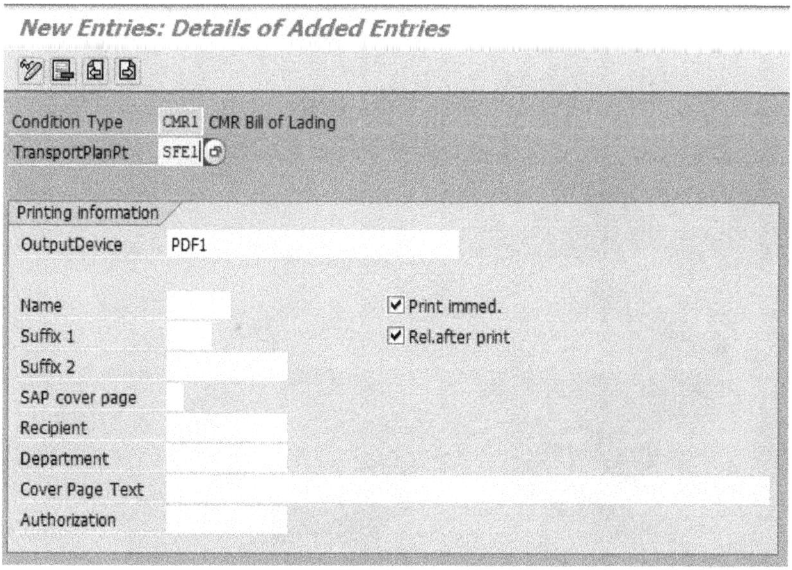

New Entries: Details of Added Entries

| Condition Type | CMR1 | CMR Bill of Lading |
| TransportPlanPt | SFE1 | |

Printing information

| OutputDevice | PDF1 | |

Name		☑ Print immed.
Suffix 1		☑ Rel.after print
Suffix 2		
SAP cover page		
Recipient		
Department		
Cover Page Text		
Authorization		

Fig 42

Now, since we have configured the basic functions let us create a shipment using VT01n to demonstrate the functionality:

Before we move further we will complete picking, packing of the delivery document.

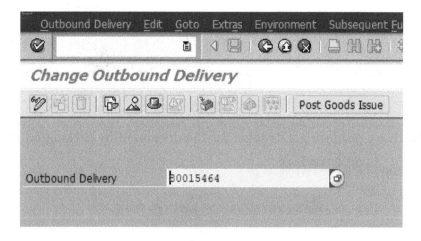

Fig 43

We picked the entire quantity available for delivery i.e. 100 for this case.

Fig 44

Next, we will do the packing using the packaging material 1000702 (material type: VERP). This can be done through  icon on the top of the overview screen.

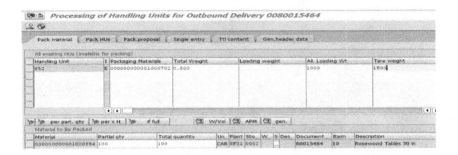

Fig 45

Next, we perform goods issue for the document by clicking on the button Post Goods Issue .

Fig 46

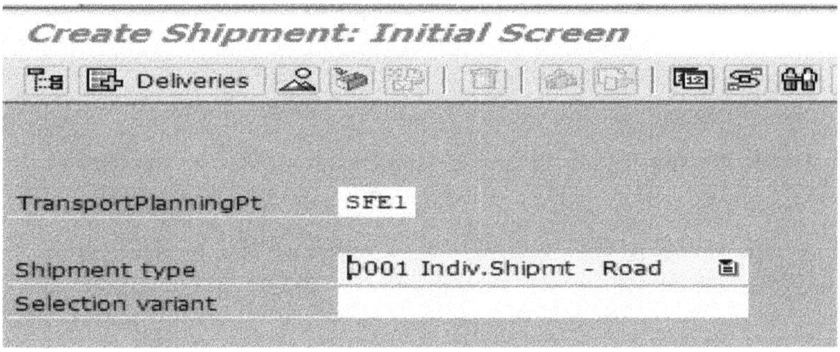

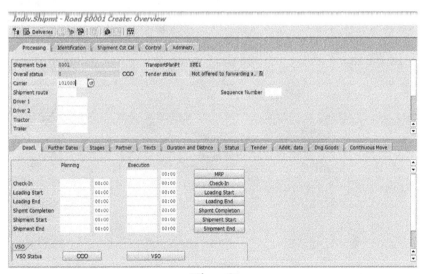

Fig 47

Transportation Planning Point: SFE1
Shipment Type: 0001

Fig 48

The carrier is the forwarding agent responsible for handling of shipment.

The overall status is indicated by numerical value as well as traffic light code indicator as shown below:

- No traffic light:

No planning activities have been performed

- Red light:

Transportation planning is complete

- Yellow light:

Loading at the plant has either started or is complete

- Green light:

Shipment has been processed and is in route or has arrived

Next, we add delivery/deliveries to the document using
⊞ Deliveries button in top left corner and using the selection
parameters. We used shipping point(SFFT) in our case.

We can see in stages tab that no entries are present since planning
activities have not begun.

Deadl.	Further Dates	Stages	Partner	Texts	Duration and Distnce	Status	Tender	Addit. data

St..	Departure point	Destination	FwdAgent	Forw.agent	S..	Shippin..	Distance	Uo..	L	Leg indi..	In..

Fig 49

In the partner tab, we can see the forwarding agent is determined:

Deadl.	Further Dates	Stages	Partner	Texts	Duration and Distnce	Status	Tender	A

Partn.Funct.	Partner	Name	Street	Postal co..	Cty
SP Forwarding age.. ⊞	101000	⊕ronto Logistics Servic..			

Fig 50

Once the planning process is done the route and stages get
automatically determined.

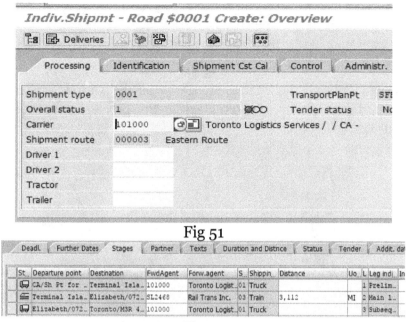

Fig 51

Fig 52

The packaging can be done through  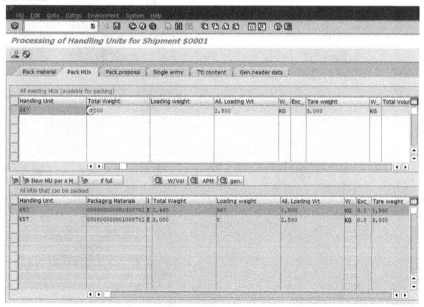 on the top of the overview screen.

Fig 53

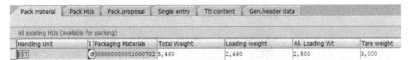

| Pack material | Pack HUs | Pack.proposal | Single entry | Ttl content | Gen.header data |

All existing HUs (available for packing)

Handling Unit	I	Packaging Materials	Total Weight	Loading weight	All. Loading Wt	Tare weight
557	⊕	00000000001000702	5,460	2,460	2,500	3,000

Fig 54

You can observe the change in status as the various stages of transportation planning takes place in the processing as well as status tab.

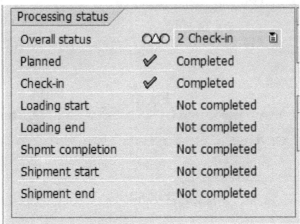

Processing status

Overall status	✺	2 Check-in ▤
Planned	✓	Completed
Check-in	✓	Completed
Loading start		Not completed
Loading end		Not completed
Shpmt completion		Not completed
Shipment start		Not completed
Shipment end		Not completed

Fig 55

Processing status

Overall status	✺	7 Shipment end ▤
Planned	✓	Completed
Check-in	✓	Completed
Loading start	✓	Completed
Loading end	✓	Completed
Shpmt completion	✓	Completed
Shipment start	✓	Completed
Shipment end	✓	Completed

Fig 56

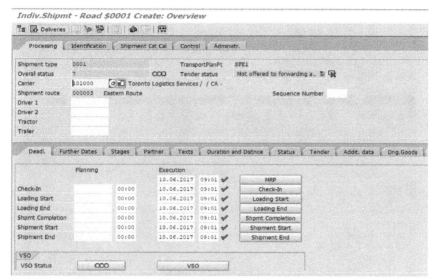

Fig 57

We can notice the output generated via Goto -> Output path or via

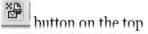 button on the top

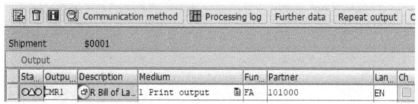

Fig 58

Finally, the shipment can be saved.

Fig 59

The output of the shipment document can be viewed through Shipment -> Output path as shown below:

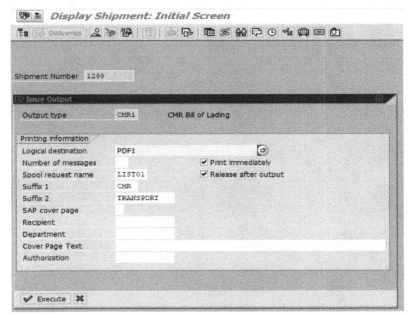

Display Shipment: Initial Screen

Deliveries

Shipment Number 1299

Issue Output

Output type CMR1 CMR Bill of Lading

Printing information

Logical destination	PDF1		
Number of messages		✔ Print immediately	
Spool request name	LIST01	✔ Release after output	
Suffix 1	CMR		
Suffix 2	TRANSPORT		
SAP cover page			
Recipient			
Department			
Cover Page Text			
Authorization			

✔ Execute ✖

Fig 60

CANADA

LSP Inc.   Company
Los Angeles Branch   Toronto Logistics Services
5000 Terminal Way
TERMINAL ISLAND CA   90731
UNITED STATES   CANADA

LSP Inc.
5000 Terminal Way
TERMINAL ISLAND CA   90731

/
CANADA
2017.06.10

658   1   Rosewood T   3,000.0   0.0
                          Rosewood   Table   960.0   0.0

Fig 61

CREDIT MANAGEMENT (C/U)

Credit management is to monitor credit status of customer so as to take decision on continuing or reviewing credit related decisions like increasing credit limit or blocking delivery to the customer.

Define Credit Control Area (C)

Menu path: SPRO→Enterprise structure → Definition → financial accounting → Credit Control Area

Click ⊕

Fig 1-Double click on credit control area, to select or create /copy new one

Update group - this determines how credit value should get updated at the time of order, delivery and billing.

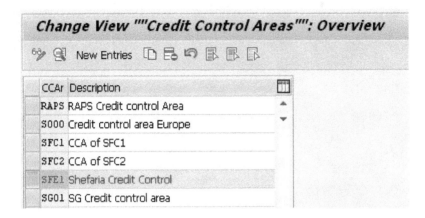

Fig 1

Risk category (Fig 2) – Risk category entered in the related control area of the customer's credit master record, which is automatically created when a customer is created in a company code.

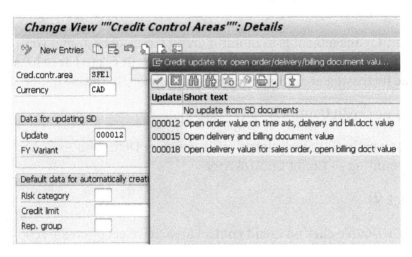

Fig 2

The credit master record is automatically maintained when at least one of the following fields is maintained for the corresponding control area.

1) Define Risk Category (C)

Menu path: : SPRO → Financial Accounting →Account Receivable and Accounts Payable →Credit Management →Credit Control Account →Define Risk Categories

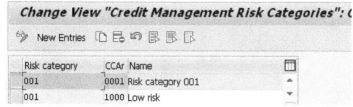

Fig3

2) Via the customer master record, you can allocate every customer to a credit risk category. This is used if automatic credit control is used.

3) Menu path: Customer master - Environment – credit management

Credit representative group (C)

Credit limit - This credit limit is not a total credit limit for the control area.

Credit restriction will be effective for new customers, too, as soon as the customer has been created. If no credit master record has been maintained, there is no credit limit.

Assigning Company Codes to a Credit Control Area:

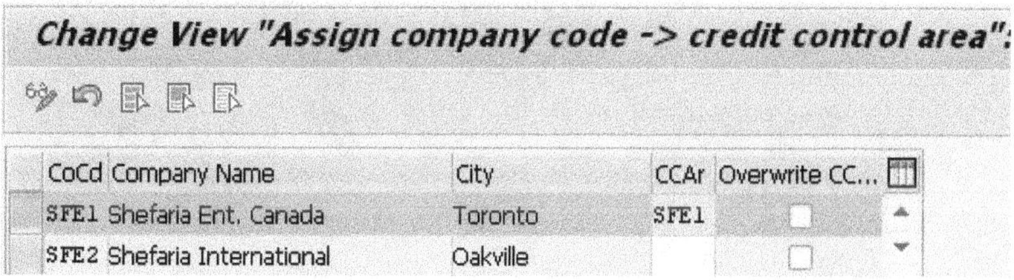

CoCd	Company Name	City	CCAr	Overwrite CC...
SFE1	Shefaria Ent. Canada	Toronto	SFE1	☐
SFE2	Shefaria International	Oakville		☐

Change View "Assign company code -> credit control area":

Fig 4

SPRO > Enterprise Structure > Assignment > Financial Accounting > Assign Company Code to Credit Control Area (C)

Fig 4: we can see Company code SFE1 is assigned to Credit control area SFE1

Assigning Sales Area to a Credit Control Area:

SPRO > Enterprise Structure > Assignment > Sales and Distribution > Assign Sales Area to Credit Control Area
Fig:5 Sales Area is assigned to Credit control area SFE1

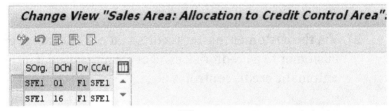

Fig 5

Define Credit Groups

SPRO > Sales & Distribution > Basic Functions > Credit Management and Risk Management > Credit Management > Define Credit Groups

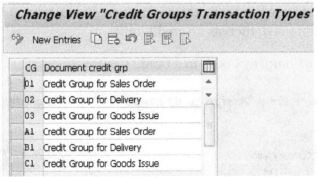

Fig6

Type of Credit check (C)

There are major two types of credit checks can be performed. They are

• No credit check

• Simple credit check or Dynamic check for a particular order type.

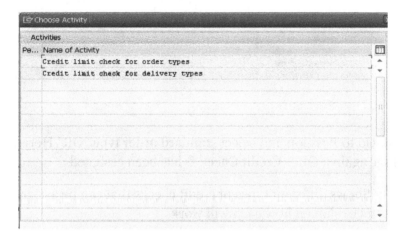

Fig 7

Menu path: SD – Basic Functions → Credit Management / Risk Management→ Credit Management / Risk Management settings→Credit Management→Assign Sales documents and delivery documents, will see pop-up as below (Fig 7)

Fig 7 Select "Credit limit check for order types" and double click

SaTy	Description	Check credit	Credit group	
OR	Standard Order	D	01	
TAF	Standard Order (FPI)			
TAM	Delivery order			
TAV	Standard Order (VMI)			

Change View "Sales Document Types - Credit Limit Check": Overview

Fig 8

Fig 8: Go to Position and select standard order type "OR" Here we can see against OR – Credit Check D has been assigned

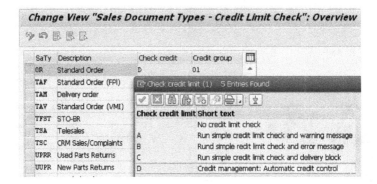

Fig 9

Fig 8: Go to Position and select standard order type "OR" Here we can see against OR – Credit Check D has been assigned

Fig 8:- Shows different types of credit checks that can be assigned, below its explained how each will work

If credit limit exceeds, system responds giving

A. Warning message in sales order.

B. Warning message and a delivery block (which will allow order to be taken but get blocked for delivery).

C. Error message that will not allow you to save the order.

D. Automatic Credit Check credit has value "D"

Credit limit check can take place @

Sales order entry

Delivery

Goods issue

For this, Automatic credit control defines "Document Credit Group" for each Sales Order, Delivery and Goods issue.

Define Automatic Credit Control (C)

IMG Path: Sales and Distribution -> Basic Functions -> Credit Management/Risk Management Settings -> Credit Management -> Define Automatic Credit Control

New Entries: Details of Added Entries

CCA	RkC	CG	Credit control		Curr.	Update
SFE1	003	01	SFE1 CREDIT CONTROL1		CAD	000012

Document controlling		Released documents are still unchecked	
No credit check		Deviation in %	
☐ Item check		Number of days	

Credit limit seasonal factor			Checks in financial accounting/old A/R summary		
%	From	To	☐ Payer		
☐ Minus			Permitted days	Permitted hours	

Checks

	Reaction	Status/Block		
☐ Static	B	✓	✓ Open orders	✓ Open deliveries
✓ Dynamic	B	✓	Horizon	M
☐ Document value		☐	Max.doc.value	

Fig 10

351

The below example is one of the scenario which shows how Credit Management works (U)

Fig 11

Goto→FD32→Pass Customer 601256→Press Enter after selection all segment as above fig 10

In central data you can manage maximum credit limit for that customer as below and save it.

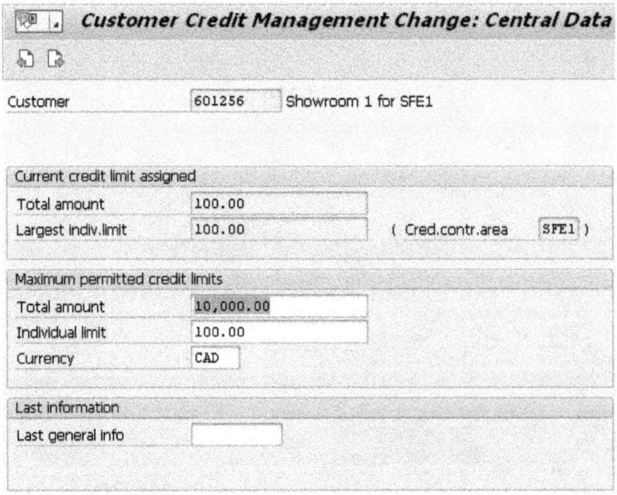

Fig 12: Total & Individual Limit maintained

Now go to VA01, enter all details customer, sales areas etc. and try creating order:

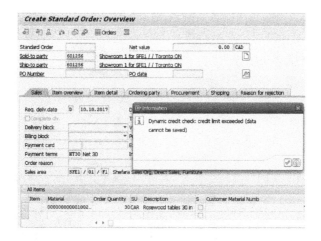

Fig 13

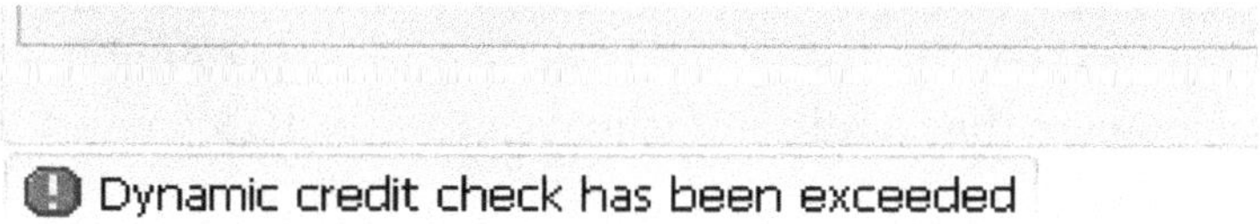

Dynamic credit check has been exceeded

Fig 14

We can see from above figures 12 & 13 that as per configurations done system will throw pop up with information and also will not allow to save the order.

MATERIAL LISTING & EXCLUSION (C/U)

Material Listing & Exclusion is a list where it is mentioned which set up materials a customer can by (those material present in the LISTING) and which set up materials a customer can't buy (those material present in the EXCLUSION). The Material Listing & Exclusion uses the condition technique.

Instructions: Follow Menu Path: SPRO → IMG→ Sales and Distribution → Basic functions → Listing/Exclusion.

Click ⊕

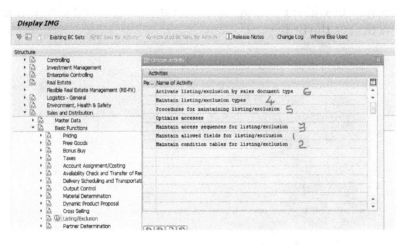

Fig 1

The material listing & exclusion is based on the condition technique. All steps are marked as per sequence to be followed (fig 1).

Assuming that the Fields & condition tables are created/already available.

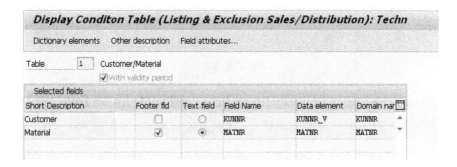

Fig 2 : Example for Condition table

Step 1 : - Maintain Access Sequence for listing/exclusionChoose access sequence A001- **LISTING** and choose Accesses option from

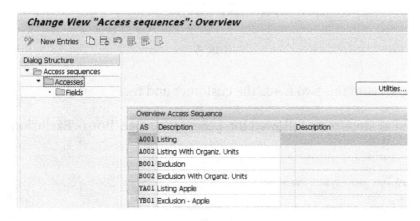

Fig 3

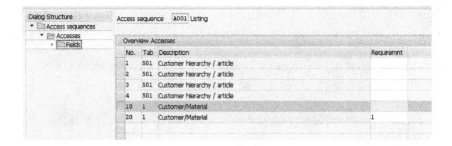

Fig 4

Choose the access line 10 with and choose Fields option from left side

Fig 5

Fig 5 - contains two fields the customer and the material.

Similar steps to be followed for access sequence B001- Exclusion as well

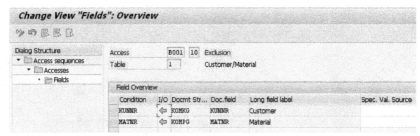

Fig 6

The next step is to create the condition type for listing and exclusion and assigning them to the access sequence. Choose the option – Maintain listing/exclusion type.

Step 2:- The next step is to create the condition type for listing and exclusion and assigning them to the access sequence.
Choose the option – Maintain listing/exclusion type

Change View "Conditions: Types": Overview

New Entries

Overview of Condition Types

CTyp	Name	AS	Description	
A001	Listing	A001	Listing	
B001	Exclusion	B001	Exclusion	
YA01	Listing Apple	YA01	Listing Apple	
YB01	Exclusion - Apple	YB01	Exclusion - Apple	

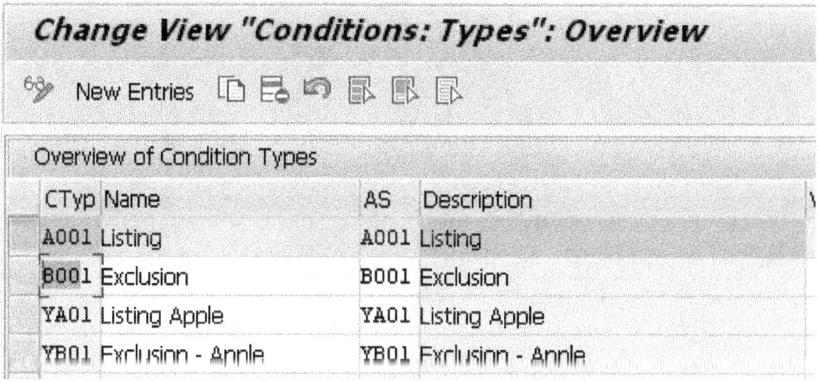

Fig 7 – Condition types A001 & B001 maintianed.

Step 3:- Next step is to create/define the listing/exclusion determination procedure.

Choose the option Procedures for maintaining listing/exclusion.

New procedures can be created by using the New Entries button. Here already two different procedures are already created one for listing-A0001 and one for exclusion-B0001(Fig 8)

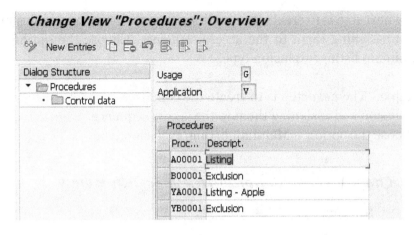

Fig8

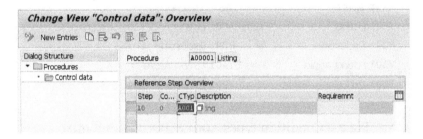

Fig 9

Select each procedure and check the control data

Fig 9 – Control data for Procedure A00001 – Listing

The inclusion condition type is added to the procedure

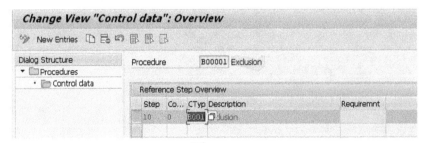

Fig 10

The exclusion condition type is added to the procedure.

Step 6 - The last customizing step is to assigning the listing procedure and exclusion procedure to the sales order type.

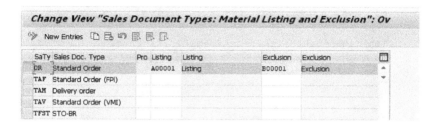

SaTy	Sales Doc. Type	Pro	Listing	Listing	Exclusion	Exclusion	
DR	Standard Order		A00001	Listing	B00001	Exclusion	
TAF	Standard Order (FPI)						
TAM	Delivery order						
TAV	Standard Order (VMI)						
TFST	STO-BR						

Now we will be creating condition types for listing/exclusion.

Transactions- VB01/VB02/VB03 can be used to create/change/display condition records. (U)

1. MATERIAL LISTING EXAMPLE (U)

Goto → VB01→Select A001 condition type (Fig 12)

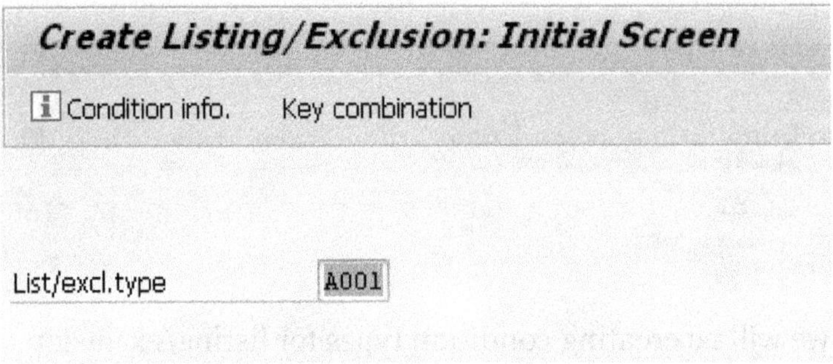

Create Listing/Exclusion: Initial Screen

i Condition info.   Key combination

List/excl.type   A001

Fig 12

Added customer and material as below and saved (Fig 13); this is listing which means only those materials which are listed are allowed for sales for this customer.

Create Listing (A001) : Fast Entry

Customer	601256	Showroom 1 for SFE1
Valid From	05.10.2017	
Valid to	31.12.9999	

Customer/Material

Material	Description	
000000000001000654	Rosewood Tables 30 in	▲
☑		▼
☑		

Fig 13

Now we are trying to create a Sales order with customer 601256and material 1000654 which is LISTED for that customer and Material 1002459 (the same material which was used to create order for same customer in SO /RO sales document examples).difference

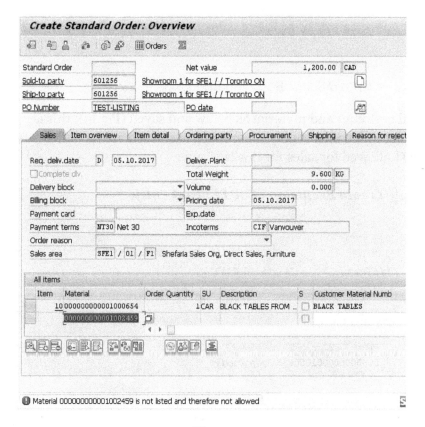

Fig 14

Fig 14 – we can see system is not allowing to save order as there is one material which is NOT LISTED and used .

Now going to VB02→Pass condition type A002→Pass customer

601256 and material 1000654, execute → Select and delete the line so that there is NO Material LISTING valid for that customer.

MATERIAL EXCLUSION EXAMPLE (U)

Goto → VB01→Select B001 condition type

Add customer and material as below and saved (Fig 15); this is listing which means only those materials which are Excluded are NOT allowed for sales for this customer.

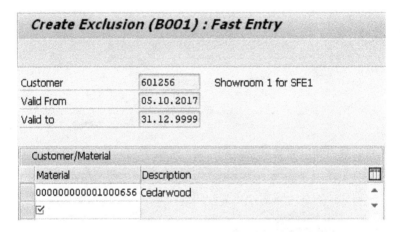

Fig 15

Now we are trying to create a Sales order with customer 601256

and material 1000656 which is Excluded for that customer and Material 1002459

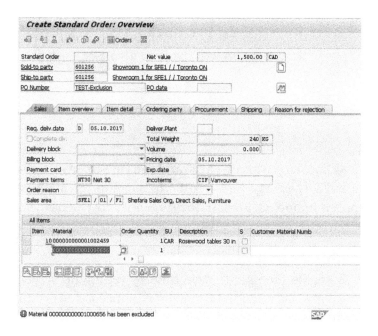

Fig 16

From Fig 16 (above) we can see system is not allowing to save order as there is one material-1000656 which is excluded but being attempted to be used in this order.

CROSS – APPLICATION AND GENERAL COMPONENTS IN SAP (U)

1. VARIANTS (U)

Strictly speaking, variants are variations of screens – both, input and output. They are not cross application components but 'common' components. Most of the screens in SAP behave similarly for the purpose of creating variants. The purpose of variants is twofold:

- To enable the user to save time by setting up screens with roughly the same data that may be needed every time the transaction is run
- To let different users who may be using the same transaction have their differentiation from each other in terms of inputs and outputs by naming their variants as suitable to them.
- Variants are best explained by an example.

1. Selection/Input Variants

Let us call a standard SAP transition to look up account balances FBL3N:

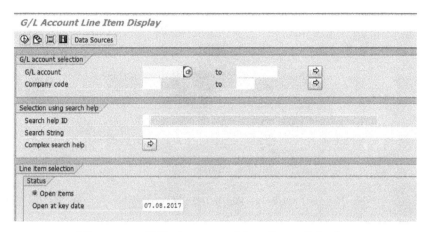

Figure 1: G/L Account Line Item Display

Let us assume you as an accounts person, is responsible for the company code SFE1 and for G/L accounts 100000 to 199999. A simple variant can be set up with these values:

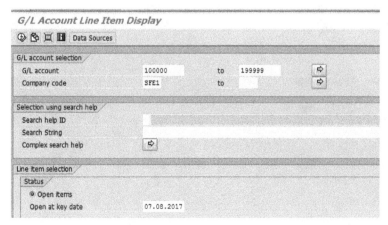

Figure 2: G/L Account Line Item Display

Save the values either by clicking on ⊞ or:

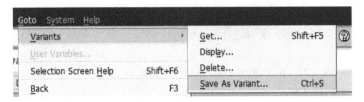

Figure 3: Variants options

Give it a name:

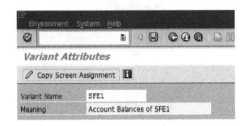

Figure 4: Variant Attributes

And save it:

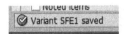

Figure 5: Variant Saved message

Next time when you call the transaction FBL3N simply click on

the button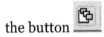

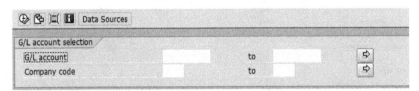

Figure 6: Find Variant

And enter the name of the variant if you know it:

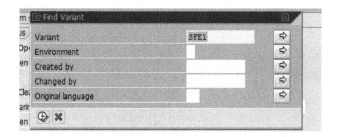

Figure 7: Find Variant

Or simply execute the above window to get a list of all and double click to choose the one you want:

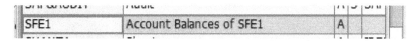

Figure 8: Find Variant

The figures you entered at the time of creating the variant will come on the screen so they don't have to be entered every time.

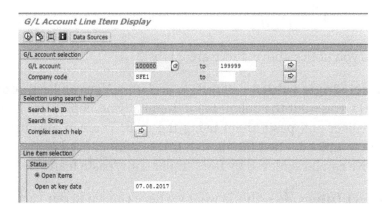

Figure 9: G/L Account Line Item Display

The above was a simple example of a variant. The inputs can be further defined using the feature of multiple values using the button

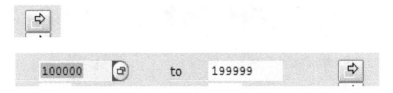

Figure 10: Multiple Selection

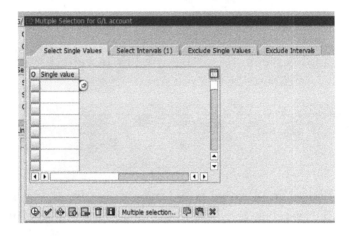

Figure 11: Multiple Selection

As you notice above, there are 4 tabs:

1. **Select single values** – here, G/L accounts. You can keep adding the G/Ls you want the balances for, manually or, copy them from a spreadsheet and paste them using the icon. You can also use the button to upload a text file though this is seldom used as the same objective can be achieved by the simpler copy/paste feature.

2. **Select Intervals** – this is what we have chosen in our variant:

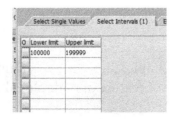

Figure 12: Multiple Selection

368

As seen above, multiple intervals of different ranges can be chosen.

3 and 4 – Exclude single values and exclude ranges – work exactly the same way as 1 and 2 except these are for excluding the G/L accounts while 1 and 2 were for including them.

2. Output/Display Variant

Let us stay with our variant and execute the report using the button Execute:

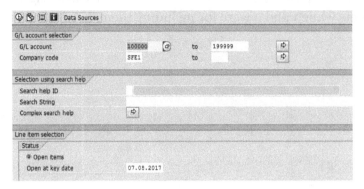

Figure 13: G/L Account Line Item Display

Some kind of a layout emerges:

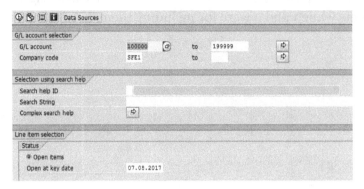

Figure 14: G/L Account Line Item Display

The above is the display of the report based on some parameters. Let us see what they are and how this can be customized to our requirement.

The first is how to display. As seen above, this is an Excel friendly layout. It can be changed to a more generic layout using:

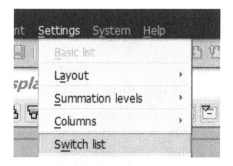

Figure 15: Setting options

G/L Balances
G/L Account * *
Company Code SFE1

St	Doc. Date	DocumentNo	Type	Cost Ctr	LCurr	Amount in local cur.	Texts	Text	Account	User Name	Reference
	30.07.2017	90036885	RV		CAD	350.00			105100	IDES0164	0090036885
	30.07.2017	90036886	RV		CAD	150.00			105100	IDES0164	0090036886
	28.07.2017	5000000136	WE		CAD	135,000.00			134000	IDES014	
	22.07.2017	1400000153	DZ		CAD	20,250.00			105100	IDES014	
	22.07.2017	1400000153	DZ		CAD	900.00-			105100	IDES014	
	22.07.2017	1400000154	DZ		CAD	1,060.00			121000	IDES013	
	22.07.2017	1400000157	DZ		CAD	50.00			121000	IDES0164	
	22.07.2017	1800000226	DR		CAD	1,000.00			105100	IDES014	

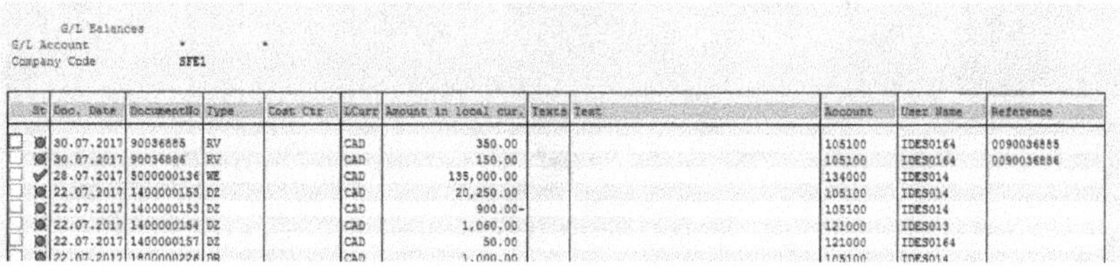

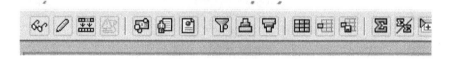

Figure 16: G/L Account Balances

Most people will prefer the Excel type grid so we work with that:

Identify a few of these Windows based icons and work with them:

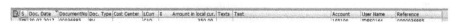

Figure 17: Based Icons

The SAP specific ones, refer to how the layouts can be created and saved:

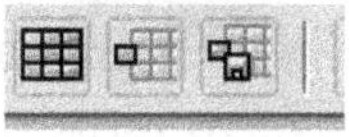

As we notice, the columns currently available to us in this report are:

Figure 18: Available columns

The source of these columns are SAP tables – in this case, accounting tables (next section, ideally, to be visited once you have finished the rest of this book).

If you wish to add/delete or re-arrange any of these columns, click on . 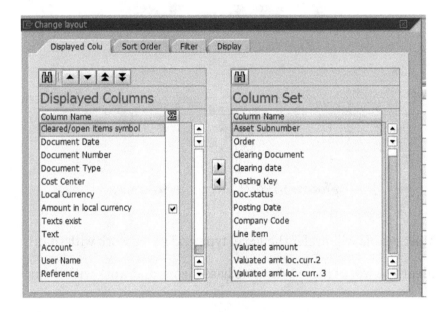 :

Figure 19: Change Layout

As you notice, the section on the left is the list of the columns displayed in the order from top to bottom > left to right in the report. The right section is the list of more fields/columns available though it is not necessary that all of them hold data. If you wish to see something new/additional or want to hide any, just double click on it and it flips from one column to the other as clicked.

The keys [ ] are useful to find, or move up or down the list.

Once you are satisfied with what you require in your report and want to save it with the ides of recalling it every time (same way as the input variant), click on 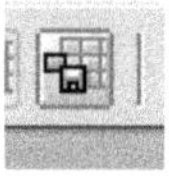:

Give it a name:

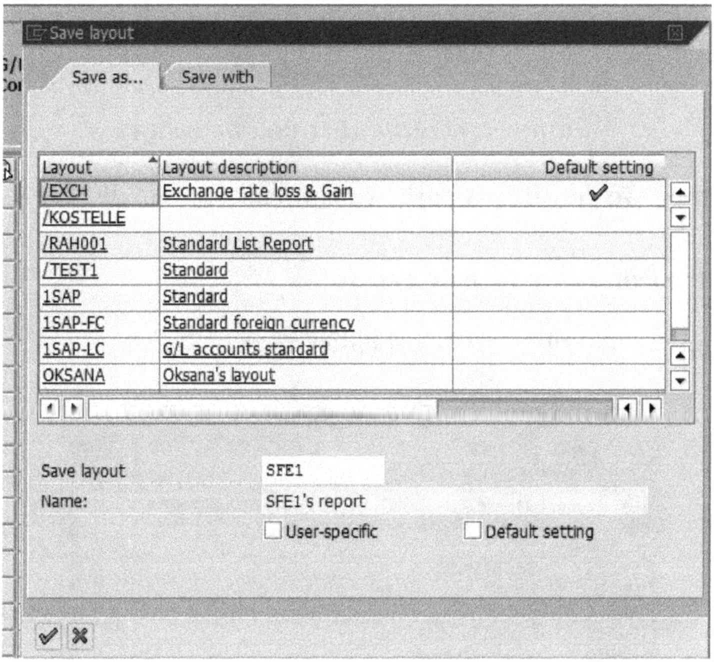

Figure 20: Save Layout

You can use the buttons:

Figure 21: Save option

To save as specific to you OR as a default layout. It is HIGHLY recommended NOT to save as a default layout otherwise everyone will see only that as a default and will have to change it to their requirements which will not be a very useful thing for other users. So we save this as user specific:

Figure 22: Save Layout

Figure 23: Layout saved message

Next time we run this report, we can call for our display variant

using the icon [icon]: (See fig 17)

Click on the hyperlink SFE1 as below:

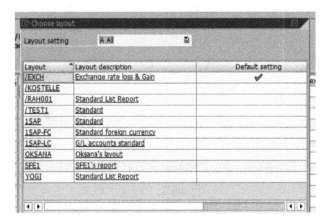

Figure 24: Choose Layout

The message displayed at the bottom is:

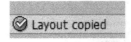

Figure 25: Layout copied message

This ensures whatever you had asked for in the layout SFE1 is not on the screen displayed for you.

For the most part, this variant functionality in SAP is exactly the same across all screens and all modules thereby making your life infinitely easier.

Not only do variants help you save time, they can also present you with data relating to the documents themselves for example. by checking any particular line, you can go straight into the document and even change it for whatever is possible to be changed.

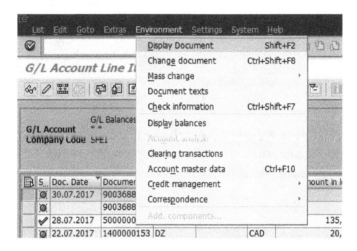

Figure 26: Environment options

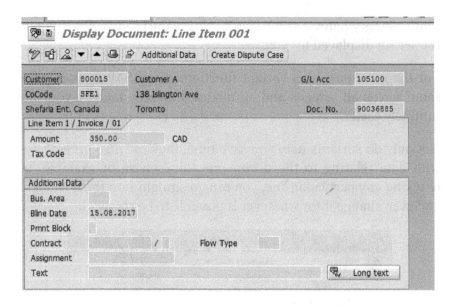

Figure 27: Display Document

Lots of other data is visible through the variants so you are saved the enormous amount of time in opening up different sessions to look up any transactions or documents.

2. TABLES IN SAP (U)

Most of the data in SAP resides in tables and structures, primarily in the former. The latter can be read only by technically knowledgeable people but the former is available to all, subject to authorizations. We will peek into how the tables exist in SAP and how they can be read and data extracted from them.

Tens of thousands of tables exist in SAP well apportioned over the different modules. In FI, the few important ones are:

BKPF - Accounting Document Header
BSEG – Accounting Document Line items
LFA1 - Vendor Master (General Section)
T001 - CCs
BSID - Accounting Secondary Index for Customers
BSIS - Accounting: Secondary Index for G/L Accounts
BSIK - Accounting Secondary Index for Vendors
LFB1 - Vendor Master (CC)
BSAK - Accounting: Secondary Index for Vendors (Cleared Items)
BSAD - Accounting: Secondary Index for Customers (Cleared Items)
LFBK - Vendor Master (Bank Details)
KNB1 - Customer Master (CC)
BSAS - Accounting: Secondary Index for G/L Accounts (Cleared Items)
SKAT - G/L Account Master Record (CoA: Description)
AVIK - Payment Advice Header
SKA1 - G/L Account Master (CoA)
KNC1 - Customer master (transaction figures)
KNBK - Customer Master (Bank Details)
VBKPF - Document Header for Document Parking
TTYP - Object Types for Accounting
LFC1 - Vendor master (transaction figures)
T052 - Terms of Payment
BSIP - Index for Vendor Validation of Double Documents
LFB5 - Vendor master (dunning data)

The transaction code to look up tables is SE16N:

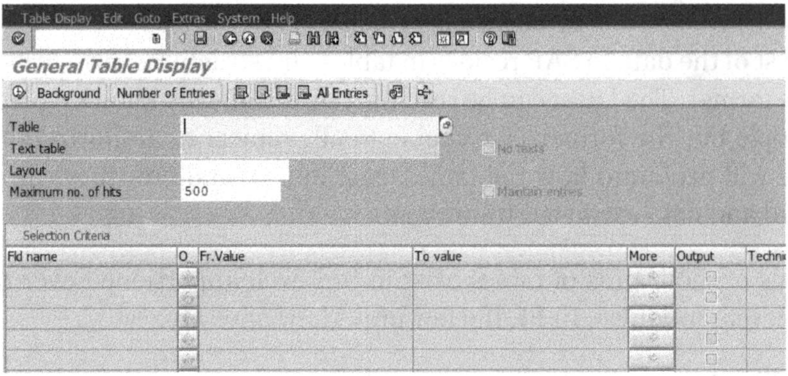

Fig 1

Enter the name of the table you want to look up and Hit Enter again:

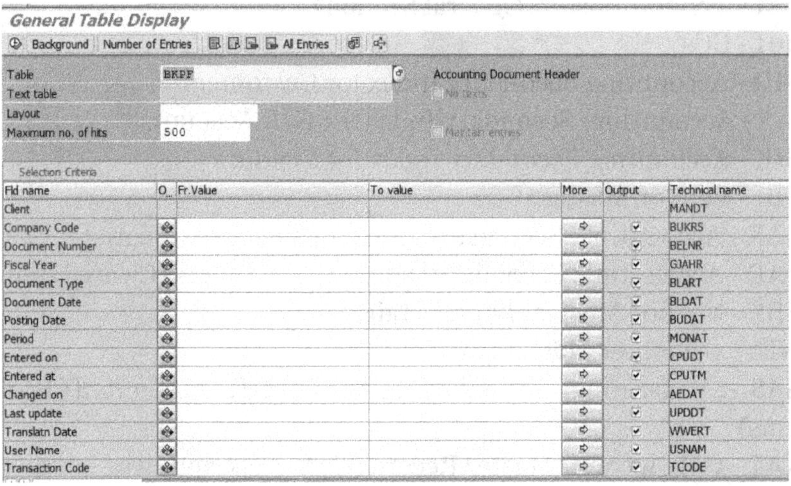

Fig 2

On the left are the names of the fields which are for most part, self-explanatory, on the right are their technical names for those who are more involved in using tables in programming. Enter input data you need to find the results for.

On the right, check the fields that you really want to see in your result as too much information can be clutter and also cause the program to take more time in executing. You can use the scroll bar on the right to look for more fields if required:

Fig 3

Use the keys ▤ ▤ to select or deselect the all fields if needed and then select the ones you need individually.

The button 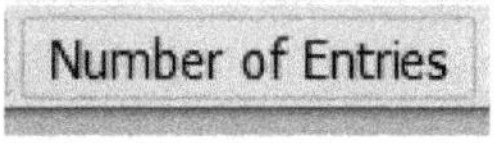 Number of Entries tells you the # of entries in the table for the input data you have entered.

If the result is expected to take a long time, then this can also be run in the background using  Background by setting up a job for it whose results can be downloaded later.

Unless you are sure the total will be less than 500, it is advisable to wipe out this number so you can get the entire list. The default can be changed in the option below though wiping it out is always the best option unless you are looking for only some sample data:

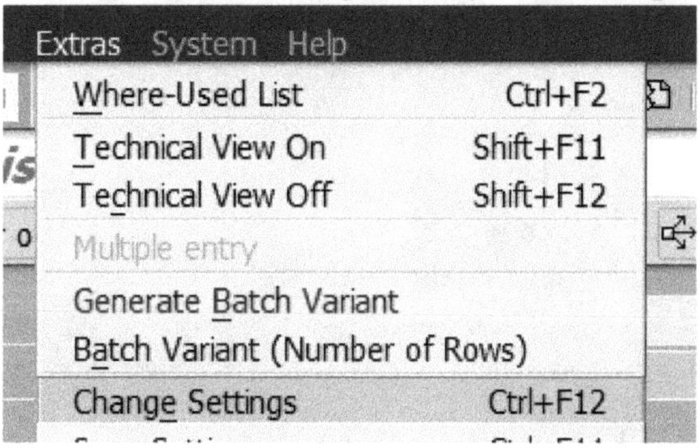

Extras	System	Help		
Where-Used List			Ctrl+F2	
Technical View On			Shift+F11	
Technical View Off			Shift+F12	
Multiple entry				
Generate Batch Variant				
Batch Variant (Number of Rows)				
Change Settings			Ctrl+F12	

Fig 4

379

Let's say we want to see only the company code, document number, date of posting and document type, so check only those boxes on the right as 'outputs'. If we want to look for all accounting entries made by any user ID for a certain period, enter these 2 data elements in their respective fields:

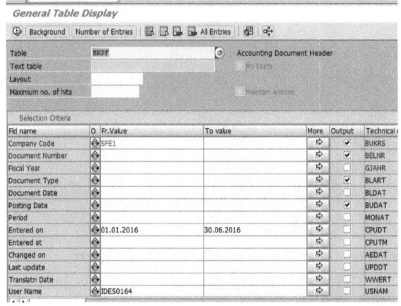

General Table Display

Background | Number of Entries | All Entries

Table	BKPF		Accounting Document Header
Text table		No texts	
Layout			
Maximum no. of hits		Maintain entries	

Selection Criteria

Fld name	O	Fr.Value	To value	More	Output	Technical
Company Code		SFE1		⇨	✔	BUKRS
Document Number				⇨	✔	BELNR
Fiscal Year				⇨	☐	GJAHR
Document Type				⇨	✔	BLART
Document Date				⇨	☐	BLDAT
Posting Date				⇨	✔	BUDAT
Period				⇨	☐	MONAT
Entered on		01.01.2016	30.06.2016	⇨	☐	CPUDT
Entered at				⇨	☐	CPUTM
Changed on				⇨	☐	AEDAT
Last update				⇨	☐	UPDDT
Translatn Date				⇨	☐	WWERT
User Name		IDES0164		⇨	☐	USNAM

Fig 5

Execute (F8):

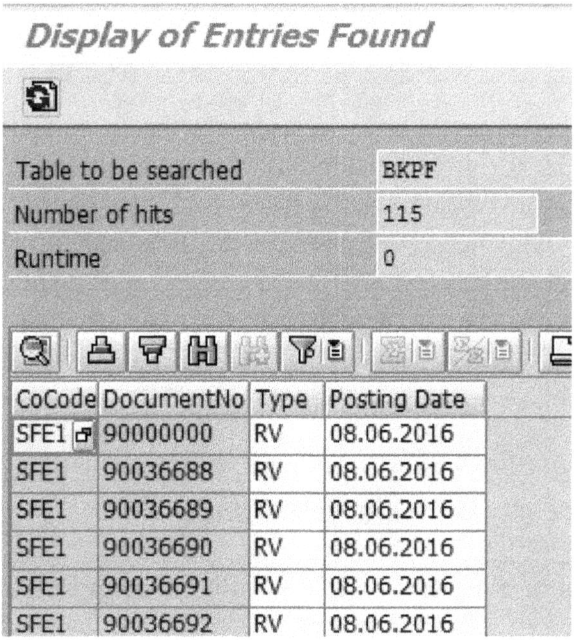

Display of Entries Found

Table to be searched	BKPF
Number of hits	115
Runtime	0

CoCode	DocumentNo	Type	Posting Date
SFE1	90000000	RV	08.06.2016
SFE1	90036688	RV	08.06.2016
SFE1	90036689	RV	08.06.2016
SFE1	90036690	RV	08.06.2016
SFE1	90036691	RV	08.06.2016
SFE1	90036692	RV	08.06.2016

Fig 6

We can either scroll through this list or download it using ⬚. The rest of the screen icons should be familiar. In this way, all tables can be looked up for the required data.

3. QUERIES IN SAP (U)

Queries in SAP link tables to give users results based off their unique requirements. There are 2 kinds of queries; one is a quick view (SQVI) which everyone has access to and the other is structured queries (SQ01) which require greater skills to develop and execute. Another main difference between the two is that a Quick viewer is available only to the person who creates it while the more structured queries can be made available to everybody using the appropriate user groupings.

In this training, we will cover the Quick viewer, as the access to the latter may be very limited in most organizations.

The concept of queries is simple – find one or more fields that are common to 2 or more tables and link the tables by those field/s to 'query' them. Then input your selection in one and get the outputs from that and the other table as desired in one single report instead of multiple lookups. However, this link needs to make sense in a few ways:

- The fields being linked must lead up to a unique value else SAP won't find a correct match or will find multiple matches
- There should not be any redundancy of data i.e. the data being linked must have consistency and clarity
- No unnecessary joins should exist between these tables or that can lead to inconsistent results or no results

As an example, we will use 2 tables from the previous section:

LFA1 - Vendor Master (General Section)
LFB1 - Vendor Master (CC)

The intent of our query is to find the vendor data in the CC section along with the vendor address. From our knowledge of the tables, we know the vendor address exists in LFA1 and the CC data in LFB1.

Since the common key that holds them together is the vendor code itself, we will use it in the join.

To get to the quick viewer use transaction SQVI or the menu path:

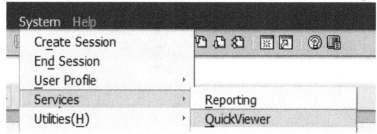

Fig 7

Give it a short name till 15 characters:

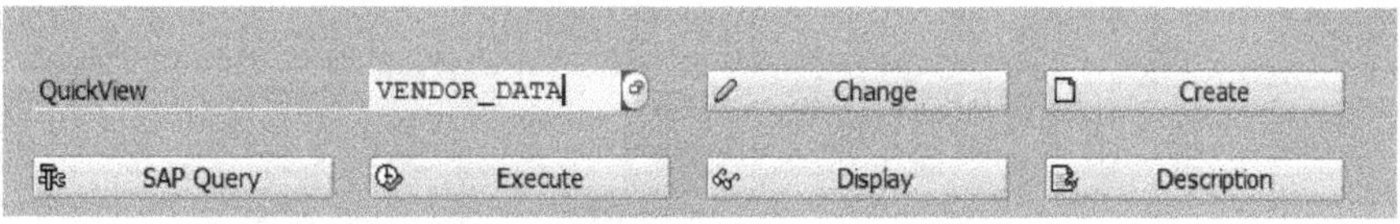

QuickView	VENDOR_DATA		Change		Create
SAP Query	Execute		Display		Description

Fig 8

Click on Create ☐ Create

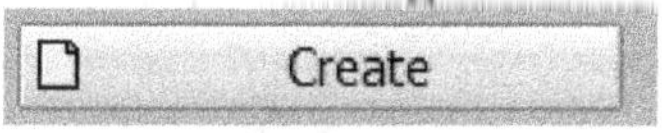

Now you have the ability to give it a longer description/Title:

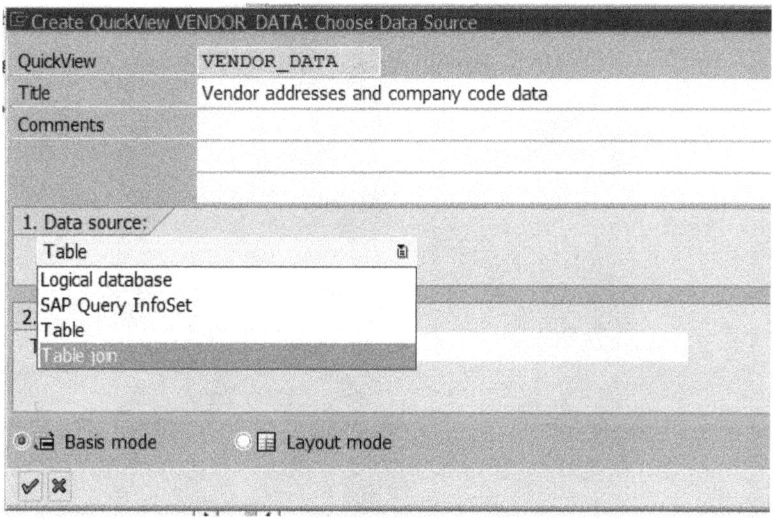

Create QuickView VENDOR_DATA: Choose Data Source

QuickView	VENDOR_DATA
Title	Vendor addresses and company code data
Comments	

1. Data source:

Table

Logical database
SAP Query InfoSet
2. Table
Table join

◉ Basis mode   ◯ Layout mode

✓ ✗

Fig 9

383

Choose Data source as Table join.

(a) Logical database are complex data structures that have been provided by SAP for some important sub areas like pricing, purchasing, accounting documents etc. and are normally used only by IT as they require more complexity to develop

(b) SAP Query Infoset is used in the more structured queries mentioned in the beginning of this section

(c) Table read would be same as SE16N as in the previous section and using it as a query is meaningless if you have access to SE16N

(d) Table join – this is what we will use and is the most common way of creating a quick viewer

Say OK to come to this screen:

Fig 10

There is a window that appears as a navigation pane which helps to see at a glance when many tables are being used for interconnection:

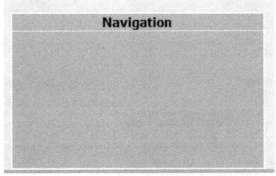

Fig 11

Our first task is to insert the tables we will be using. Use the icon

to do that:

Enter the name of the first table when the window comes up:

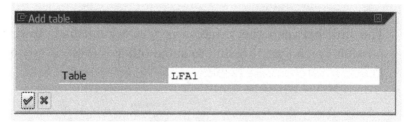

Fig 12

Hit Enter and it should be now available for use along with all its fields:

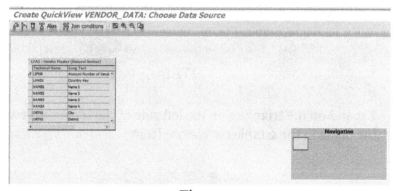

Fig 13

Repeat the insert for the other table LFB1 and SAP will link them together automatically based on the most important field, which is LIFNR (Vendor #):

Navigation

Fig 14

The link between the 2 tables is now established. It is also possible to change this link to some other if there is any other field that can be more helpful.

Click on Green arrow to step back

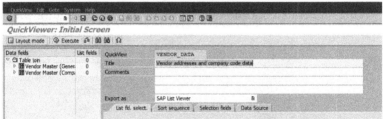

Fig 15

Expand on the triangles on the left side of the screen to reveal all the fields in the 2 tables to choose from

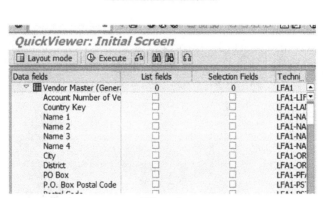

Fig 16

We now have 3 options wrt the fields of these tables:

1. List fields i.e. show the value in this field in the result – List Field. Then check it.
2. Selection Fields i.e. we use a field to only input what we need as a selection criteria. Then check it.
3. Do both i.e. use it as a selection criterion and also have its data it in the resulting report.

In our case, we will use the following fields in the general area of the vendor:

Data fields	List fields	Selection Fields	Tec
▽ ▦ Vendor Master (Gener;	5	1	LFA
Account Number of Ve	☑	☑	LFA
Country Key	☐	☐	LFA
Name 1	☑	☐	LFA
Name 2	☐	☐	LFA
Name 3	☐	☐	LFA
Name 4	☐	☐	LFA
City	☑	☐	LFA
District	☐	☐	LFA
PO Box	☐	☐	LFA
P.O. Box Postal Code	☐	☐	LFA
Postal Code	☑	☐	LFA
Region (State, Province	☑	☐	LFA

Fig 17

And the following in the CC data:

QuickViewer: Initial Screen

⊞ Layout mode | ⊕ Execute | 6⊡ | ⊞ ⊞ | 6⊡

Data fields	List fields	Selection Fields	Te..
▽ ▦ Vendor Master (Company	5	1	LFB1 ▲
Account Number of Vendo	☑	☐	LFB1 ▼
Company Code	☑	☑	LFB1
Personnel Number	☐	☐	LFB1
Date on which the Record	☑	☐	LFB1
Name of Person who Crea	☐	☐	LFB1
Posting block for company	☐	☐	LFB1
Deletion Flag for Master R(	☐	☐	LFB1
Key for sorting according t	☐	☐	LFB1
Reconciliation Account in G(	☑	☐	LFB1
Authorization Group	☐	☐	LFB1
Interest calculation indicatc	☐	☐	LFB1
List of the Payment Metho	☐	☐	LFB1
Indicator: Clearing betweer	☐	☐	LFB1
Block key for payment	☐	☐	LFB1
Terms of Payment Key	☑	☐	LFB1
Our account number with t	☐	☐	LFB1

Fig 18

387

Again, use the scroll bar at the right to see the other fields in the tables.

Save the query. It is common to get a window like this below and in which case, just hit Enter since it is only an info message in Yellow:

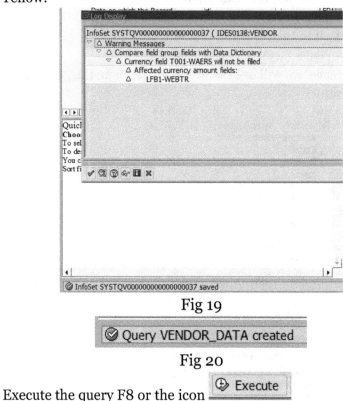

Fig 19

⊘ Query VENDOR_DATA created

Fig 20

Execute the query F8 or the icon ⊕ Execute

Alternatively, step out and go to SQVI again. This new query will now be available for you to use every time:

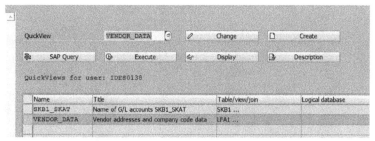

Fig 21

Select and execute:

Vendor address and company code data

Report-specific selections			
Account Number of Vendor or		to	
Company Code	SFE1	to	

Output specification	
Layout	

Fig 22

Recall we had selected only 2 fields as input criteria – Vendor Number and the CC and so only those ones show up in the above selection screen.

From here, this selection screen works the same way as in all other transactions in SAP. Since we do not want to look for any vendors in any Co Code other than SFE1, then we enter SFE1 in the Co Code and execute again:

Vendor address and company code data

Vendor	CoCd	Acctg clerk	Name 1	City	PostalCode	Rg	Vendor	Date	Recon.acct	PayT
100863	SFE1	WR	GreenLand Corporation Ltd.	TORONTO	M6N 1B4	ON	100863	06/18/2016	211000	0008
100864	SFE1	WR	Concor Corporation Ltd.		M6N 1B4	ON	100864	06/20/2016	211000	0003
100865	SFE1	WR	Suculant Ltd.		M6N 1B4	ON	100865	06/20/2016	211000	
100844	SFE1	WR	FA Property Canada	Ontario		ON	100844	05/28/2016	211000	0003
100845	SFE1	WR	Ontario Supplier	Ontario		ON	100845	05/28/2016	211000	0003
100846	SFE1		Bolt Supply Company vendor for SFE1				100846	05/28/2016	211000	0003
100847	SFE1		Dubak Electric				100847	05/28/2016	211000	0001
100848	SFE1		Val Electric			ON	100848	05/28/2016	211000	0001
100849	SFE1		Data Enterprise for Devika	Toronto			100849	05/28/2016	211000	0003
100850	SFE1		SP Plus				100850	05/28/2016	211000	0001
100851	SFE1		Jazmin				100851	05/28/2016	211000	0001
100852	SFE1		STONE VENDOR FOR SFE1	TORONTO			100852	05/28/2016	211000	0003
100853	SFE1		xyz company	TORONTO	M6N 1B4	ON	100853	06/02/2016	211000	0003
100854	SFE1		ABC for sfe1	Toronto			100854	06/03/2016	211000	0003
100855	SFE1		Wood for SFE1				100855	06/03/2016	211000	0003
100856	SFE1		QQQ Company Ltd.	TORONTO	M6N 1B4	ON	100856	06/04/2016	211000	0003
100857	SFE1		WEY Campany Ltd.		M8N 7Y6	ON	100857	06/05/2016	211000	0003
100858	SFE1		Bum Company			ON	100858	06/11/2016	211000	0003
100859	SFE1	WR	Free Polution Corporation Ltd.		M6N 1B4	ON	100859	06/14/2016	211000	0008
5000000085	SFE1		Health Corporation Ltd.		M6N 1B4	ON	5000000085	06/15/2016	211000	0008
100860	SFE1	WR	BGW Corporation Ltd		M6N 1B4	ON	100860	06/16/2016	211000	0003
100838	SFE1	WR	Wood vendor for SFE1	Oakville			100838	05/10/2016	211000	0003

Fig 23

This list can be now downloaded the same way as we have done at other times. It can be modified to hide columns you do not need and it helps to save the layout if you will use the query frequently. Queries can also be modified the same way by adding/deleting fields or even adding tables using the Change Query button from the main SQVI screen.

GLOSSARY OF TERMS

BOM	Bill of Material
CC	Company code
CoA	Chart of Accounts
CS01/02/03	Create, Change, display Bill of Material
DC	Distribution Channel - the way goods are sold - e.g. retail, wholesale etc
DIV	Division, represents a business area/segment in a company
F.27	Look up, generate or print customer statements
F-02	Reclass entries
F1	Help Key
FD01/02/03	Create, change, display customer master from FI perspective
FD10N	Display customer balance
FI	Financial Accounting
Financial statement Versions	SAP terminology for P&L and Balance Sheet

FK01/02/03	Create, change, display vendor master from FI perspective
FK10N	Display vendor balance
FS00	Area Menu for creating G/L accounts
FSG	Field Status Group
GR	Goods Receipt
IR	Invoice Receipt
LIV	Logistics Invoice Verification
MB03	Display material document
MB1C	Post initial stocks directly
ME01/03	Maintain (includes create and change) and display source list
ME11/12/13	Create, Change, display Purchasing Info records
ME21N/22N/23N	Create, Change, display Purchase Orders
ME41/42/43	Create, Change, Display RFQ
ME47	Enter vendor quotations in the system
ME49	Compare Quotations from vendors
ME51N/52N	Create, change Purchase Req
MI01/02/03	Create, change and display physical inventory document
MI05	Change inventory count

MI07	Post inventory recount document
MI10	Enter count w/o physical count document
MI11	Recount inventory
MI20	Compare physical with book stock
MIGO	Post Goods Receipt
MIR4	Display accounting document of LIV Material document
MIRO	Invoice Receipt
MK01/02/03	Create, change, display vendor master from MM perspective
MM	Materials Management
MM01/02/03	Create, change or Display material respectively
MMBE	Overview of Stocks
MRRL	Evaluated Invoice Receipt (to auto create payables)
P.Org	Purchasing Org; the highest object in MM, responsible for purchases on behalf of the c. code
PIR	Purchasing Info record
Posting Key	Key used by SAP to segregate based on customer or vendor, type of posting, debit or credit
PP	Production Planning
PR	Purchase Requisition
QM	Quality Management

RFQ	Request for Quotation
Sales Area	A unique combination of SO, DC and DIV
SAP	Pronounced ess-aye-pee, formerly called Systems, Applications, Products in Data Processing
SCM	Supply Chain Management
SD	Sales & Distribution
SE16N	Look up tables
SFE1	Company code being used in this manual for demo/training
SO	Sales Organization: Representing the company code, it is the highest object in SD
Source List	Listing of approved vendors for a certain product
SP02	Look up spools generated by yourself
SQ01	Central query - visible to all users
SQVI	Quickview visible only to the user who creates it
T-code	Transaction Code
VA01/02/03	Create, Change, Display Sales Order
Variant	A variation of input and output screen as desired by the user to simplify information
VB11/12/13	Create, change, display material determination
VD01/02/03	Create, change, display customer master from SD perspective
VD51/52/53	Create, Change, display customer-material info record

VF01/02/03	Create, Change, display Billing Document
VF11	Cancel Billing document
VK11/12/13	Create, Change, display pricing record
VL01N/02N/03N	Create, Change, display Delivery
VL09	Reverse Goods Issue from delivery
VT01N/02N/03N	Create, Change, display Shipment
XD01/02/03	Create, change, display customer master Centrally (all views)
XK01/02/03	Create, change, display vendor master Centrally (all views)

MAIN SYMBOLS

Symbol	Meaning	Extended meaning/ Function
/n	New	Before the t-code, replaces the existing screen with the new t-code
/o	Another	Before the t-code, replaces opens up a new screen with the new t-code
	Session key	Opens up a new session – up to 6 can be opened simultaneously in the latest version, at the time of writing
	Execute button or F8	Executes the program to give results based on what the user has selected on the input screen
	Navigation keys	Goes one step back (also F3), goes completely out of the transaction and cancels the current screen, respectively
	Page scroll	First page, previous page, next page and last page respectively
	Find on current page	Find and find again respectively, useful when you have long lists of documents and want to find any particular one

	Click on top extreme left to get to this window	Creates new session or stops current transaction. Very useful if you started a transaction but forgot to use /o and want another window open to run another transaction. Also useful to cancel the current transaction if you gave incorrect input parameters and it is taking too long to fetch the results.
F1	Help	
F4	To look up values	For configurable objects, we can choose only what is available. Pressing F4 enables us to look up this list to choose from it.